The Orphic Moment

SUNY Series, The Margins of Literature
Mihai I. Spariosu, editor

The Orphic Moment

SHAMAN TO POET-THINKER IN
PLATO, NIETZSCHE, AND MALLARMÉ

Robert McGahey

STATE UNIVERSITY OF NEW YORK PRESS

Published by
State University of New York Press, Albany

For information, address State University of New York Press,
State University Plaza, Albany, N.Y., 12246

Production by Bernadine Dawes
Marketing by Dana Yanulavich

Front and back cover: "Sous l'aile dombre, letre appliquait une active morsure" (Plare IV
of "Songes"), lithograph, 1891, 22.5 x 16.9 cm., Stickney Fund, 1920.1689. And photo-
graphs © The Art Institute of Chicago. Odilon Redon, French, 1840–1916, cover-fron-
tispiece from "Dans le rêve," Mellerio 26, lithograph on tan wove paper, 1879, 30.2 x 22.3
cm, Stickney Collection, 1920.1555.

Library of Congress Cataloging-in-Publication Data

McGahey, Robert, 1946–
      The orphic moment : shaman to poet-thinker in Plato, Nietzsche,
and Mallarmeé / Robert McGahey.
            p.   cm. – (SUNY series, the margins of literature)
      Includes bibliographical references and index.
      ISBN 0-7914-1941-X (hc). – ISBN 0-7914-1942-8 (pb)
      1. Poetics. 2. Orpheus (Greek mythology) 3. Plato—Contributions
in poetics. 4. Nietzsche, Friedrich Wilhelm, 1844–1900—Aesthetics.
      5. Mallarmé, Stéphane, 1842–1898–Criticism and interpretation.
      I. Title. II. Series.
      PN1035.M34   1994
      801'.951—dc20
                                                                          93–46495
                                                                          CIP

10 9 8 7 6 5 4 3 2 1

to my mother and father

Contents

Foreword

The image of Orpheus is truly one of the great, fertile, inspiring, and confounding myths in our heritage. What is it to be dismembered, to sing out of that fragmentation, to be islanded (isolated)? What kind of necessity compels us to transgress the absolute law and eternally lose our cherished loves and desires to a realm outside or beneath the consoling light of familiar life? Who is this Orpheus—an historical theologian, a figure of myth, a founder of religion, a poet, or nothing but a figment appearing like a ghost throughout our history? With Orpheus we are obviously placed insecurely and yet fruitfully on a boundary, not knowing exactly where we are, but finding there an unusual bountifulness of imagination and piety.

This is an extraordinary book on Orpheus, one that is willing to circumvent explanations and fixed positions. Itself it teaches us how to live and imagine Orphically on the invisible and impossibly thin line that separates and unites all opposites. As in Rilke's sonnets that celebrate Orpheus, it invites us to appreciate and enjoy the musical tension that is created by the tuning of polarities. As he observes the phantasmic appearances of Orpheus over the centuries, Robert McGahey writes with authority, sculpting out a precise place and time that is the Orphic moment, and he also straddles the difficult but necessary ambiguity of historical time and poetic eternity. The sheer joy of the book comes in part from the multiple fugal counterpoints of many schools of poetic and philosophic sensibility.

The point of writing about a figure like Orpheus is not to expose him to our intellectual curiosity and self-serving need to dissect—a caricature of true Orphic fragmentation—but rather to evoke him and his song. In this sense, Mr. McGahey writes as an Orphic musician; not one who plays literally on a lyre, but one who calls forth the harmonic and tuneful voice of being itself.

—THOMAS MOORE, author of *Care of the Soul* and *Soul Mates*

Acknowledgments

Before entering the "well-roofed cave" of the text, I wish to grate-
fully thank those who have enabled me to lay its foundations:
Arthur Evans, for leading me back to Mallarmé, and for unfailing
encouragement and support through early difficulties; Elizabeth
Sewell, who gave me Orpheus, and who has taught me more than
she knows; and Bobby Paul, for deftly guiding me through a dissertation prospectus hearing when I was truly "prospecting." Special thanks are due to my two chief dissertation readers: Walter
Strauss, for his timely response, in mid-summer, to an SOS from
an unknown Emory ILA student, and for his incisive criticisms
and prompt responses ever since then; and in memoriam to my
dissertation director, William Arrowsmith, who managed to
make time for my project in the midst of severe illness and a myr-
iad of competing demands. Our talks were so engrossing that
there were times when I wasn't sure where his thoughts ended
and mine began. I want to acknowledge here my general indebt-
edness to his ideas.

During the process of revising the mansuscript for publication, several people have been extremely helpful. I especially
want to thank my "mystery reader" Marshall Olds, whose penetrating—but still anonymous—remarks I had the great fortune of
paraphrasing in front of him at a reception for Walter Strauss in
the spring of 1992, after we had each read papers in Walter's
honor. Reynolds Smith provided continual encouragement, and

wisely steered my manuscript to SUNY Press. Larry Alderink
read the introductory "Greek" chapter, and made numerous helpful suggestions. Ted Johnson provided invaluable help with the
knotty problems of translating Mallarmé's "poëmes critiques." At
SUNY, Mihai Spariosu kindly reread each of my revised chapters
as I produced them, making my task of working at the "margins
of literature" immeasurably easier. Carola Sautter and Bernadine
Dawes deftly led me through the maze of academic publishing.
My copyeditor, Carol Newhouse, did a splendid job.

Finally, reaching as far down in the well as I can, I want to
thank my wife Judith for enduring.

Introduction

This study will examine the figure of Orpheus as he operates both explicitly and implicitly in the poetics of Plato and Mallarmé, each a key figure in a moment of transformation of western language and thought. Building upon an analysis of the *daimon* as a *way between* the modes (*nomoi*) of Greek thought, I use Nietzsche's brilliant recasting of the Dionysos/Apollo polarity in *The Birth of Tragedy* as a frame through which one may see the *daimon* Orpheus reappearing at the end of the nineteenth century. During the fifth century B.C., Apollo and Dionysos were involved in a remarkable rapprochement at the great temple of Apollo at Delphi, an Olympian peace that was concurrent with the rise both of Orphism and of images of Orpheus in literature and the plastic arts. Orpheus has been seen (Guthrie, *Orpheus and Greek Religion*) as a religious reformer who mediated these brother-gods.

Just as he was present there, at the moment when the Apollonian forms of Western culture were being encoded, so does he appear again at the opposite moment represented by the language-crisis at the end of the nineteenth century, an era that inaugurated the breakup of those forms. It is a moment characterized not only by an eruption of Dionysos, dramatized in the *Birth of Tragedy*,[1] but also by a reappearance of Orpheus, a kind of nuclear particle emitted by the Bacchic god's dance with his contrary, Apollo. Orpheus, residual in the mythic creations of Plato despite the philosopher's burning his poetry and banishing the poet from the *Republic*, is a figure ignored in Nietzsche but realized in the life, poetry, and letters of the Symbolist poet who was his exact contemporary.

The Greek *daimon* Orpheus has a rich history of connection with poetry, beginning with his reputation among the Greeks as the original, or eponymous, poet. Since the poet, the lyrist, accompanied himself by the lyre, this archaic poetry was also music. As *mythos* gave way to *logos* in the fifth to fourth centuries, the original music (*mousike*: compare muse and Musaios, Orpheus's son) was sundered, transmuted into the children of myth: poetry and philosophy. In the transformations of this "axial period" (Jaspers), Orpheus is a key operator, carrying forward the older, shamanic mode of thought and being into the youthful logocentric age, as I will attempt to show in chapter 1.

The relationship between Orpheus as figure of legend and the religious reformation of the fifth century commonly called "Orphism" has always been somewhat problematic. There is a curious gap involved here, a slippage between Orpheus the myth and Orphism as a religious-philosophical movement. Unlike Charles Segal (in his recent book, *Orpheus: the Myth of the Poet*), I include Orphism as well as the Orpheus of literature and art in the first part of my study, and I take the slippage as an essential quality in Orpheus's nature: Orpheus is "gap" as well as border and bridge, as I suggest in chapter 1. Ivan Linforth (*The Arts of Orpheus*) regards the slippage as being so loose that he calls Orphism a "rumor"—or a later fabrication of the Neoplatonists.[2] The behavior of Onomacritus, Orphic reformer in Athens who was caught revising the official copy of the Orphic theogonies, also indicates the *daimon*'s tendency to act by insinuation, rumor, and trickery.

In a more formal sense, Orpheus as mediator of mantic Apollo and manic Dionysos (Plato's distinction in the *Phaedrus*) acts in his daimonic capacity as a *way between modes*, just as the human is daimonic, walking the tightrope between beast and divinity. This is precisely the model for the tribal shaman, and I argue that Orpheus was shaman before he became eponymous poet. Musically, the modes are Dorian and Phrygian, but in a larger sense the modes involved are whole worlds that the two gods represent, properly envisioned as the Olympian and the chthonic. I develop this model at the end of the first chapter, following the work of Usener and Cassirer (*Language and Myth*).

When first encountered in the archaic era, Orpheus comes to us out of the shamanic mists. When first mentioned in Greek texts of the sixth century B.C., he is already "famous Orpheus." A sixth-century *metope* at Delphi shows Orpheus seated in the Argos along with another figure and playing his lyre. Later references speak of Orpheus as having accompanied Jason and the Argonauts on their journey, providing the *oima* ("way-song") for their passage through the *symplegades* (the "clashing rocks"—very like Scylla and Charybdis in Homer). Jack Lindsay (*The Clashing Rocks*) places this figure within the shamanic tradition out of which, in his opinion, tragedy grew. The eponymous poet was originally a shaman, for each wielded a telltale possession: a lyre fashioned out of the carapace of a tortoise. The shaman's incantation (*epoidos*) becomes the tragedian's *oima*, which teaches the tribe—later the *polis*—how to move among conflicting demands in an existence that is basically tragic. Lindsay's identification of a "shamanist contradiction" is basic to my thesis. It helped lead me to recognize a continuity among Orpheus on the Argos, Empedocles and Herakleitos as shaman-philosopher-poets, Plato as inventor of philosophy yet unwitting Orphic poet, through Mallarmé as shaman and poet-thinker, a magician rowing his own cauldron amidst the alchemical fires that gave birth to the modern at the end of the last century. Lindsay's notion of the "shamanist contradiction" parallels my emphasis upon the poet-as-instrument, the identification of the poet with his lyre.

The shamanic contradiction, in my amplification of the idea, is a given, a fundamental contrariety of the soul. It occurs because of the "mixing" of the titanic and divine within the human (the lesson of the Rhapsodic Theogony, in which Zeus refashions men out of *titanos*, the clay formed of the ash of the titans, who had just eaten the infant Dionysos). Plato's image of the soul, as we shall see in chapter 2, is always multiple, with inner tensions: (1) the bipolar soul of the *Phaedo*, (2) the tripartite soul of the *Phaedrus* (charioteer, white and black horses), (3) the tripartite image from the *Republic* (lion, man, beast of many heads).[3] With the *rhapsode* of the *Ion*, there is no contradiction, because the "divining power" has not yet come forth. He is like the "Aeolian harp" of the romantics, the wind-harp invented in the seventeenth century, passively sounded by the divine winds passing through his "light and winged" being. The divining

power, which is within the mind (*Phaedrus* 242 b–c), but involving
the entire being of the poet, is the defining characteristic of the
Orphic poet, a "new being" built on the old figure of the shaman.
The original melody that is produced by this divination is played
through his body, for the body is his instrument. This melody
cannot be heard by the physical ear; it is beyond sense. In this
respect, "Orphic music" is like the music of the spheres. It is an
inner music that is itself a "way," charting a soul-path for the poet-
shaman (thus the psychopomp is self-led), just as the music of the
heavenly spheres charts their respective orbits. But the playing
out of this divine melody through the titanic flesh creates a contradictory kind of music of such power that the singing Orphic
poet shatters his body. The mind, the "head," breaks loose from
the instrument, the skeletal frame strung with sinews. Orphic
poetry is the music issuing from the contrariness of the
soul/body; "poetry thinking itself," (Elizabeth Sewell) or singing
itself, enacts a contradiction. That very contradiction, when lived
and played through, creates an exquisite music.

　　The renewal of interest in archaic Greece by the *Frühromantiker* in Germany set the stage for Nietzsche's challenge to the
philological establishment at the end of the nineteenth century.
What I have called Mallarmé's "Orphic moment"—rekindling in
France the tradition of Orphic poetry, which has continued unin-
terrupted since then—is framed within the same decade by Nietzsche's analysis of Dionysos and Apollo as brother-gods whose
joint labor establishes the warp and woof of art. This process too
is a *Widerspruch* (contradiction), the action of "contraries" in
Blake's terms. When Nietzsche says that Apollo and Dionysos are
"forces of nature . . . operating without the intervention of any
human subject," he is speaking of these gods as if they are opera-
tively akin to natural law (*physis*), rather than cultural law
(*nomos*).[4] Consonant with his role in the Greek fifth century,
Orpheus in late nineteenth-century Europe provides the medial
way between modes. For Nietzsche's analysis overlooks Orpheus,
who appears on the border between these gods.[5] Orpheus/Mal-
larmé is an evanescent figure, dancing into being at the boundary
of interaction between these powerful forces. The moment is
highly charged and synchronous, a mythic recurrence reshaping
the texture (a *retrempe*, as Mallarmé would say) of European arts
and letters, constituting as well a striking coincidence in biogra-

phies of the two men, Nietzsche and Mallarmé ("Brothers in Decadence," chapter 3).

My thesis with regard to Mallarmé (chapter 4) is that the symbolist poet embodies a precise moment of the Orpheus myth, which I shall examine on four related levels:

1. It is the *kairos*, an opportune occasion that he shared with Nietzsche: that of the accelerated breakdown of the forms of Western culture in fin-de-siècle nineteenth-century Europe. This moment is the inverse of the moment of creation of those forms in classical Greece. Using Nietzsche's aesthetic construct, the Apollo-Dionysos contrariety, as frame for this moment, I suggest that Orpheus/Mallarmé appears when the Apollonian world of *Schein* disappears back into its ground, the *Ur-Eine*, which is Dionysos. Orpheus shadows the *limen* (border) between their two realms. This is a fleeting moment that Nietzsche misses, identifying instead with Dionysos the "crucified."

2. Mallarmé's Orphic moment is an internal event, perhaps precisely to be reckoned by the prose poem "Le démon de l'analogie" (1865). This moment, the poet poised at the window of an antique lutenist's shop in Tournon, is the beginning of a *sparagmos*, after which he is painstakingly "restrung." I shall follow this Orphic metaphor, the poet-as-instrument, through several poems and the poet's major critical works, the "poëmes critiques."

3. The moment is a particular stage of Orpheus's mythic pattern: when the scattered limbs first begin to stir back into life.

4. Closely related to this third aspect of the moment is a subtle but characteristic oscillation, a "volatilization" (Mallarmé, "Les dieux antiques") expressing an ontological realm experienced not from the personal viewpoint of the poet, but impersonally. This oscillation is expressed by a tensive quality of language that surfaces throughout the poetry, letters, and "poëmes critiques." The tensive quality is like a reflex, registering the shudder as Orpheus passes between the gaping void of the Dionysian *Ur-Eine*, with its immense gravitational pull, and the rigid frame of an Apolline form that has lost its suppleness.

The characteristic oscillation in Mallarmé's verse operates in miniscule within a larger pattern established by Plato, as demonstrated in a study of the reciprocal ebb and flow of the tides of eros in the *Phaedrus*. This latter phenomenon appears against the background process of *hydrostasis* demonstrated in the *Phaedo* (chapter 2).

In chapter 5, I compare the poetic universes of Plato and Mallarmé, attempting to show that an idealism remains in Mallarme, only of a very different order than Plato's. This is a position bewteen those of Guy Delfel (*L'aesthetique de Mallarmé*) and Jacques Derrida (*Dissemination*). Whereas Delfel has argued for a Platonic idealism in the French poet's work, Derrida has deconstructed all such idealist scenarios.[6] I also argue here that the French poet's "Igitur" constitutes a replay of an Orphic mystery: the ritual *sparagmos* of the infant Dionysos by the titans in the Rhapsodic Theogony. Mallarmé's Hamlet-like stripling hero performs his Orphic duty as theurgist, reinscribing the Orphic theogonies for a decadent age, incidentally repromoting the goddess Nyx to her deserved status as mother of the gods.

In conclusion we will look at the continuation of this Orphic moment in the work of the Orphic critic Maurice Blanchot, briefly contrasting his orphic and homeopathic perspective with that of an "allopathic" critic, Jacques Derrida. Blanchot identifies "Le regard d'Orphée" as the "center" of his key work, *L'espace littéraire*: the point when Orpheus looks back into the oppressive darkness for Eurydice, who is the "work of art." She is also a "second night" within Night, the hidden spring of art that the Romantics intuitively sought among the "Brood of Night": including sleep, dream, and death.

Blanchot's center, like the Mallarméan center, is a vortex, a void with the overwhelming gravitational pull of a black hole. In Mallarmé, this center is the Néant (nothingness), which he calls his "Beatrice." The void is the principle that vivifies the "anterior heaven where Beauty flourishes," the anti-world in which Mallarmé finds the continued existence of something very like the Platonic forms. The Néant of Mallarmé is an active principle, more like the Night of the Orphic theogonies. This is the quality that Nietzsche suggests in his remark, "if you gaze long enough into an abyss, the abyss will gaze back into you."[7] This active quality of the negative, with its tremendous gravitational power, is far different from the simple lack or inert absence of the Derridean aporia. Another cosmos shines darkly through these holes, belying the skillful but sophistic critic's arguments that there is nothing beyond the rim of the linguistic universe.

The Mallarméan center, which Blanchot understands so well, cannot be attained or clearly seen. It continues steadily to retreat before the effort of consciousness to colonize it. My observation of Mallarmé's poetics is that they enact a dance on the threshhold of this dark, hidden, enormously dense retreating center—a dance of an evanescent but recurring moment: the poet's Orphic moment. Through this dance, the sympathetic reader is drawn repeatedly to that threshhold, where one awaits the crossing of worlds, the knitting of the loom of the Fates clicking in muted tones just beyond him. At times, the poet is magisterial, as when referring to himself as one "qui déchaîna l'Infini," abrogating to himself the power to undo the Great Chain or the Spindle of Necessity by which the worlds are hung. More often, though, he brings us to awareness of this center through infinitely subtle indirection, and this is more characteristic of the moment of the Orphic dance.

Orpheus is the smallest, indivisible moment of decay of material form into energy. He is the moment of volatilization.

He is the flicker of fire on the walls of the Cave and the rumor of ocean wave from the conch.

Orpheus is the boundary between Dionysos and Apollo, appearing when one is absorbed into the other.

Orpheus is the sunset and the sunrise: those moments when the sun just touches the principle of darkness (Mallarmé, "Dieux antiques").

He is as sweet as honey, as bitter as ash (see Lévi-Strauss, From Honey to Ashes*).*

Orpheus is immediate as the song of the cricket, distant as the last angelus of the swan.

"Orpheus . . . is a vast den of a thousand monsters" (Vico, New Science*). He is the moment of transition from the titanic to the human.*

Orpheus is "philosophy personified" (Bacon, "Wisdom of the Ancients"); therefore through him philosophy would keep its "persons."

Orpheus is the artist, and Eurydice his art (Blanchot).

Orpheus is literature and its asymptotic relation to Being.

> Under a juniper-tree the bones sang, scattered
> and shining . . .
> And the bones sang chirping
> With the burden of the grasshopper, saying . . .
> —T. S. Eliot, "Ash Wednesday"

Prologue

Eunomus and the Cicada

In the early morning darkness, figures move about. It is pitch-black, no moon. At the center of the theater, on the edge of the choral ground, a lone lyrist appears, strumming and humming a sparse melody. Today at Delphi Eunomus will compete for the privilege of joining other great lyrists: Musaios, Amphion, Orpheus. The occasion is the funeral of the great serpent Python, who has been slain by the Olympian, Apollo, and must be mourned properly. By midday, quitting their labors in the fierce heat, a great crowd has gathered. Eunomus launches his song. In the middle of his performance, a string breaks, and a cicada who was twittering on the edge of the stage jumps onto the lyre. Not missing a beat, Eunomus shifts modes, including in his lay the cicada's ancient song.

So Clement, the Alexandrian evangelist to the Athenians, informs us. To Clement this little miracle does not testify to the power of the Locrian's song, but to the piety of the cicadas, singing "a spontaneous natural song" to the "all-wise God." The cicada chirps in, not due to the magical influence of the lyrist, but "of its own accord." By casting doubt on the interpretation of this little episode, Clement would render even more ludicrous the Athenians' lingering assent to "worthless legends, imagining brute beasts to be enchanted by music."[1]

1

The cicadas, according to Plato in the *Phaedrus* (258e ff.),
are the vestigial traces of an earlier race of men, a race who lived
before the Muses. When the Muses appeared, and song was introduced into their midst, many of this race were so entranced that
they forgot to eat, feeding instead on their own song, until they
died "without noticing it" (259c). The cicadas, sprung from this
race of men, indeed need no food, singing from birth to death,
after which they go and report to the Muses those men who have
honored each of them. Following Plato, then, Eunomus's cicada
is merely recognizing its own essence in the lay of the bard, joining his chord in a spontaneous act of sympathy. This is no miracle
at all, but an expression of sympathetic magic: like follows like.

The cicada sings continually, unable to restrain its pleasure
in song. At the other extreme is the swan, who sings only at
death. Considering the milieu where our study begins—that of
fifth-century Greece, where a strong and deep current of belief in
metempsychosis is swelling—this is a song of anticipation. Indeed,
as Plato relates through the myth of Er in the *Republic*, the soul of
Orpheus "selects the life of a swan, because for hatred of the
tribe of women, owing to its death at their hands, it was unwilling
to be conceived and born of a woman" (*Republic* 10. 620a).

The work of Orpheus is between these two extremes: grati-
fication in the present moment, celebrated in the ceaseless song
of the cicada, and austere postponement of joy in the swan. The
two join in the image of Orpheus's prophesying head, where the
cicada's spirit of lyric sweetness and the swan's hope for life in
the Beyond conjoin. These two modalities are also spanned by
Orpheus's lyre, a figure for the work of culture, but more specifically a figure for charging the "gap" between primordial
metaphor and ordered gestalt. This is the fundamental job of
myth: binding the potential energy inherent in the continuing
gap between phenomenon and meaning.

Orpheus as Gap, Border, and Bridge 1

Focussing of all forces on a single point is the prerequisite of all mythical thinking. . . . When, on the one hand, the entire self is given up to a single impression, is "possessed" by it, and, on the other hand, there is the utmost tension between the subject and its object, the outer world; when external reality is not merely viewed and contemplated, but overcomes a man in sheer immediacy, with emotions of fear or hope, terror or wish fulfillment: then the spark jumps somehow across, the tension finds release, as the subjective excitement becomes objectified, and confronts the mind as a god or daemon.

— Ernst Cassirer, *Language and Myth*

One could read this statement in an early work of Ernst Cassirer, propadeutic to his monumental *Philosophy of Symbolic Forms,* as his "founding myth," that moment of essential insight in which the germ of a lifetime's work lies: here, the near-identity of myth and language. Throughout these pages, and again in his summary work, *An Essay on Man,* which looks back upon the body of his opus, he speaks of these two symbolic modes in a single breath.[1] Despite the development since Cassirer in this century of powerful analytic tools for prying apart myth and language, I want to accept this linkage because of the play, what Maurice Blanchot calls the "looseness in the mechanism," it allows.[2] The process that Cassirer describes in his early little book is basic not only to "mythical thinking," but also to the making that goes on in all language acts: what the Greeks called *"poiesis."* When the Orphic critic Elizabeth Sewell speaks of Orpheus as "poetry thinking itself," she refers to something other than the mimesis the Greeks traditionally associated with the activity of the poet or *rhapsode.*[3] Though Cassirer's statement sounds a bit like the mimetic transfer that Eric Havelock sees as the essential pre-Platonic mode of acculturation, that is, "possession" of the "entire self," involving the *thumos* (appetitive self) with its emotions fear, hope, terror and awe, I see the "mythical thinking" that Cassirer describes as characteristic of original thinking of any sort.

This genealogical thinking, which must always go back to its origins to "think itself," requires honoring both the appetitive self and the reflective processes of *nous*, the divining rod within the mind. It is the thinking involved in the Platonic *anamnesis* (recollection) of the soul, and it is a shift from the poet's traditional operation by *mimesis*. Poetry and philosophy are the children of myth, and in the poet-philosopher, they seek a passionate reunion, one that has never been better described than by Plato in the *Phaedrus*. Paradoxically, Plato's own poetry, the myths that he weaves into the text at key junctures, insinuates itself into the dialogues long before he boldly throws out the archaic poets as sirens that the well-ordered state can ill afford to sanction (*Republic* 10). Indeed, he ends that book with one of the more remarkable pieces of *poiesis* in the dialogues, the myth of the warrior Er, who returns from a shamanistic trance to describe life after death.

Cassirer's remark, which serves as our touchstone, contains a second place of looseness or hedging: "the spark jumps somehow across." Across what? Reading further, the mystery remains: "as soon as the spark has jumped across, as soon as the tension and emotion of the moment has found its discharge in the word or the mythical image, a . . . turning point has occurred in human mentality: the inner excitement which was a mere subjective state has vanished, and has been resolved into the objective form of myth or of speech."[4] "Word or mythical image," "myth or speech"—again, there is slippage; he hedges. Like many original thinkers, Cassirer builds his entire edifice on instinctively undefined axioms. It seems to me that his are these: (1) that language and myth are a single symbolic mode, so closely intertwined that they cannot be separated, and (2) that there is a threshold in human experience on the nether side of which one stands victim of a "mere subjective state," whereas after crossing it, the experience is "resolved into the objective form of myth or speech."[5]

This study is about the close relation of myth and language, in particular how language *functions as myth* in the poetry of Stéphane Mallarmé, the remarkable French symbolist poet whose work revolutionized the course of modern poetics. At the same time it is about a moment: one suggested by the image of the cricket's jumping into the gap created by Eunomus's broken string. In the largest sense, this moment is the [——] across which language as *poiesis* moves in "fixing" the experience wherein the

god or *daimon* is named. Like Cassirer, I could simply leave the
object of "jump across" unnamed, respecting its infinite potential
as an essential openness at the center of this naming process. But
imaging it, I will call it a "gap": a space that can be seen as channel, point, or iota; chasm, gulf, or vortex. Plato says in the
Timaeus that the "marrow of all sciences" is the art of generating
"middle terms." Our gap is the perennial open center where middle terms come into generation. From this silent, hidden, and
prelogical center arise analogy and metaphor, in which each of
the authors appearing in this study excels: Plato and Nietzsche,
boldly; Mallarmé, with great subtlety.

Crossing the Gap

> ORPHEUS, who reduces the wild beasts of
> Greece to humanity, is evidently a vast den of a
> thousand monsters.
> —Giambattista Vico, *The New Science*

Another name for this gap or space is Orpheus, who appeared in
the Greek sixth to fifth centuries, an era transitional between the
oral, formulaic culture of the Homeric epic and the invention of
literature. Orpheus is a paradoxical figure who is considered to
be the very type of the Greek poet—older than Homer and Hesiod, even though they predate his appearance in both written and
plastic record. Vico's Orpheus is a "poetic character," a class
name for the civilizing figure whereby the fierce Thracians
became humanized, or Hellenized.[6] Though a "moment" to the
poetic mind, Vico says that it nevertheless took a thousand years
("a monstrosity of Greek chronology"). Orpheus is the poet of
the divine age (Kronos' age of gold): the first of Vico's *ricorsi*, as
Homer is another "poetic character," a collective noun for the
Greek oral poet on the border between the heroic age and the
third Vichian age, that of men in the grips of history.[7] But in
Vico's curious way of putting it, Orpheus is both the "reducer" to
humanity *and* a den of monsters. He is a figure for a humanizing
capacity located within and emergent from something monstrous. This dual nature, located at the very birth of the human
(in Vichian terms), looks ahead to the Orphic anthropogony and

its emphasis upon the "mixing" of titanic and divine in the human as characteristic of the Orphic turn. Vico's den is Plato's cave, as we will consider below.

Orpheus and Shamanism

One of the chief characteristics of Orpheus is that he always seems to unite what is oldest and newest. As a poet-singer with the power to entrance, he bears close resemblance to the oldest go-between of the spiritual and human realms, the tribal shaman. Several works of the last forty years focus on the close relation between Greek religion and the shamanistic cultures extending from the north of Greece into Thrace, Scythia, Siberia, Alaska and thence into the North American mainland.[8] Characteristic traits of the shaman identified in these sources include: bilocation, flying on an arrow, survival for long periods under the earth (suspended animation), androgyny, assuming the form of an oracular bird (usually a crow), and a prophesying head surviving the body after death.[9] The shaman's instruments include the lyre—fashioned of sheep gut and the carapace of the tortoise—the drum, and the rattle. What is most important about the shaman, however, is his ability to insinuate himself into the energy patterns of the complex web of life and death in which humans live. In this process he becomes a channel of divine energies, a conductor for the "peculiar mode of activity" that is the daimonic.[10] As this channel, he is an instrument for enacting sympathetic magic, the principle that, according to its adherents, holds together the universe. The phenomenon that I shall later call the "poet as instrument" (chapter 4) rests upon this same principle.

Based upon the widespread evidence of the Orpheus motif in North America, Europe, and northern Asia, Orpheus appears as a shamanic figure involved in a mission of retrieval of a lost or stolen soul.[11] The shaman is a Paleolithic figure, whose powers grow out of a highly individualistic spiritual culture rather than out of the collectivist Neolithic model, where the entire society is involved in the enactment of a ritual built around the ever-dying, ever-rising son and consort of the Mother Goddess.[12] In the latter, the survival of sun, seed, or savior is a resurrection miracle of world-shaking proportions. With the Orpheus motif, on the other hand, the underworld journey is a matter of simple retrieval; overcoming the forces of darkness and death to be sure, but with a modest goal on a personal scale. Though involving enchantment, the vulnerabliity, limitations, and even some bumbling comic aspects keep Orpheus close to the realm of human achievement and expectation. He is a magus, not a savior.

Bordering Greece on the north, Thrace (or Phrygia—modern Rumania), was always viewed by the Greeks with some suspicion as "wild." At the crossroads between West Asia, the northern "shamanistic" lands, and Mycenae and Greece to the south, it was a religio-cultural melting pot. Associated with Thrace, Orpheus is a figure in whom it is tempting to see a blending of northern shamanism, Mycenaean Dionysian religion, and the Apolline cult widely thought to have migrated from Lydia (modern Turkey). Whereas W. K. C. Guthrie sees him as an "Apolline missionary" sent north to quell the raging Dionysian cult that had enthralled the Thracians, the Greek habit of viewing him as something foreign, an "alien drop" in the Greek bloodstream as Erwin Rohde put it, seems to confirm that he is indeed a Thracian figure.[13] The views of E. R. Dodds and Mircea Eliade that he is an eponymous Thracian shaman who mediates Mycenean-West Asian religion and northern shamanism (viz., Dionysos and Apollo) seem to make the best sense. Several historical Greek figures may be viewed as belonging to the shamanist type, including Parmenides, Pythagoras[14] and Empedocles, whom Dodds calls "the last belated example of a species which . . . became extinct in the Greek world."[15] The Phrygian figures Abaris and Aristeas, however, have the most extensive documentation.[16] It is interesting that the first references to shamanistic possession appear in the sixth century, where Orpheus, with his singing head, turtle-lyre, and underworld journey, appears as one of numerous Phrygian figures. Some view him as a double of the Phyrgian daimonic/shamanic figure Zalmoxis.[17]

Jack Lindsay (*The Clashing Rocks*) sees a continuity in the shamanic tradition, with the tragedian building upon the prototype of the shaman. The tragedian is an ally of the pre-Olympian tribal groups ("Pelagians," among others) in contest with the Olympians and the advanced *polis*-forms.[18] His hero is an individualist of the "defiant shaman type" such as Prometheus, especially in Aeschylean tragedy. To Lindsay, the shamanistic experience is

the initiation-experience of the Mysteries raised to a higher inten-
sity.[19] The Mysteries are then the common link between the Paleolithic shaman and the tragedian of the classic age.[20] They also
link the shamanistic cultures with the philosophy of Plato, as we
shall see in the next chapter.

The shaman, originally a possessed instrument of the spirit (the
divine afflatus), develops a "bifocal consciousness," so that he
becomes the interpreter (*choros*) for them.[21] As Lindsay puts it,
the shaman becomes a tragedian when "possession becomes
poetry."[22] But the two states continue to exist side by side, creating a tension experienced within the consciousness of the Orphic
poet, a tension that grows out of what Lindsay calls the "shamanist contradiction": "The shaman feels himself a wholly free and
independent person; yet he is at the same time nothing but the
mouthpiece of forces beyond himself."[23] Or in the words of the
Odyssean bard Phemios, "I am selftaught. The god has implanted
in my heart songs of all kinds."[24]

In conclusion, Lindsay notes that at the end of the classical
period the "old shamanist power" remains in only two roles: the
Dionysiac missionary and the poet-musician.[25] These are precisely the two separate traditions which Guthrie and Ake
Hultkrantz see combining in the figure of Orpheus: the religious
reformer and the legend. The two figures come together via the
common element of incantation (*epoidos*). This term is related to
the archaic Odyssean word *oima*, designating "song as way,"[26]
linking the older tribal shaman with the lyric and dramatic poet
of the classical era. Thus the voyage of the shaman, the initiatory
spirit-journey into the underworld through a narrow and harrow-
ing passage (the "clashing rocks"—*symplegades*—of his title) is a
song-way. Lindsay sees the voyage of the *Argo* as a shamanic journey which probably rests upon the oldest stratum of Greek pre-
history. Orpheus, whose voice and lyre provide the *oima*, or later,
epoidos that leads the band through the clashing rocks (compare
the "horns of dilemma" motif), appears then to be a very ancient
figure.[27]

Lindsay's association of the lyric dramatist with the Dionysian dithyramb suggests that the tragedian carries the spirit of

tribal shamanism into the classical era. But Mircea Eliade rejects the view that sees Dionysos in association with shamanism. For him the shaman is Apolline, not Dionysian. Following Guthrie and Dodds, Eliade sees Apollo originating in the northern shamanic belt, coming down into Greece via Scythia and Phrygia. He is thus Hyperborean, descending from "ultra-north," the place where he retreats from Delphi every winter. Apollo shares some of the characteristics of the shamanic figures Abaris, Musaios, Aristeas, and Zalmoxis, including traveling on an arrow and bearing a lyre fashioned of turtle's carapace and sheep-gut. But he does not manifest other shamanic aspects: bilocation, survival of long terms under the earth, and the prophesying head.

Dionysos shares even fewer shamanic qualities, though the drum—which is part of the Phrygian mode, associated in the classical era with Dionysos—suggests a connection between the god and the northern shamanic cultures. But the consensus of religious historians is that Apollo comes from Asia Minor (Lydia), Dionysos from Mycenaea, and therefore that neither is from the shamanic north—though Apollo may well pass through that territory en route to Greece. Again, some see Zalmoxis and Dionysos/Zagreus as the same god, placing Dionysos at once above and below Greece. What makes most sense to me is that Orpheus as shamanic figure, though appearing in the Greek records relatively late, antedates both of these gods. That he is a mediating figure—as in Guthrie's calling him an "Apolline missionary" to the Phrygians and their cults of Dionysos/Zalmoxis, or in Lindsay's remark about the link between the shamanic figure and the "Dionysian missionary"—need not be contested. He *is* a medial figure, but not necessarily one newly hatched. Like Phanes and Eros, he is a link between the oldest and the newest. This is in accord with the views of both Cornford and Burkert, who see the religious phenomenon called "Orphism" as the revival of an ancient religion as well as a reformation.[28]

Orpheus as Melding of Old and New

As noted above, at every point of Orpheus's history, both in the earliest appearances and in subsequent revivals, he represents the old and the new at once.[29] Thus he becomes a major figure in

the era of Hellenistic syncretism as the reputed author of the so-
called Orphic theogonies, as a latter-day Moses and as the Greek
incarnation of Hermes Trismegistus.[30] In the Christian Era he
becomes the pacific shepherd, a type or double for Christ. In the
Renaissance, he is the magus, both the model operator of
Ficino's "natural magic"[31] and the principal figure (along with
Eurydice) in the spectacular rise of the opera in the first decade
of the seventeenth century in Florence. He and Eurydice reap-
pear as figures of the love-death in the Romantic era, after which
they undergo a continual development into the modern era, as
the themes of love, death, and night are replaced by the act of
creation/sacrifice by the Orphic poet out of the void: Mallarmé's
Néant. This final transposition will be the focus of the latter half
of this book. Our task now, however, is to get a glimpse of
Orpheus in his fifth century context.

The Greek fifth century

The fifth century was a time of enormous strife and revolutionary change. Along with a political situation dominated by civil
war "absolutely unprecedented in its savagery: city against city,
man against man, father against son,"[32] with accompanying atroc-
ities, including possibly the first instance of genocide, traditional
myth underwent a rapid decline as carrier of what Gilbert Murray called the "Inherited Conglomerate." The old integrated culture disentegrated, supplanted by the arts of the Sophist,
including criticism of the gods, the installation of theogonies
that rivaled Hesiod's, and the invention of new myths.[33] *Nomoi*,
the traditional laws that governed human behavior, came to be
seen as human inventions subject to change, not the inalterable
decrees of the gods. Though not in the first generation or so, this
eventually opened the way to atheism, which was one of the consequences of the invasion of Athens by Protagoras (450 B.C.), who
brought the Sophist's ruthless mode of questioning, following the
strict antithetical thinking of Parmenides, into the center of the
polis. In this climate of changing allegiances, the Sophists entered
as hired teachers, each offering his *logos* as the best to advance
the careers of young men. The new agon became that between
the rival *logoi* of the Sophists. Plato's invention of the *philosophos*
came against this background of shifting loyalties.

Orpheus between Apollo and Dionysos

It is against this strife-ridden background that Orpheus makes his appearance. When the founder of the Orphic mysteries at Athens, Onomacritus, forges Orpheus's name upon some of the state theological documents, he goes beyond the Sophists in questioning the authority of the traditional gods, behaving more like one of the Orpheotelestai whom Plato excoriates in the *Phaedrus*. The theory that Orpheus was an imposter, a hoax perpetrated upon the state of Athens, has had many supporters ever since Wilamowitz studied the evidence for his existence and found it severely wanting. I also see something of a trickster element in Orpheus, and as such he plays the role of mediator, a hybrid figure between Apollo and Dionysos.

We recognize these gods as divinities with whom whole realms of being came to be identified: Apollo as the Olympian principle and Dionysos as the chthonian. Something like this characterization of Apollo and Dionysos recurs in Nietzsche's *Birth of Tragedy*, though the general model reaches back at least to Plutarch, with recrudescences in Robert Fludd, Marsilio Ficino, and Friedrich Schelling.[34] But in the fifth century, these divisions were not so obvious. It was during this time that a remarkable *rapprochement* occurred between the increasingly popular cult of Dionysos and the established cult of Apollo at Delphi. The grave of Dionysos was reputed to have been moved to Delphi, within one hundred feet of the oracle itself. During the winter months during which Apollo went on his retreat to Hyperborea, the *dithyrambos* was sung at Delphi, replacing the Apolline paean. A vase painting from about 400 B.C. shows the two gods holding out their hands to one another.[35] Macrobius recorded two striking instances of their mingling in fragments from Aeschylus and Euripides. Aeschylus speaks of Apollo "the ivied, the Bacchic, the prophet"; and Euripides invokes "Lord Bacchos lover of the bay, Paean Apollo of the tuneful lyre."[36] Orpheus's concurrent appearance at their meeting point in Phrygia is for many related to this *rapprochement*, which is how I view Guthrie's remarks on Orpheus as an "Apolline missionary" to the Thracians.

In order to understand Orpheus as the figure who arises as the *limen* of their respective domains—both in the classical Greek context and in the later context (chapter 3) as the missing third or ignored moment in Nietzsche's formulation of the contrariety Apollo-Dionysos—it is important to attempt a brief sketch of the place of these gods in the Greek fifth century. I will then proceed to give a summary of the legend of Orpheus, noting where Apollo and Dionysos enter into it, followed by a review of the ways in which Orpheus may be seen as their mediator. Finally, I will end this section with a comparison of Orpheus and Dionysos as foreshadowing the analogous relation between Mallarmé and Nietzsche.

Apollo

Apollo's worship has at least three prehistoric components: Dorian-northwest Greek, Cretan-Minoan, and Syro-Hittite. The Greek habit of viewing him as coming from Lydia-Anatolia reflects the latest of these three.[37] In the earlier pre-Greek form, Apellon, he is closely tied to the *apellai,* annual gatherings of the tribe or phratry, including one at Delphi, which grew to be one of his two great, Panhellenic cult centers. He is intimately associated with one of the most important actions taken at these men's gatherings: the initiation of youths who have come of age.[38] In this respect, he is quite similar to his twin sister Artemis, who is associated with the initiation of girls into womanhood. Apollo's patronage of the initiation of adolescent males broadened in the classical era to include athletic and musical contests as well. As modeled in the *kouros,* he emblemizes the Greek worship of youthful beauty, poised on the threshhold of manhood.

Apollo has special renown as an archer, which is another feature he shares with Artemis. She, however, is goddess of the hunt, whereas Apollo's bow is twinned with the lyre. Like the lyre, the bow sings when plucked; like the bow, the lyre flings its arrow-songs unerringly at their targets.[39] In contrast with Artemis, who is goddess of wild nature, Apollo is a city-god; his lyre "sang the stones into place" at Troy. One of Apollo's most common epithets is "striking from afar," which characterizes both his death-dealing arrows and the reach of his healing paeans. But though he was god of healing, he was also the sender of plague. Writers of antiquity spoke of the sweetness of death by his silver arrows. His distance, reserve, and aloofness are key characteristics and mark him as opposite to Dionysos, who gets painfully close to his worshippers.[40]

Apollo is the great lawgiver of Magna Graecia, concerned, as W. K. C. Guthrie says, with the "statutory aspects of religion."[41] More than any other god, he is Panhellenic, and his oracle at Delphi was consulted as arbitrator of many a dispute. Via his oracle, he was the promulgator of legal code, but Delphi was also consulted with regard to such basic matters as where to found cities. The oracle at Delphi was an archaic shrine of Earth (Gaia) where he supplanted her by slaying the Python, though he retained the prophetess (Pythia) who proclaimed the oracle. He was preceded by a goddess at his other cult-center, too: the island of Delos, site of his birth by Leto, where his twin Artemis ruled before him (and assisted at his birth, since she was there first).[42]

As lawgiver, Apollo has an even older and deeper connection to the rules concerning homicide: how the attendant pollution (*miasma*) from such an act could be ritually purified. This concern for purification (*katharsis*) reinforces his association with the purity of the young initiate; *katharsis* is a way to return to the earlier condition of purity after it is lost. Apollo himself makes an annual retreat to the mythical land of the Hyperboreans, in the far north whence he supposedly came, as a kind of ritual renewal of his purity.[43] The society of Pythagoras, with its elaborate set of regulations to assure purity in every aspect of life, is perhaps an extreme example of an "Apolline" society.

Pythagoras's work with mathematics, music, and harmony is also characteristically Apolline. Though other gods have hymns and various connections to music, Apollo is *the* musical god par excellence. Harmony, balance, proportion, moderation: these are all qualities that we tend to think of as quintessentially Greek, yet they are more especially hallmarks of the Apolline. Around the sixth century, a series of injunctions were recorded on the walls of the temple that encode his values. They include these two: "nothing in excess" and "know thyself." The latter connotes not what it came to mean after Socrates but simply "know thy nature"; that is, know your limits as a human being. In this sense, it is Apollo who defines the key Greek notion of *sophrosyne*.[44] Apollo's limits, however, are simply those of the visible universe. With characteristic reverence, Walter Otto speaks of Apollo in his aspect as sun god (after the epithet *Phoebus*), paraphrasing the *Orphic Hymns* and Skythinnus to form the magnificent image of Apollo holding the universe together with the tones of his lyre, his solar rays acting as the plectrum.[45]

Dionysos

Though scarcely mentioned in Homer, Dionysos is an even older deity in the Greek context than Apollo; he is mentioned in Linear B, the Minoan alphabet found at Pylos which is the oldest deciphered record we have of Greek speech. Here he is already associated with wine, which remained central to his identity. Other data attesting to his early appearance in Greece include the following: a cult shrine dedicated to him at Keos since 1500; an association with the Anthesteria (one of his chief festivals) common to both the Athenians and Ionians, indicating that he predated the Ionian migration, and the exceedingly ancient form of the *dithyrambos*, the characteristic hymn to the god.[46] Before Linear B was deciphered, his absence from Homer was interpreted to mean that his cult had not become very well established in Greece in the archaic era, but now the sense is that this absence reflects a class difference. Apollo is a god of the nobler class, whereas Dionysos is a god of the common folk (especially the women), and Homer writes for, and thus portrays, the former.[47] In the era with which we are concerned, the sixth to fifth centuries, Dionysos is always seen as an invader, a foreign intruder. Guthrie thinks that the whole group of myths having to do with Dionysos's disruptive entry into cities and villages, challenging the local authorities to admit his cult, is aetiological, following the path of his westward course from Asia and Phrygia.[48] The pattern is one of refusal, followed by Dionysos's turning the women into raving Maenads who occasionally hunt down and destroy their own children. This is the model which Euripides gives in the *locus classicus* for Dionysos, *The Bacchae* (first performed about 400). The extraordinary phenomenon of the Maenads—adult women who heed the call of his drum and *aulos*, leaving their husbands and children to join in rituals of catching, tearing apart (*sparagmos*), and tasting the raw flesh (omophagia) of young wild creatures—is one of his most characteristic touches.

In their complementary aspect, the women (also called "Thyiades"), were nurses to the infant Dionysos, Dionysos Liknites, who was carried in procession in a *liknon* (linen-covered basket) as the "heart" that Athena had saved from the Titans' omophagia during his spring festival, the Anthesteria. As part of this rite, one of the Thyiades lifted the cover of the basket to revive the infant god by performing an "unspeakable act" (*arrheton*).[49] A similar kind of *hieros gamos* at the Anthesteria at Athens was the ritual marriage of the city's queen, the Basilinna, with Dionysos in the god's cave-temple on the city's outskirts.[50] Only a priestess could accompany the Basilinna into the god's inner chamber, where their ritual union was also "unspeakable."[51]

The Anthesteria (Ionia/Attica) was the chief festival of Dionysos and the site of one of his most famous mysteries. It was preceded by the Lenaia, specifically dedicated to the new wine crop, and like all of the Dionysian festivals, an intoxicated period of license, precursor of the Roman carnival. This pair formed the first of four basic Greek festivals dedicated to Dionysos. The Agrionia (Dorian/Aelolic) was a time of dissolution and inversion. This festival commemorated the Minyades, who, after refusing Dionysos's worship were maddened by the god, ending with the murder of one of their own children, Hippasus, son of Leucippe.[52] The birth of Dionysos at Thebes is also associated with this regional festival.[53] The rustic Dionysia was commemorated by the sacrifice of a goat, a phallic procession, and a satyr-play. The antics of this lighter festival formed the basis of comedy.[54] The Greater Dionysia, Katagogia, was a commemoration of the god's advent by boat from the sea, also celebrated in Athens.

In addition to these state festivals, there were private, localized *orgia*, which were trieteric, that is celebrated every other year. Carl Kerenyi gives a fascinating account explaining these *orgia* as tied to the cycle of Sirius, the Dog Star. Their beginning was signaled by the first rays of the star entering the Idaen birth-cave of Zeus/Zagreus in early July.[55]

Central to Dionysos is his identification with the procreative element: he is wet with the sap of the evergreen, the juice of the vine, and sperm.[56] He is the Greek version of the dying-rising god and as such is beautifully fitted for his burgeoning role in the sixth century as a mystery-god.[57] He also enacts the identity wine = blood, playing a double role as the wine coming from the death of the grape, and the infant king who rises up anew (phallically) after *sparagmos*. In the myth of his second birth from Zeus's thigh, there are overtones of castration and death (issuing from a "thigh wound"—where thigh is euphemistic of genitals) as well as of homoeroticism.[58]

Walter Otto, whose *Dionysus: Myth and Cult* defines, in Guthrie's words, the "German" Dionysos at the same time as providing his latest cult document, speaks of Dionysos as *der kommende Gott*: "the god who comes."[59] He emphasizes the unpredictability of the god and an underlying connection with madness. Otto sees Dionysos's arrival and departure as sudden, best symbolized by the accompanying din and silence. For him the Phrygian, which was the Dionysian mode, was binary, characterized by the juxtaposition of shrieks and silence. We will presently see an excellent example of this in the "concerto" by which Orpheus dies. As the "god who comes," also called the "loosener," Dionysos is at the other extreme from Apollo. Apollo is always distant and aloof, the god of boundaries.[60] Dionysos is a destroyer of boundaries; he erupts into the center of the lives of his followers, getting into their blood.

Summary of the Orpheus myth

The interplay between Dionysos and Apollo, with Orpheus as a kind of mediator, may be seen in the following summary of the main lines of the legend of Orpheus. As I shall note in enumerating the mythemes, I am including some of the material which was first "fixed" in Virgil and Ovid, thus expanding the nexus of the myth beyond the fifth to fourth centuries. Though there is some disagreement about the era in which Eurydice first appears, and more disagreement over the reasons Orpheus shuns the company of women after his unsuccessful bid to rescue her, these differences are far less profound than the scholarly disagreement over the existence of Orphism and the authorship of the Orphic theogonies, as we shall see below.

1. Orpheus is born of Kalliope and Oiagros (in some versions, Apollo is his father). Kalliope is a Muse, "she of the beautiful voice." The Muses live high on the slopes of Olympus and are associated with Apollo. Oiagros was a river god but also king of Thrace, home of the religion of Dionysos. His father Charops was a pupil of Dionysos.

2. Orpheus is paired with Eurydice (Eurydike, "the wide-ruling" [Jane Harrison]), interpreted as a variant of Persephone but sometimes seen simply as a dryad (tree spirit). By some accounts, they have a son, Musaios. In other accounts, Musaios is Orpheus's father. (Musaios is widely mentioned as a religious reformer and shaman, but these accounts are independent of stories containing Orpheus.)

3. In a famous episode, Orpheus charms the forest beasts, the trees, and the birds—even the stones—who all gather round him transfixed by his singing, as he accompanies himself on the lyre. The lyre is from Apollo (who got it in turn from Hermes). In all the ancient depictions (primarily vase paintings) his head is thrust back as he sings, as if in ecstasy. This episode is repeated in the accounts of the voyage of the *Argo*, where it is the seabirds and dolphins that he charms.

4. Eurydice, chased by Aristeas (a beekeeper, aligned with Apollo), steps on a viper, which bites her on the heel, and she dies. A sorrowful Orpheus persuades Hermes to lead him into the underworld in an effort to bring her back (Virgil).

5. Once in the realm of Hades, Orpheus again takes out his lyre and sings, moving everyone to tears. Sisyphos sits on his rock, transfixed. Ixion's wheel stops turning. The Danaides' leaky vase stops overflowing. For the first time, the Fates cry. Hades and Persephone are persuaded to release the shade of Eurydice, but on condition that Orpheus not look back at her until he reaches earth again. As Orpheus, Eurydice, and Hermes approach the upper world, Orpheus, thinking to have lost her, turns around for reassurance, whereupon Hermes turns to guide her back, this time forever. After losing Eurydice a second time, Orpheus is griefstricken.

6. As a consequence, he goes into "celibate" retirement, "shunning the company of women." He climbs Mount Pangaion daily to worship Apollo as Helios. The Thracian women complain that he has lured away their warrior-husbands (Aeschylus *Bassarides* fragment).[61]

7. While these warriors are worshipping inside Apollo's temple, their angry wives—turned Maenads—steal their husbands' weapons, piled outside the temple, and assault Orpheus.[62] He continues to sing, warding off the first blows, but they overpower his music with their own wild Phrygian shrieking, piping, and

clapping; then they kill him with stones, spears, and in some versions, agricultural implements they have taken from workers in
fields nearby.

8. The Maenads then tear him to pieces in a ritual *sparagmos*, throwing the body parts in the sea (or they are retrieved by
the Muses, who bury them) while the head and lyre float down
the Hebrus, eventually landing on Lesbos. There the lyre rests in
the sanctuary of Apollo, the head at the shrine of Dionysos.

9. The head continues to prophesy, until Apollo, made jealous by this intrusion on his function, silences it (usually by burial). When it first arrives, however, he saves it from being
swallowed by a snake, which he strikes to stone, its mouth agape.
Eventually the lyre makes its way to the heavens, where it
becomes the constellation Lyra.

10. Dionysus angrily pursues the fleeing Maenads, spelling
them into a grove of trees. (Mythologems 7–10, all Ovid).

From this summary account, one can see that Dionysos and
Apollo are involved with the myth of Orpheus from the begin-
ning. As son of Oiagros, he is associated with Dionysos, who
taught Oiagros's father Charops. Rival versions, though, have
Apollo as his father (occasionaly even Musaios, his apocryphal
son, is given as the father, doubling the connection with the
Muses, who are traditionally associated with Apollo). Under
Orpheus's spell, the Thracian warriors and their wives exchange
places, the men going off pacifically to worship at the temple of
Apollo, while their wives steal their weapons (and perhaps the
leopard skins with which the wild Thracians are typically
depicted, thus assuming the Maenad costume) as they storm by
on their way to murder Orpheus.[63] Supposedly, says Aeschylus,
they are angry because Orpheus, spurning women since his
unsuccessful descent, has led their warriors into homosexuality (I
will return to this important aspect shortly). From here on, the
dialectic of the Apolline and the Dionysian becomes intertwined
increasingly thickly. The story of Orpheus's death is the enactment of a concerto: the solo voice, accompanied by the lyre
(often used for the stately Dorian mode, associated with Apollo)
against the concerted performance of the Maenads: shrieking,
drumming, sometimes wailing on the *aulos*, in the Phrygian
mode.[64]

As murderers of Orpheus by ritual *sparagmos*, the Maenads treat him as their lord and prey. In the manner of his death, Orpheus reveals his underlying kinship with Dionysos. And with Ovid's finishing touches, his head and lyre float down the Hebrus until coming to rest on Lesbos at the shrine of Dionysos. But Dionysos's turning the Maenads into a grove of trees (a "Phrygian" silencing—see note 64) as punishment for their crime indicates a continuing differentiation from the pacific lyrist. Strangest of all, we have the detail of Apollo's appearing at *Dionysos'* shrine to save Orpheus from the yawning jaws of a huge serpent, echoing the motif by which Apollo secures Delphi. But later, returning to command Orpheus's head to silence, he seems to have changed his mind. It almost seems as if, in these final movements, Apollo and Dionysos are in collusion—which is exactly the point. Later, in the context of Schelling, Schopenhauer, and Nietzsche, we will see Orpheus as the reconciliation of opposites—that is, as Nietzsche suggests, of Apollo as the *principium individuationis* and Dionysos as the primal chthonic ground, the *Ur-Eine*. Here, though, what we seem to have is a subtle kind of cult battle.

Orpheus and Dionysos

Though Orpheus is widely seen as mediator of these two gods and their realms, he is usually interpreted as being closer to Dionysos. Genealogy and burial place are two cardinal aspects informing us of the essential nature of Greek heroes and *daimones,* and each of these indicates a deep likeness between Orpheus and Dionysos. However, as Jane Harrison says, "Orpheus reflects Dionysos, but at almost every point seems to contradict him."[65] There is something in Orpheus's nature that is perverse, in a way that Dionysos, as seed, sap, and sexual fluid, can never be. Nietzsche speaks of the triumph in Greek tragedy of saying "yes to life" as an essentially Dionysian phenomenon.

In *Eros and Civilization*, Herbert Marcuse speaks of two essentially different culture-heroes: Prometheus, the proud, assertive yea-sayer, stealing the gods' energies, and Orpheus, author of the Great Refusal.[66] To Marcuse, Orpheus's homophilia is as foundational as Prometheus's theft of fire, establishing a particular pattern of sublimation modeled upon the refusal of Dionysos's gifts. One might call this refusal an inversion, to take

up Freud's term for the homosexual. "Invert" is usually seen as
yet another dated Freudian misnomer, but in this case, it seems
apt—particularly if one gives credence to Marcuse's theory. It also
fits the structuralist interpretation (see note 63): Orpheus's
actions may be seen as a series of *inversions* that mediate Dionysos/
Apollo, male/female, tame/wild, and so forth.[67]

Orphism and the Orphic Theogonies

A few twentieth-century scholars have believed there actually was
a historical man named Orpheus. One is W. K. C. Guthrie, whose
book *Orpheus and Greek Religion* remains the basic, indispensable
survey of Orpheus and Orphism. Guthrie sees Orpheus as an
Apolline priest: a missionary who acts to calm the Dionysian cult,
whose strength in Phrygia had begun to alarm Attic peoples. Jane
Harrison's belief in Orpheus included accepting his followers'
claims that he was a cosmogonic poet. Most scholars, however, do
not find evidence for a historical Orpheus, reading him as a hero
of legend, perhaps shamanic.

The significant argument, however, is not over the identity
of the figure but over the existence of a bona fide religious movement called "Orphism." The word *Orphism* is a neologism,
coined, according to Brian Juden, by Nietzsche's friend Rohde
(*Psyche*).[68] Here is the issue: is the group of attitudes and activi-
ties, however loosely organized, designated by the term also a late
invention? The chief positions here are represented by Guthrie,
who argued for the presence of such a movement in the fifth to
fourth centuries, and Ivan Linforth, whose *Arts of Orpheus* (1941),
following Wilamowitz, presents a minimalist case, concluding
that the amorphous body of beliefs called "Orphism" was a
"rumor": merely the fabrication of neoplatonists of the Hellenistic and subsequent eras (including those of Proclus an entire
milennium later).[69]

However, if there was no such thing as "Orphism"—and I do
not hold the sword with which to cut through the tangle of arguments—there were *Orphicoi*, "orphic folk," and *Orpheotelestai* (wandering priests), who carried around trinkets, amulets, stock
prayers, and the like, which they sold to (usually) poor people—
much like mendicant friars peddling medals of St. Sebastian. And

there were also the trappings of a cult. Unlike the traditional Greek cults, anchored to the graves of heroes, oracles, and the like, the *Orphicoi* had manuals and hymnbooks in which their hero was said to have written praises of the gods and new cosmogonies. This made the (presumed) cult more portable and more open to revision and reflective thought during moments other than the administration of *teletai*. It also contributed to its democratization, something that it had in common with the cult of Dionysos (the god overseeing telestic madness).[70]

Associated with this Orphic religion, one strand of a "protestant" movement in the fifth to fourth century that accompanied the greatest changes in religious life and belief that Greece had known, were rewritten cosmogonies and an Orphic anthropogony, "neatly explaining to the devotee why he felt wicked and guilty."[71] The Orphic theogonies are mostly known to us by the compilation of hymn fragments called the "Rhapsodic Theogony," recorded in the first century B.C. (henceforth called "Rhapsodies"). Though these have long been criticized as later interpolations along the lines of those perpetrated by Orpheus's priest Onomacritus, the relatively recent discovery of the Derveni papyrus (at Thessaloniki in the sixties) has pushed back the dates of known compilations of Orphic theogonies to at least the middle of the fifth century.[72] They are widely accepted as rival theogonies to the canonical theogonic poem of Hesiod. Details vary, but the main lines and most replicated details are given in the Rhapsodies, which will form the basis for my summary. Though Orpheus as a mythic figure is more significant to my study, there are nonetheless elements of these Orphic theogonies that bear upon my thesis as well and, in fact, give glimpses of occasional unity between what are widely perceived to be disparate subjects: Orpheus the lyric enchanter and Orphism, displayed in part via the theogonies. Knowledge of both is necessary background for reading Plato and Mallarmé as "Orphic" poets.

Nyx, Phanes, the primal egg

The chief, striking difference between Hesiod and the Rhapsodic Theogony is that the universe begins with Nyx (Night), who plays a pivotal position. A birdlike creature with huge black wings, she lays the original Orphic egg "in the lap of darkness."[73] As the uncreated original, she thus takes the place of Chaos in Hesiod. After the birth of Eros/Phanes, hatched from the egg, she receives his scepter. Only Night can then see Phanes, the "shining" who appears in the space between the two halves of the shell, the *aither* above and the gulf below (which later become sky and earth, Uranos and Gaia) for there is nobody else to perceive him. She is the "nurse of the gods," two generations later becoming counselor to Zeus, who begs her advice on how to reconcile the "one and the many" (admittedly a problem more philosophical than practical, indicating the "hidden agenda" of the Orphic reformers). Nyx advises him to swallow Phanes (all of visible creation) and, after "mingling" its elements with his own organs, to regurgitate the whole anew (looking ahead to Mallarmé, a *retrempe*, "re-saturation"). This is the cardinal solution to the Orphic cosmogonists' desire that he become the demiurge, the connecting link between the reigns of Night and the Orphic Dionysos who succeeded Zeus. But though she becomes a powerful, pivotal figure in the *Rhapsodies*, Nyx is left behind when Zeus swallows Eros.[74]

Dionysos and the Titans

The concern over demiurgy, then, unites Eros/Phanes and the infant Dionysos on his throne in the Idaen cave, bequeathed to him by the father who bore him from his thigh. This sets the stage for the second key shift in Greek myth wrought by "Orpheus," the anthropogony. For no sooner does the infant Dionysos, the *Orphic* Dionysos, mount his throne than the *kouretes*, white-faced daimonic male dancing figures, turn upon the infant and redirect their din, originally protective, at their infant lord.[75] The guardian *kouretes* have become bloodthirsty Titans who divert him with toys and then kill him. While he is enthralled by a mirror, they rip him apart, roast him, boil him, and then eat him. Thus Dionysos, the shuddering progenitor, the "loosener," is reduced in the Orphic version to an infant tricked into death by the play of a mirror. This sparagmos and omophagia of Dionysos is followed by Zeus's enraged destruction of the Titans by a lightning stroke. According to Pausanius, he fabricated man from clay (*titanos*) and their remaining ashes. The human is thus a radically "mixed" creature, part Titan, part divine.[76]

What is common to all of these revised accounts (exempting the traditional one, the *dromenon* at the *liknon*; see note 76) is that the male demiurge tries to assert a power similar to parthenogenesis, celebrating his dual potency as progenitor as well as vessel for birth. Thus Zeus bears two of his most beloved offspring, Athena and Dionysos, from his own body and, in a detail of the Derweni papyrus, appears to swallow the phallus of Uranos after Kronos has "done a great deed" to him. According to this version, instead of Kronos swallowing his own children (the Hesiodic account-with Zeus hid away in the ever-handy cave), Zeus swallows the severed genitals of his grandfather and thereby gains the procreative power of the entire universe and its gods.[77]

A Model: Momentary Gods, Functional Gods, and *Theoi*

In closing this chapter, I will return to Cassirer to look at the phenomenological sequence in which the gods appear, for his model in *Language and Myth* will help us to structure the relationships among Orpheus, Dionysos, and Apollo. There, Cassirer summarizes the stages of development of the gods in the work of the religious historian Usener.[78] The first stage of this development is the experience of *Augenblicksgötter*, "momentary gods," objectifications of a fleeting, though powerful experience of *religiosum*. Such deities exist only in the "one indivisible moment," and only for the one experiencing subject.[79] These atoms of religious experience are similar to Jane Harrison's *erotes* and *keres*, localized *daimones* flitting about a certain place, the Greek forebears of the *genius loci*, the Roman spirit of place.[80] Usener's formulation in terms of moment emphasizes time over place, though *occasional poetry*, the matrix through which the Greek lyric poets commemorated notable occasions in the life of the *polis*, unites both senses.[81]

Cassirer goes on to report two more strata of deities from Usener's research, *Sondergötter*, "functional gods,"[82] and finally *theoi*, gods with proper names, where the god is not merely a function but capable of independent action and exhibits a personality. In each of these steps there is an accretion in sphere of influence. The name of a deity, while first denoting function, governing the hearth, the harvest, marriage, and so on, comes over time to lose the exclusivity of that function, taking on other nuances of meaning until a "new Being" is produced, one that continues to develop by a "law of its own."[83] Though exclusivity of function ceases for these last deities, they are nevertheless subject to necessity: each must follow its own law. Thus each *theos* in the Greek pantheon has a particular quality and style as well as sphere of operation. These spheres often overlap (and the human can be caught between gods, as was Hippolytus, for example), but the styles do not. When the poets named the gods, as Herodotus put it, they were fixing a style, a tone, a mood as much as anything else. Naming the god is not arbitrary; it requires a grasp of something essential about that *theos*, a law of its being. One might speak of the gods as *modes*. A mode is a law (*nomos*), for a way of being. Though apprehended in language, it is a "force of nature" to use Schopenhauer's expression.[84]

The Daimonic

Like the gods, the members of the vegetable and animal kingdoms function modally: they are one thing and can act only according to its laws. Their behavior is fixed and repetitive. With human beings, and with beings between the human and the divine, what modern biology calls "fixed drive-states" are no longer operative.[85] Instead we have the *daimonic*. The daimonic has to do with the ability to move between modes. It has tremendous range and suppleness, what the Neoplatonists loved to call "plastic." The archetypal *daimon* is the great god Eros, who fills the entire universe, having as he does the potential to interconnect all of its parts. As more local powers he is the *erotes*, little winged carriers of the contagion "love." The latter are much more like Baroque "cupids," except that they are thin and supple ("wasplike" to Jane Harrison's imagination), rather than dumpy and cute. As special cases, the gods Hermes and Dionysus, each in his own way, function daimonically. Hermes, for instance, is the very principle of hidden connection. He is the "god of ways," patron of merchant and thief alike, as well as god of boundaries, including that between public and private space in the form of the phallic "herm," the original door-knocker. More especially, he is a psychopomp, guide of souls bound for Hades.

Still another class of *daimon* is the "demigod." In this group are border creatures like the blind seer Tiresias, as well as heroes, including both Herakles and Oedipus. Orpheus is part of this group. In her *Prolegomena*, Jane Harrison speaks of the movement in the Hellenistic era away from the classical *theoi* and back into *daimones* as more supple figures of the divine energies.[86] Something like this continues to be the case in the modern age. Our century has a peculiar affinity for the daimonic figure, ranging from Oedipus and Tiresias to Orpheus, and as such seems to be a continuation of Mallarmé's "interregnum": an age between the gods' banishment and dubious return.[87] The daimonic, appearing as these demigods, is a recognizably human entity; not divine, but bordering upon it. When Nietzsche spoke of the "death of God," he spoke prophetically of the rapid decline of a particular image of the divine. But the divine spirit feverishly continued to seek channels for expression, one of which was the *daimon* Friedrich Nietzsche. Another was Orpheus/Mallarmé. This last figure unites the full range from "momentary god"[88] to Orpheus as a protean god-in-formation, ever a "new myth": unfinished, tentative, prospective. As the figure in the evanescent moment, he unites that "one indivisible moment" with the divine spirit of immanence that the daimonic alone can provide.[89]

Do not be misled by "immanence," though. What is indwelling is not a montheistic deity but the *daimon* as an implicit fatality. As Herakleitos put it, character is destiny (*daimon*), and destiny is character. It was Nietzsche who restated the archaic Greek sense given in Pindar's epigraph: "Become the thing that you are." This sense of an indwelling fatality—indeed, an *entelechy*—is perhaps the most important sense of *daimon*. One's fate is given as a kind of seed wrapped in one's physical vessel, a kind of homunculus: a destiny that, if fully lived, becomes a new being. Schopenhauer spoke of each human being as a new species. By following one's own *daimon*, a person becomes that divine thing, a human being who fulfills his or her own law. This, as Nietzsche continually reminds us, is an instinct, not a cultural law (*nomos*). In this sense, its realization is similar to that of a *theos*: it follows the law of its nature and can do no other. The key difference, though, is that whereas the god-modality defines an entire world, the inner law (*daimon*) of the individual projects one solitary fated path. In the Greek (and Nietzschean) sense, one consciously *embraces* this destiny, relentlessly seeking it out (as King Oedipus does). Nietzsche's term for this quality is *amor fati*: loving one's fate. This is the sense of himself proclaimed at the head of his last work, *Ecce Homo*: "Why I am a destiny."[90]

Following the basic and somewhat simplified pattern of the daimonic as the way between modes, Orpheus may be construed as a *daimon* moving between the realms of Apollo and Dionysos. Though Nietzsche's characterization of their realms deviates in some major ways from that of the classical era, I will use it as a frame setting the stage for the appearance of Orpheus/Mallarmé. For that "moment" as I call it—although it is steeped in the entire tradition of Orpheus from his earliest appearance—is recontextualized by the Nietzschean restatement of the forces involved in Greek tragedy as "music" in *The Birth of Tragedy from the Spirit of Music*. The life of Orpheus/Mallarmé also manifests a progressive acceptance of the poet's destiny: the poet learned to accept his fate to lie awake every night, the furniture writhing before his fevered mind. Like Nietzsche, Mallarmé learned to love his fate and to "become the thing that [he was]."

But with the appearance of Orpheus as an oscillation, the moment of the return of the scythe of history in the fin de siècle atmosphere of Nietzsche and Mallarmé, we have jumped far ahead to another reversal of the sort that Plato described in the *Politicus*: the myth of the reabsorption of the race, growing backwards into its mother, the earth.[91] Characterizing and following the shape of this oscillation in Mallarmé will be the chief concern of this work. However, I want initially to sketch the Orphic turn as it appears in Plato. For, as Guthrie says, it is chiefly through his works that we learn of Orpheus.

Plato's Orphic Universe   2

> That which differs with itself is in agreement: harmony consists
> of opposing tension, like that of the bow and the lyre.
>   —Herakleitos

Attunement

In the *Phaedo* Socrates argues against the widely held belief that
the soul is an attunement, insisting that the materials of the soul—
the instrument, its strings, and their untuned notes—are all prior
to the attunement, and therefore that the attunement is a "composite" thing growing out of a prior unity. Though as always
Socrates carries the day (in this last discourse before his execu-
tion by the state of Athens for consorting with strange gods), I
am not convinced by this particular argument. The image of
human souls being in some way "attuned" or rhythmically
ordered, then undergoing a fouling of pitch, rhythm or harmony,
is too pervasive in Plato's writings to leave the matter as politely
as Socrates' grieving disciples do on this last morning.[1] Socrates'
implicit alternative image—an inert untuned instrument—is so far
from exhibiting the vitalism of an eternally living substance that
I must mark it as one of the more awkward casualites of Socratic
dialectical victory.

    It is not Socrates' logic that I question here but rather his
negligence toward a fundamental aspect of the life of the soul in
the human universe, one that Herakleitos suggests with his image
of the bow and the lyre. The body, seen by the Orphics as the
soul's prison, is also its house or temple; and with its skeleton and
sinews (and the marvelous sounding chambers of the head and
chest) forms a kind of instrument, which Shakespeare's remark,

"For Orpheus' lute was strung with poets' sinews," attests so forcefully. The very body against which men strain shapes the stretching and refining of the soul that is required to reach the perfection that the Orphics, Pythagoreans, and Plato's own Academy so eagerly sought. To do this requires stringing opposite forces against themselves, thus creating a harmony out of a contrariety. This involves Lindsay's "shamanist contradiction" put into a musical metaphor, which I shall argue is a fundamental requisite of the Orphic poet.

The dualism that Herakleitos's remark seeks to resolve has a deep heritage that Rohde finds going back at least to the Homeric era. To the Homeric poet *psyche* is a mere essence, associated with the physical body and its functions, but not in any sense ruling it. At death, this essence, like breath or smoke, awakens to its immaterial life as an *eidolon*, a shade or image. This belief has some similarity with the Egyptian idea of two distinct souls, one for earthly life (*po*), the other for life after death (*ba*). However, the division to the Homeric mind is not so formal. As Rohde points out, Homer gives conflicting testimony with respect to which is the "real" man: the bloodless shade, or the willing self that directs the body's activity during life. And at the end of the Homeric era, *psyche* and *soma* are still used fairly interchangeably. In the sixth century, *psyche* comes to be equated with the appetitive self, *thumos*. This shift helps establish the ground for the Ionian physicalists' description of all life in terms of attraction and repulsion of material elements (later, with Democritus and Leucippus, elementary particles).

Empsychon: The Garden of Beasts Within

In the fifth century, the belief in the psyche as an eternal entity that both preexists and survives the physical body at death moves from popular religious belief into the theological and philosophical arena. But the dualistic strain continues. Philolaos, a student of the Pythagorean school, speaks of the soul both as an independent, imperishable entity and as a harmony of contraries, as Herakleitos does.[2] Pherecydes speaks of two souls: *psyche* as a vital warmth that is reabsorbed into fire at death and *daimon*, which is the immortal occult self. Parmenides (ca. 475) and Empedocles (494–44) both saw the soul as an independent, preexistent being.[3]

Empedocles gave spectacular witness to the doctrine, saying, "Thus I myself was once a boy, and also a maiden, a bush, a bird, and a voiceless fish in the salty flood" (fr. 117).[4] Like Pherecydes, Empedocles saw the individual beings who dwell not only in men but also in the other creatures of nature as *daimones*, strangers to this earthly vale of grief, thrust into a "Meadow of Disaster." The soul-*daimon* is not made of the elements, who "cast it about one to another";[5] "they all hate it" (fr. 115).[6] Psyche, on the other hand, is material, identical with the blood, which is the heart's thought.[7]

As we noted in the introductory chapter, Dodds sees this rise of metempsychosis to the forefront of Greek thought in the fifth century as concurrent with an influx of northern shamanism into Greek religious life.[8] But to him the significant change was less the maturation of the idea of metempsychosis than Plato's thoroughgoing "reinterpretation of the old shamanistic culture-pattern" into the terms of the *Republic*; the Guardian is modeled upon the old tribal shaman (as is the *poietes* for Lindsay). The "crucial step," he notes, is "the identification of the detachable 'occult' self, which is the carrier of guilt feelings and potentially divine, with the rational Socratic *psyche* whose virtue is a kind of knowledge."[9] The rational Socratic *psyche* is "most like" the Ideas, the world of Forms, and as such could not have been subject to the "attunement" of multiple elements, as it was for Philolaos. But Socrates had his mysterious *daimonion*, which is more like the "occult self" of Empedocles, Pythagoras, and Pherecydes. And though Plato moves in the middle dialogues to achieve the "identification" to which Dodds refers, the radical dualism by which the Orphics equated the body with the tomb and the soul with the Beyond tends to overshadow this accomplishment, whose monistic consequences remain to be drawn by Plotinus. Empedocles' perceived war between the elements of *physis* and the Stranger-soul continues to hold a dominant affective position in Plato's works. The "rationalist" we sometimes see in the dialogues is something of a scholarly conceit, an amalgam of a Socratic figure and a Plato seen through post-Enlightenment eyes. Even after the influx of Ionian and Socratic rationalism, the old dualistic tendency remains a persistent feature of Greek religious thought.[10]

Still, something has shifted in this period, perhaps best summarized by a new term in the fifth to fourth centuries, *empsychon*: "a *psyche* is within."[11] Instead of being manipulated by extrapsy-

chic gods and *daimones,* as in the archaic period, Greek man,
ruled by the *empsychon* as an eternal indwelling soul, now takes
responsibility for his own actions, and he is thus responsible in an
afterlife for the acts committed in this one. In Plato, the struggle
in which man had been seen as a plaything of the gods becomes
an interior drama, fought by a soul that still has a tendency to be
ruled not by reason (*nous*) but by the appetitive self (*thumos*). So in
the *Phaedo* he sees the soul as basically dual. In the *Phaedrus,* he
gives a tripartite image, the soul envisioned as a chariot pulled by
two contrary steeds (reason and appetite), commanded by a charioteer (*Phaedrus* 246b). Even more provocative is the image from
the *Republic* (588c–e) of yet another tripartite soul, that of a lion
(the appetitive will), a man (reason), and a many-headed beast,
made of alternate wild and tame heads. The task given with this
last image is for the man in us, in alliance with the lion, to master
the "huge and manifold beast" (590a), as the kingly soul must rule
the Republic.[12] This inner man is like a "farmer who cherishes
and trains the cultivated plants but checks the growth of the wild"
(589b), thus the alternating "wild and tame" heads of the initial
metaphor are a crop within the potential moblike confusion of
the soul, the sober and just parts to be cultivated by culling the
worldly, passionate ones. Plato has taken the image of the warring
steeds of the *Phaedrus* and multiplied it, thus breeding a whole
beastly necklace, which is fitting in a work that discusses how to
subject the inchoate state to the kingly principle within. At the
same time, though, he admits that the dualistic principles that we
have been attending grow thickly, side-by-side, within the soul.

As Plato grapples with images in which to express the now-
interiorized life of the soul, the old model of possession-states
keeps reintruding itself, and the scene in the *Iliad* where Athena
shows up in the midst of battle to have a word with Odysseus is
introverted into a battlefield of the soul, where an underlying
Strife often still seems to be the father of soul-life. These dualistic—or, in the case of the "moblike beast" (590b) of many heads,
pluralistic—images of the soul in the dialogues are evidence of
the continuing necessity of image-thinking, though now as an
action of persons or beasts within, rather than an invasion of
gods or *daimones* from without. On the other hand, Plato's
famous view of the gods supervising the various forms of mania
is a capital instance of the persistence in his thought of the

archaic view. Consonant with Pindar and Archilochus, Plato sees these four manias as the gifts of the gods, each form ruled by a different god: mantic (prophetic madness), Apollo; telestic madness, Dionysos; poetic madness, the Muses; and last, the highest of all, erotic mania, Aphrodite and Eros (*Phaedrus* 265b). Mania, then, is another variation of states of possession, for through these states the gods speak via the human being possessed by the specific mania. We have thus come full circle: the *empsychon* must still make room for the invasion of *theoi* as *maniai*.

Mimesis and Anamnesis: The Great Divide?

Plato's quarrel with poets in the tenth book of the *Republic* represents a crucial shift whose ramifications extend all the way through the *paideia*, the traditional means of passing down Greek culture.[13] According to Eric Havelock's influential analysis, cultural learning prior to the Platonic revolution in pedagogy consisted in rhythmically employing the whole body in a total mimesis of the words and actions of the *rhapsode*, who was merely passing on what he had learned in the same way.[14] Plato's emphasis upon *anamnesis*, learning by recollection, brought to life through Socrates' maieutics, was a direct and thoroughgoing challenge to this mode of *paideia*.[15] In the Socratic dialogues, received opinions were challenged, and the ultimate arbiter of the truth in any given situation was the soul's assent within each man's breast (which had a "check" in Socrates' *daimonion*). Seizing upon the revolutionary nature of this shift, Havelock argues plausibly that *anamnesis* routs mimesis at the Academy, giving birth to modern critical thinking.

Or so we have been taught. Plato/Socrates indeed was instrumental in inaugurating a different kind of thinking, but the changes may not have been so great as Havelock would argue. The head does not exist apart from the body, and the *thumos* (affective will), which was of central importance in ordering the old *paideia*, is still crucially active, as Plato's image of the lion as one of the parts of the soul—dwarfing the "man" within the man—indicates. Body-learning and body-thinking, as several "Orphic" poets have since affirmed, are still important to the thinker-poet, whose primary teacher has become the eternal indwelling soul. They provide her *context* (as does the "Inherited Conglomerate" for the individual).

In the early and middle dialogues, Plato tends not to emphasize what has been conserved of the old "Inherited Conglomerate,"[16] but by the time he writes the *Laws*, he has been disillusioned by his experience under a tyrant and has come to embrace many aspects of the traditional ways of the *polis*, so that even Dionysos is welcomed, within bounds and thus in an "Orphic" manner.[17] Boyancé emphasizes this counterthesis in *Le culte des Muses chez les philosophes grècs*.[18] His position is a welcome bow in the direction of continuity, but he pushes it to an extreme, so far that Dionysos becomes a kind of Pythagorean figure.[19] Still, one of his more telling observations is that it is the Muses who are represented over the entrance to the Academy, and he mounts a credible argument that their important feast days were singled out for inclusion in the Academic year.[20]

It is in this area—that of the Muses and their relation to Plato and his Academy—that Boyancé is most instructive. There was an entire chain of inspiration involved in the process of dispensing the afflatus that informed the words the poets breathed, and the Muses were its beginning link. Following them came the inspired bard (*thespis aoidos, Odyssey*; *poietes* in Plato's era), then the recitor or *rhapsode*, and finally the audience.[21] The remark about the *rhapsode* Ion (section epigraph, below), suggests that Plato wanted to get rid of the poetic "lightweights": those whose delicate magnetism was so sensitive it would turn and mirror every passing wind. But in the tenth book of the *Republic*, Plato makes it clear that he wants his Republic rid of Homer and Hesiod, who, as *poietes*, are one step closer to the Muses. We are left, then, with the Muses themselves. For if Plato banned the poet—both *poietes* and *rhapsode*—but not the Muses from his ideal state, he must retain a certain piety for them as bestowers of the poetic form of mania.

Looking at the *Phaedrus*, we find that though the Muses remain important as the inspiration for one of the four manias (265b), the poet as beneficiary has been demoted in the hierarchy of births which Socrates presents as the "ordinance of Necessity" to a place far down the list, sixth (just below a "prophet or Mystery priest" and just above an artisan or farmer); whereas the first position is given to "a seeker after wisdom or beauty, a follower of the Muses and a lover" (248d–e). A "follower of the

Muses," then, is a philosopher or a lover, not a poet in the traditional sense. The Muses have been separated from both the *poietes* (bard) and the *rhapsode*, and wedded to the philosopher-lover. This is essentially Havelock's argument, and it is the section in which his rhetoric is most passionate. In fact, he adopts a figure, "Paideia," who personifies the entire Greek tradition, saying that she must learn a new role and a new language if she is going to acquire the loyalty of this new breed, the philosopher.[22]

Havelock's "Paideia," though, is too general a figure to double for the Muses and the particular mimetic pathway that they initiated. Nor is she, nor the Muses themselves for that matter, quite so malleable as Havelock would suggest. I believe this is no simple substitution in the mimetic chain, but a wedding of what had been known as *poietes* to the new figure, the *philosophos*. Orpheus, son of the Muse Kalliope, is one possible model for this new kind of poet-philosopher. Though Plato scorns the "Orphics" and compares Orpheus negatively with Alcestis in the *Symposium*, he, unlike the traditional poets Homer and Hesiod, is not banned from the *Republic*. His poetic modality is not mimetic: he has his root in Kalliope and therefore partakes of her being. The song he sings is the inner song of creation, and is an analogue of the "song" that Socrates taught each individual seeker to listen for. On the eve of meeting his illustrious pupil, Socrates had a dream in which Plato visited him as a swan, the animal in which Orpheus chose to be reborn in the account of Er (see below). I suggest that there is a sense in which this swan figure replaced the poets banished from the *Republic*.

The Shamanic Contradiction: Pathway of the Orphic Poet

> For a poet is a light and winged and sacred thing, and is unable ever to write until he has been inspired and put out of his senses, and his mind is no longer in him . . . the gods take away the mind of these men and use them as their ministers, just as they do soothsayers and godly seers, in order that we who hear them may know that it is not they who utter these words of great price, when they are out of their wits, but that it is the gods themselves who speak and address us through them.
>
> —Plato, *Ion*

> The mind has within itself a kind of divining
> power.
>
> —Socrates, *Phaedrus*

We generally think of Plato as a philosopher. Havelock credits him with inventing the profession.[23] We also remember that Plato banished the poet from his ideal *polis*, the Republic, because he was a trafficker in shadows (*eidola*) of truth rather than the truths themselves, the "Ideas" (*eidoi*). But Plato began his career as a composer of tragedies, and burned his verse only after coming under the influence of his master Socrates. And though he burned these youthful productions, he never fully banished the poet in him, who as composer of myth was indispensable to Plato's ability to paint his image of "that great animal," the universe. Throughout the dialogues there is a subtext, through which we listen to the Orphic poet in Plato, the conflation of the young tragedian who burned his verses and the poet banished from the *Republic*. Implicit in Plato is a new kind of poet who sings his own melody, not that placed in him by the Muses.

Speaking in the *Ion* of the *korybantiontes,* the epileptically entranced followers of Dionysos, Plato says that they "have a keen ear for one tune only, that which belongs to the god by whom they are possessed," adding that they ignore the songs of the other gods.[24] In the chain of inspiration, each link interprets (as Plato explains) its predecessor. Its power lies in the strength of the sympathetic attraction, or "magnetism." Its weakness lies in the puppetlike dependence upon the "one tune only." But this is one necessary pole of the magnetic attraction/repulsion involved in the shamanic contradiction. The other pole lies in Socrates' characterization of the divining power that enables him to give a new sense to the command of the Delphic oracle: "know thyself." To restate then, the shamanic contradiction: the poet (*poietes*) speaks as a mouthpiece of the gods; he is a channel for the divine *logoi*. But at the same time, there is a power of divination within the mind itself that is accessible through the process of recollection, the *anamnesis* performed by the soul in seeking out her own origins. This divinatory power Plato clearly differentiates from the power of the seer to read signs in the flight patterns of birds or in the entrails of sacrificial animals. The latter soothsayers are "sane"—just like Lysias, the author in the *Phaedrus* of a sophisticated speech on the superiority of the calculating lover to the lover who is maddened by Aphrodite and Eros. Both the lover and the poet, however, are mad with a heaven-sent mania that is far superior to any skill (*sophos*).[25]

Orphic Music: Er and the Music of the Spheres

Mircea Eliade, in his discussion of Greek variations on the shamanic theme, suggests that the myth of Er (at the end of the *Republic,* book 10) is the most nearly shamanic of Greek accounts.[26] In this remarkable *récit,* Plato describes the extended travels in the nether realm of Er, a Pamphylan warrior who undergoes a kind of shamanic trance during the twelve days that lapse between his death in battle and the laying of his funeral pyre. During this journey, Er witnesses the differing fates of good and bad souls in the underworld.[27] Both the souls in transition between lives and the planets running their courses come under the same rule of Necessity, imaged as the spinning managed by the three Fates. The Spindle of Necessity, upon which the revolving spheres of the planets hang, is also the adamantine rod under which the souls must pass as their fates are confirmed. These fates, though spun by the Fates, are freely chosen by the assembled souls from among the lots cast by the attendant prophet after he receives them from Lachesis. After choosing their lots, the souls get from Lachesis the *daimon* who is to lead them through their next life, after which each is led under the hands of her sister Fates to have its destiny "ratified" (Clotho) and rendered "irreversible" (Atropos) (*Republic* 620e). Since the fate of each soul is both determined by the gods (spun by the three sister Fates, administered by attendant *daimones,* also "gods") and freely chosen, we have yet another example of the shamanic contradiction at the fundament of human life.

Around the Spindle of Necessity are concentric hollowed whorls that form the bed and pathway for the planets in their journey. At the head of each planet is a siren who sings one note (all of them together forming a harmonious octave, which includes all sounds). The sister Fates are also "sirens"; the fate-webs that they spin have a kind of music. So each life has its own inner music sung by the guardian *daimon* it receives to embody and administer its fate. However, both the Music of the Spheres and the inner music of the soul are unheard as long as self-knowledge, self-"attunement," is lacking.

The process described on the cosmic scale of Er's vision is quite similar to that which Lindsay describes as the original shamanic journey of the "Clashing Rocks"—the *symplegades*. Er and the Argonauts (including Orpheus) undergo the classic shaman's journey back through the channel leading to earthly life. From this vantage point, they describe the underworld and heavenly realms that lie before and after earthly life. Central to the ability to make this journey is possession of the *oima*: the "song-way" (or "songlines") that is itself the journey.[28] The journey *is* the song. It is a song that is unheard except by the poet-shaman, who has trained himself to be its channel. Orphic music, then, is attuned to the Music of the Spheres as well as to the inner music of the soul; they both come from a common source. Plato states this even more clearly in the *Timaeus*, where the souls of beings are said to equal the number of stars, the "visible gods" whence they transmigrate (*Timaeus* 42d–e).[29]

It may seem ironic that Plato, who paints a remarkable inner vision of the universe, and who can hear the inner music described at the end of the tenth book of the *Republic*, does not want to hear what the poet has to sing. But the poet's song plays upon the passions, which can so easily lead one astray. He wants to protect the citizens of his ideal *polis* from the rhythmic singsong that enslaves the soul to someone else's melody. As did Odysseus' men passing through the straits of Scylla and Charybdis, he stops up his ears so that he can, like the shaman Er, make it through the narrow passage under the adamantine Spindle. In claiming to hear nothing he is like Socrates, who always insists that he knows nothing (*asophos*), yet by diligently listening to his own soul, knows essentially everything. The great eschatological myths reveal that Plato has a tremendous sense of inner vision. But he also hears a melody, his own original melody. The mythic image of Orpheus's song awakening the animals, the plants, and the shades is the image of the poet-shaman singing the original song to which all of creation responds, as if hearing its own inner melody.

Just as the planets in their orbits are hung upon the axial Spindle of Necessity, human beings are strung upon a necklace of the gods.Thus, in a remarkable passage from the *Laws*, Plato speaks of the "thread of song and dance" upon which we are strung:

> No young creature whatsoever . . . can keep its body or its voice still; all are perpetually trying to make movements and noises. They leap and bound, they dance and frolic, as it were with glee and again, they utter cries of all sorts. Now animals at large have no perception of the order or disorder in these motions, no sense of what we call rhythm or melody. But in our own case, the gods of whom we spoke as given us for companions in our revels have likewise given us the power to perceive and enjoy rhythm and melody. Through this sense they stir us to movements and become our choir leaders. They string us together on a thread of song and dance, and have named our choirs so after the delight (*chara*) they naturally afford. (*Laws* 653e–654a)

The gods as "companions in our revels" and "choir leaders" evoke Dionysos and Silenus. Like possessed Maenads, we are strung on a "thread of song and dance." The divine inner thread in this passage is identified with rhythm and melody, not the *logos*. This is true not only in the *Laws*. In the *Phaedrus*, which I shall presently examine in some depth, Plato invents a fable in which the cicadas are described as descendants of an earlier race of men. These men were so mesmerized by song when introduced into their midst by the Muses that they forgot to eat and starved singing (see below, p. 42).

Socrates's simile (*Symposium* 215e) about the marketplace statues of Marsyas, *sileni* who contain images of the gods arranged concentrically, god within god, also strikingly conveys this sense. The outer "prison" of an ugly body belies the soul's beauty within. This central deathless thread, in contrast to the mortal somatic sheath, is divine. Working in a polytheistic context, Plato does not go so far as to identify this deathless thread with God (as do the Hindu *Upanishads*), but it is *athanatos* nevertheless. Depending upon the desired stress, this divine inner thread is variously imaged as the gods, a web woven by the Fates, the immortal soul (or the *daimon* who carries the fate), and a thread of song and dance. All of these may be equated with one

another and with the shamanic *oima* or *epoidos*. The thread upon
which we are strung is the song-way, but only the poet-shaman
knows how to play it in such a way as to travel to and fro. The
cicadas, shriveled vestigial men that they are, poetically indicate a
variant of the one-way path.

Plato's Orphic Universe: Setting

By now it should be clear that Plato's "Orphism" is implicit.[30] His
stance vis-à-vis the *Orpheotelestai* was harsh, calling their hymnbooks and manuals of *teletai* "a hubbub of books" containing for-
mulas with which they presumed to purchase their clients
dispensation from their sins and, therefore, a trip to the Abode
of the Blest (*Republic* 364e).[31] Though critical of the popular,
diluted form of Orphism, Plato nevertheless agreed with the new
theology at its core. This core included focus upon the individual
soul as terminus of the Delphic oracle's charge to "know thyself";
metempsychosis, with an emphasis on the differential fates of
good and bad souls; and an insistence upon purification, *katharsis*.[32] The last, however, taken in Plato's sense was a matter not of
arbitrary, externalized rites but of learning to "practice philosophy" as he had learned from his master, Socrates.

   Plato not only agreed with the core of Orphic theology but
also built upon its images. The images of the necklace of the gods
and of the divine soul sheathed like the gods within the statues of
Marsyas are variants of the most basic Orphic image of all,
summed up in the phrase *soma* = *sema*: "the body [is] the tomb." In
an analogous fashion, he imaged the universe as a cave within
which the soul, a winged *daimon*, was trapped. Plato's imaginative
vision of the cave in the *Republic* builds upon Empedocles's
remark, "We come under this roofed-in cave."[33] The image of the
original Orphic egg ingeniously expresses both of these senses, for
its membrane, when opened to reveal the greatest *daimon* of all,
Eros/Phanes, became the *aither* above and the gulf below. He is
thus the soul-principle surrounded by the imprisoning universe,
later viewed by the Neoplatonists as noetic substance entrapped in
matter (like the Orphic Dionysos exiled within the bodies of men).

   All of these variations form an extremely fertile area of comparison with Mallarmé's poetic universe, as we shall see in chapter

5. At this juncture, however, I want to look in some detail at the setting of Plato's Orphic universe as envisioned particularly in two dialogues, the *Phaedo* and the *Phaedrus*. The outlines of this universe, which Plato gradually builds over the course run by the dialogues, are sketched chiefly in the great eschatological myths: *Gorgias* 522c–527c; *Phaedo* 107d–115a; *Republic* 10. 614a–621d; *Phaedrus* 246a–257, as Frutiger outlines them. We have already briefly reviewed one of these, the vision of Er (*Republic* 10). But, rather than dwelling with these great accounts of the fate of the soul after death, I want to examine Plato's description of the physical universe in the *Phaedo* and the detailed "phenomenology" of the soul's dynamics as it contracts the contagion brought by Eros in the *Phaedrus*. Whereas the eschatological myths portray the ascendance of the doctrine of metempsychosis, the *Phaedo* details a physical setting that continues the other strain that Plato joins to the metaphysical: that of the Ionian physicalists.[34] The *Phaedrus*, in my view his greatest dialogue, has some of both. Plato's worldview is Orphic/Pythagorean, but this perspective is woven in thoroughgoing fashion with the domain of *physis* to form mutually requisite contraries: earthly and heavenly, logical and irrational, scientific and mythic.

A Hydrostatic Economy: The Phaedo

The setting for the drama of the fluxion[35] of the soul is cosmic, bringing together the play of forces from the realm of Hades all the way up to the stars in the Empyrean above. The stars, as in Herakleitos and Empedocles, are cups, turned toward the earth, so that the fire they receive from the *aither* reflects back towards the earth. Each star has as its center and source of life a "lesser" god or *daimon*. The number of these star-*daimones* is equal to the number of souls, and their cycling through the universe thus has a fixed economy (*Timaeus*). Somewhere beyond the orb of the fixed stars is the "Abode of the Blest," where purified souls (philosophers and lovers) enjoy an eternal banquet.[36] Beneath the earth, in a geography with which we will soon familiarize ourselves, the corresponding souls of the damned lie in mud (or muck, or worse) forever. Plato captures the essential connection between these realms in this striking passage: "And it is literally true that when the eye of the soul is sunk in the barbaric slough of the Orphic myth, dialectic gently draws it forth and leads it up" (*Republic* 533d–e). The phrase "of the Orphic myth" is gratuitous, Paul Shorey's overzealous gloss exemplifying the sort of laxity about which Linforth complains so strenuously (suggesting the "Orphic" by "rumor"). But both the vision and the logic of the passage *are* Orphic, in the sense that there is a necessary connection between the things of Tartarus and the things of the Beyond: a connection whose thread the soul may follow if dialectic would gently draw her up.

Let us begin, then, with the chthonic end of things. It seems altogether fitting that in the *Phaedo,* Socrates, at his deathbed in the Athenian prison and poised on the brink of heaven and earth, describes the setting for human life in the *oikoumene* (the subcontinent of Magna Graecia) as analogous to frogs or ants sitting on the shores of ponds and lakes. The familiar world brought to us by our senses, and more importantly, through what Durkheim would characterize as "collective representations"—those opinions born of grapsing at shadows playing on the wall of the Cave—is really life in the hollows, places where the watery *aer* of the lower atmosphere drains into valleys that are more like sloughs in Plato's vision.

The "true Earth," which is still physical, is that mountainous portion of the earth that reaches up at its edges, as if yearning for union with the *aither* above. This portion Plato describes as appearing like a glittering world of precious stones, reflecting a whole palette of colors in a passage worthy of a Goethean hero.[37] The earth, dominated as it is by the lesser, feminine elements of water and earth, becomes in this dialogue a multitiered organon, with channels of vaporous material ranging from the cool *aer* of the quotidian realm of ape-frogs to the depths of Oceanus, the great river that surrounds the *oikoumene*, to the icy confluence of the underground rivers of the infernal region, culminating in the Styx. Underneath it all is Tartarus, which receives all the other currents and is regulator of the whole, for what it receives from one side of the earth it can distribute again on the other.

Remarkably, all of these various waterways are interconnected, and the resultant of forces is the homeostasis of water seeking its own level throughout the cosmos in which it courses. This is a striking incidence of the unity in Plato's conception of the sub, super, and medial with respect to "Nature."[38] In seemingly artless fashion, Plato gives simultaneously a plausible physical explanation of the chthonic realm, a chthonic explanation of upperworld events, and, through the play of the daimonic "tides" of eros, also explains the watery pulses and counterpulses of the vast *methexis,* the "medial" realm through which the soul-*daimon* courses. We shall now examine these erotic tides in some detail with the *Phaedrus.*

The Tides of Eros: A Phenomenology of Reciprocal "Winging" in the *Phaedrus*

If the *Phaedo, Timaeus,* and *Politicus* variously describe the setting of Plato's Orphic universe as an analogue of the cave as fundamental Platonic topos, the *Symposium* and *Phaedrus* focus upon the process that drives it. If in the former dialogues the Hesiodic cosmogony becomes reinscribed with the *typos* of Plato's Orphic reformation, it is in the latter that the language and tone of the mysteries assume central importance. In each of these dialogues the core process is a dialectic that begins with the stirrings of love for the divine excited by the longing for union with the earthly beloved, whose beauty is a reflection of the otherwise unimaginable beauty of the world of forms. Though each of these dialogues is remarkable, I want to focus on the *Phaedrus* because it strings the principal themes of this chapter around its invisible center. It, more than any other dialogue, demonstrates the truth of Walter Pater's superb observation that Plato is a "seer who has a sort of sensuous love of the unseen" with an "aptitude of things visible [that] empowers him to express, as if for the eyes, what except for the eye of the mind is strictly invisible."[39]

In his perspicacious commentary upon this dialogue, Paul Friedländer perceives a "concentric" structure in which the questions concerning rhetoric surround the inner core, which focuses centrally upon dialectics and psychology.[40] The whole is carefully worked, exhibiting the nature of discourse as an "animal" (*Phaedrus*) in which each of the parts has its place. Thus what I intend to emphasize, a phenomenological description of the "pulses and counterpulses of eros" (Friedländer), is indeed precisely at the center of the dialogue. As the little statues of sileni encapsulate images of the gods, so does the composite mythic structure of this dialogue girdle the central mystery of the life-springs of the soul reawakened by Eros. This structure ranges from the opening local myth of Orithyia and Boreas, followed by an effort to join the present rites under the plane tree with those of Achelous and his Nereids, to the ending, where Plato explores the more fundamental topos of the origin and probable effects of writing in the exchanges between the mythical scribe Thoth and the philosophical Egyptian king Thamus. In the interstices we find the curious little myth of the cicadas.

The Cicadas

The theme of the autochthonous origin of the human race, which has a significant place in the *Phaedo,* the *Politicus,* and, to a lesser extent in the *Republic,* also appears in the *Phaedrus* with the remarkable account of the cicadas, which Socrates relates to Phaedrus as they approach the shade of the plane tree by the Ilissus. As Frutiger points out, it is one of two myths that seem to be wholly invented by Plato. The story is that the cicadas are descendants of an earlier race of men who, upon the advent of the Muses and thus *mousike,* took such pleasure in song that they neglected food and drink, singing from birth to death, which they suffered "without noticing it."[41] This "boon which heaven permits them to confer upon mortals," however, is granted only if Socrates and his companion avoid the "bewitching Siren song" being sung above their heads by the cicada-choir.

In my opinion, this fable is a condensed version of Havelock's criticism of *mimesis*: the two men must not succumb to the pleasure of listening to this Siren song but produce their own music, feeding on nothing but *its* melody, the "supreme music" that is philosophy. The cicadas themselves, like the autochthonous men who preceded them, come out of the womb of the earth and are the embodiment of music that requires no food but its own incantation. The lack of need for food continues the core myth's theme of nourishment for the soul, where three kinds of food signify the hierarchy of needs that the soul experiences, from the "food of semblance" (248b) of the material plane; to "being," the ambrosia and nectar upon which the white horse feeds (247d–e); to the medial "beauty of the beloved" (251b), without which the other two planes would never intersect. The myth of the cicadas adroitly combines the interrelated themes of beauty and nurture of the soul in the theme of spontaneous, unceasing song: the original song of the soul in each philosopher-lover. But at the same time it declares that one may be "bewitched" by the mimesis, not of the soul's original song, but of the cicada choir as the chorus of the "Inherited Conglomerate."[42]

The Winged Mystery

Plato depicts the soul in its earthly sojourn as having shed its wings. Recovering those wings, so that it can once again range about the universe and, at Great Year's end, tether the "noblest part" to the pasturage in the meadow that nurtures wing growth, is its chief duty and pleasure. This recovery is most likely in one who is "a seeker of wisdom or beauty, a follower of the Muses and a lover" (248d). Plato gives the essence of this experience in a remarkably acute observation of the phenomenology of love as the reciprocal action of wing growth in the souls of lover and beloved. The context for this, as noted above, is a dialogue on rhetoric, the opening and closing movements of which enclose the heart of the matter. But it is also a master class given by Socrates to Phaedrus: one in which he uses his own peculiar brand of irony to the utmost. In this lesson, what begins merely as a rhetorical play on the theme of the best qualities in a lover is transformed into an opportunity for a pivotal teaching on the nature of love, divine and human, and a provocative probing of the worth and dangers of the written word.

The dialogue opens with Socrates and his young admirer under a plane tree by the Ilissus, outside the familiar city gates of Athens, in a "mythical" setting, as noted above. Phaedrus produces a speech by his lover, the rhetor Lysias, which he reads. In essence, the argument is that the passionless older lover is superior to one motivated by passion, because he will behave in a reasonable fashion toward his young beloved. Everything about this speech: that it is read, that it is full of elegant sophistic turns, and the "pernicious rubbish" (242e) of its conclusion, absolutely goes against Socrates' own values and method. But instead of over-

turning the parroted argument point by point, leading his inter-
locutor ever more deeply into Lysias' own logical traps, Socrates
puts a cloth over his head to avoid "breaking down for shame,"
and launches into a thinly veiled parody of Lysias's speech.

Now this business of covering the head is typical of one who
wants to hide from the "visible gods," but there is also the added
element of suggesting the mystery rite, which the initiate undergoes veiled. It is as if Socrates must, like the initiate, go all the way
down before he can go up. After the speech, when he reveals that
his *daimonion* gave him the "customary sign" just before this bur-
lesque of the *kathodos*, Socrates gives a second speech, this time
unveiled, followed by a prayer apologizing to the wronged god,
Eros. Though this must be primarily a piece of irony, there is nevertheless the characteristic Platonic barb of probability (hovering
between the plains of truth and falsehood) that this could be,
after all, an action for which Socrates undergoes genuine shame.
In terms of its rhetorical—even theatrical—effect, the little inter-
lude lends invaluable *gesture* to Socrates' argument: a kind of
dromenon that brings us inside for the central rites of the dialogue.

These rites are reserved for "one who is fresh from the mystery" (251a): the awe inspired by the presence of the earthly
beloved provokes the lover's urge to sacrifice to the beloved as to
one of the gods so recently left. Indeed the lover seeks to mould
the beloved into the shape of his chosen deity; and the beloved in
turn, once he has "caught" the erotic madness, sees his own form
reflected back from the lover as that deity. Thus love, in its highest form, is the mutual deification of lovers. As in the great
speech of Diotima in the *Symposium*, this dialectic continues, spiraling upward to scale the heights of heaven. But here the
process reveals itself in exquisite detail, more like a lyric poem
than a philosophical dialogue. Indeed, the description of the
awakening of passion is evocative of the "near-death" experience
in Sappho's lyric that begins, "Like the very gods in my sight is he
who sits where he can look in your eyes" and ends, "I feel that
death has come near me."[43] Like Sapphos's lyric, Plato describes
the painful ecstasy of this awakening, which the sequence of verbs
"shuddering," "sweating and fever," and "throbs with ferment"
recalls directly. As the dormant roots of the wings begin to swell
again, watered by the "stream of particles" entering into the soul

of the lover through the channels of vision, the soul feels overall like a teething child—such is the throbbing caused by the eruption of wing growth. The elements involved in this process are moisture and heat. Thus the stream of beauty, the "flood of passion," "melts" the root stumps, causing the wings to grow again. But when the beloved leaves the soul's presence, the nourishing flood subsides, the openings to the rootlets dry up and the "wing's germ is barred off," leaving the soul "behind its bars, [where] together with the flood aforesaid, it throbs like a fevered pulse, and, pricks at its proper outlet, and thereat the whole soul round about is stung and goaded into anguish" (251d–e).

This process repeats in the lover's soul, alternating joy and anguish, which she manifests in the madness of running "hither and thither," not sleeping at night, and being unable to keep still by day. We recognize in this behavior the unsettled behavior of the *tetraktys* falling into the river of earthly life from the *Timaeus* (42–43). It is also the "homeopathic" behavior of the restless child or the wine-imbibing adult, seeking in restless motion the ordered movements it once followed. But then the beloved comes once again into the soul's presence, and in the warm light suffused by one like unto a "visible god," this "physician" administers the *pharmakon* (cure), recalling to the soul her once-heavenly estate. When this happens, "she lets the flood pour in upon her, releasing the imprisoned waters" (251e).

In his fervor at the heart of this dialogue Plato mixes his metaphors (as has often been noted). Critics usually see an offending mix in the jumbled metaphor of charioteer and horses taken together with the waxing and waning of the wing. This combination does provide for strange, even ludicrous moments. As Friedländer notes but rejects, this apparent awkwardness has been taken to indicate Plato's subsequent revision or even later interpolation.[44] To me this is yet another instance of a Platonic origin for supposedly later "Neoplatonic" accretions: the deplored "syncretism" with which the Hellenistic age abounded (also found in Gnostic literature). The jumbling or metaphor mixing is part of the titanic Orphic heritage, and the present metaphor is a capital instance of its operation at the source of the Platonic tradition.

What I want to emphasize here is the bold passage across the borders between the sensorium and the divine soul, imprisoned in the body like an "oyster in its shell," yet susceptible to the flood of passion that can give it a foretaste of release. This mixing of heat, light, and moisture in the repeated descriptions of the entry and passage of the image of the beloved into the soul's outpost in the "prison house" is what I call Plato's *primary synesthesia.* Boyancé speaks of the "divers canaux et les diverses parties du corps qui sont parcourues par l'âme comme ses liens," which he allies with the notion of the "soul-breath," who thoroughly canalizes, and thus colonizes her host.[45] Thus we have the image of a flood of water created by the "melting" of the solidified wing stumps through the first influx of the beloved's radiance into this tiny cosmos, which is then "imprisoned" and, when his presence is withdrawn, "barred off." This is an instance of the Orphic/Pythagorean *soma = sema* equation, but it is also the field of operations for the soul as mistress of a primary synesthesia where all the senses meet, mingle, and exchange.

The capital element and chief means of transfer for the eros between lover and beloved is, however, fluidity.[46] When the soul of the lover is full and can hold no more of the incoming image of the beloved, that image flows away from him back toward the beloved, who receives it "as a breath of wind or an echo, rebounding from a smooth hard surface, goes back to its place of origin" (255c–d). The stream of beauty reenters the eyes from whence it came; consequently, the beloved falls in love, loving, "yet he knows not what he loves," having "caught" this return love "like a disease of the eye" from the lover.

Eventually it becomes clear whence comes this "counterlove," and the two lovers become vessels for one another: vessels that must not leak, lest the pair lose the goal of this spiraling surge of erotic tides between them. Plato describes this *telos*: "with burden shed and wings recovered they stand victorious . . . in that truly Olympian struggle" (256b). Once again, as in the *Phaedo*, the process is a kind of equilibration in the watery element's "seeking" homeostasis. This time, the reservoirs that regulate the process, instead of being the subterranean rivers which ultimately meet in the Gulf of Tartarus at the earth's center, are the two souls yoked together by canals that carry their erotic traffic back and forth across a soul-bridge that becomes upon expansion the veritable *metaxy.* By a reciprocal damming, these "yokefellows," to transfer Plato's term for the contrary horses of the chariot, raise the tides of love as in a system of locks higher and higher through the mutual rebound of love and "counterlove" until they have scaled the "Beyond." There the two indeed become one, the unseen object of their longing, and are transmuted into something at which Plato can only hint. This is his truly Aristophanic image of Pteros (252b), the winged phallus who translates the awkward metaphor of a tripartite winged chariot into sublime comedy.[47]

The Cave and the Skein

> It looks as if those who established the rites of initiation for us were no fools, but that there is a hidden meaning in their teaching when it says that whoever arrives uninitiated in Hades will lie in mud, but the purified and initiated when he arrives will dwell with gods. For there are in truth, as those who understand the mysteries say, many who bear the wand, but few who become *Bakchoi*. And these latter are in my opinion no others than those who have given their lives to true philosophy.
>
> –Plato, *Phaedo*

The play of water or *aer* through channels deep into the substratum of earth, the vision clouded by the heavy atmospheric haze, coupled with the darkness of dreary damps far from the sun's warmth and illumination: such is the geography of the *Phaedo*. This is a fundamental Platonic topos that finds its analogues throughout his work, especially exhibited in the cave motif of the seventh book of the *Republic*. Here in the *Phaedrus*, the most "sunlit" of the dialogues, we have nevertheless a series of allusions to this overarching topos, the "roofed-in cave" of Empedocles (frag. 120).[48]

The image of an oyster in its shell, which is enclosed at the epicenter of the central myth of the dialogue, is a double of the "eye of the soul sunk in the barbaric slough" (*Republic* 564e). They both dwell beneath the mire at the base of Plato's Orphicized cosmos. And both alike have the native capacity to rise out of the muck in which they are mired: the eye of the soul to realize its "divining power"; the oyster to culture its pearl. Moreover, they are like the souls of the "uninitiated in Hades," who "will lie in mud." But they are inexorably tied to their contrary, the triumphant *Bakchoi*—the souls of the liberated philosopher-lovers who have climbed out of the cave to the Abode of the Blest, for whom the "Homeric fable" of the Pteros two paragraphs later (252c) gives a metaphor of the utmost economy. Indeed, the oyster and the winged phallus give the entire range of Plato's daimonized cosmos, from *sub-limus* (Hazlitt's pun) to the sublime. Together they elicit Eros emerging from his shell (oyster/egg). The image of the twinned souls of lover and beloved, vessels for the mutual exchange of the waters of passion, with their subtle but fateful capacity to scale the heavens with regenerated wings, gives the fundamental unit that can recover the scattered body of Eros/Dionysos from the "traps of matter" into which it was exiled. But this too has its mirror in the souls of the Danaiades, condemned forever to pour water into leaky amphorae. Again, the dominant image is that of "holding water" and the process that regulates it at every level of the cosmos. Plato's cave has become a grotto.

It is the "hidden meaning" that Plato coaxes out of the rich images given in the Orphica. As Guthrie puts it, "Plato thought of the Orphic myths as the complementary mythological expression of profound philosophical truths."[49] The myths are one part of what Cornford calls the "datum" of philosphy; the other part is *physis*.[50] These are Plato's givens, things that cannot be proved, but without which his philosophical universe could not exist. As an Orphic poet-philosopher, descendant of the shaman, he must experience in his own soul the *nekyia*, as well as the heavenly peregrinations of this transmigrant. This makes him of necessity a cosmogonist, a theogonist, an anthropologist. Basic to all of these, like Orpheus himself, he is a musician, one who transposes (Frutiger, Dodds), who seeks another mode between the Dorian and Phrygian. As Shakespeare put it, "For Orpheus' lute was strung with poets' sinews"—hence the immediacy of the Dionysian, earthy music of the *Laws*.[51] But this soul-music has its counterpart in the music from afar, the heavenly music of the spheres, where Lyra sounds, struck by the rays of Apollo/Helios: the music of the *Timaeus*.[52] The closeness of the chorus of the cicadas in all its sweetness: there, in that tree overhead; there, ready to leap into Eunomus's lay—has its more distant and reserved counterpart in the song of the prophetic swan of Apollo, the "totem" bird of Socrates, Plato, and Er.

In Empedocles, the Orphic cosmos, child of Night and rising out of Chaos, becomes the fundamental topos of the cave. With Plato, this much-traversed *temenos* where the novices are swallowed, hidden, lost, tricked, and betrayed becomes a prison where the inmates sit with fixed stares, dully attending the flickering *eidola* reflected through the curtain stretched between them and the figures trudging the Stations of the Veil beyond it. One of them, the Platonic hero, picks up the end of the skein of light and travels these stations in the opposite direction, recollecting through slow but steady steps the reversal of vision that they had entailed. For this he is much maligned ("probably killed"), his reports of the ontic realm of the "true earth" in the sunlit heights beyond the Cave seeming like madness. In this instinctive motion toward the sun, the Platonic hero emerging from the Cave is a twin of Orpheus, as he "retires to a cave, from whence he rises every morning before Helios to greet his appearance."[53]

Plato's Cave—subsuming the cosmos of the Orphic theogonies, and including the *oikoumene* as grotto—is the Orphic universe that contains our inquiry into the form of Orphic poetry. He gives us as well a process for traveling its bournes: the pulse and counterpulse of lover and beloved in the improbable act of regenerating the soul's wings. In the chapters that follow, we will be investigating a precise moment in the cycle of the Orpheus legend, that of an instant in which this delicate process of regeneration begins, through the poetry, letters and poetic theory of Stéphane Mallarmé.

Brothers In Decadence: 3
Mallarmé, Nietzsche,
and the Orphic Wagner

Only as an aesthetic phenomenon can existence and the world
be eternally justified.
> —Friedrich Nietzsche, *The Birth of Tragedy*

Tout au monde est fait pour aboutir dans un beau livre. [The
whole world is made to end up in a beautiful book.]
> —Stéphane Mallarmé

Plato, as Orphic poet in spite of his own dicta, provided a bridge
across which much of the archaic cultural material of Magna
Graecia moved into the new logocentric, post-Socratic world.
With some irony, I would note also that he recombined, rewrote,
and invented myth, therefore including under the aegis of his
philosophy writing acts not so foreign to those of that rascally
Orphic "priest," Onomacritus. The greater irony, however, is that
though he bans the poet from the *Republic*, he is perhaps the best
example of the Orphic poet in the fourth century. The *mythic*
world that forms the substrate of his philosophical enterprise is a
veritable Orphic universe that provides Stéphane Mallarmé with
a small host of Orphic insignia, as we shall explore in chapter 5.

The focus of the rest of this book will be the aesthetic and
linguistic revolution of the late nineteenth century, especially the
defining role played by Mallarmé as Orphic poet of the modern.
Admittedly this leap will omit some of the key moments when the
figure of Orpheus was involved in cultural/artistic revival, beginning with Augustan Rome, notably including the invention of
opera during the waning years of the sixteenth century by Mon-
teverdi (*Orfeo*) and his colleagues in the Florentine Camerata.
These men composed four of the first five operas on the theme
of Orpheus and Eurydice.[1] But I shall argue nonetheless for a
continuity with the tradition of Orphic poetry, and with the
shamanic tradition out of which it grew. Central to this tradition
is the effort of poetry and philosophy to reunite and refind their

ground in myth, a recognizable romantic hope. Mallarmé, in his redefinition of poetics, represents a move from one side of the logocentric division back toward this common ground. A move from the other side, from philosophy toward "Maenadism" and the dithyramb, is made at precisely the same time by the French poet's almost exact contemporary, Friedrich Nietzsche.

Whereas Plato provides a topos, a universe of images that contains the labor of Mallarmé's Orphism, Nietzsche contributes a precise setting for Mallarmé's Orpheus. His construct, Apollo-Dionysos, a fundamental contrariety of "art deities" defining the world as "aesthetic phenomenon," creates a frame for Orpheus: god of an evanescent moment that the French poet dances into being. In terms of our model at the end of chapter one, Orpheus is the *Augenblicksgott* between the modal forces represented by Apollo and Dionysos. In terms of the history of ideas, however, we have a fascinating replay of the Hellenic moment; Nietzsche now enacts the role played earlier by Plato.

One of Nietzsche's most telling remarks in *Philosophy in the Tragic Age of the Greeks* (1873), is that a "chasm" separated the thought-worlds of Herakleitos and Aristotle. This chasm was bridged by Plato, the first *philosophos*, a "professional philospher" at whom Nietzsche sneered for having no ideas of his own, merely synthesizing the "giants," the pre-Socratics. But I hasten to add that in Plato the poet and philosopher were not yet entirely sundered (as they most certainly were in Aristotle). Nietzsche himself bridges the considerable distance, if not a chasm, between Winckelmann, Kant, and Schiller and the world of Mallarmé, Rimbaud, and the surrealists.[2]

Before discussing an immediate ground for Mallarmé's aestheticism in Nietzsche's *Birth of Tragedy*, I want to briefly review the philosophical and literary context that Nietzsche "overcame," to use his word. A primary cluster of ideas in this context is the new subdiscipline of aesthetics, which begins with the inquiries of Baumgartner, but whose principal players are Kant and Schiller. The shift in the cultural center of Europe at the end of the eighteenth century from France to Germany is highlighted by the seminal work of Winckelmann, whose labors initiated the "tyranny of Greece over Germany"—a tyranny that Nietzsche's *Birth of Tragedy* was to tighten through the tremendous influence of his Apollo-Dionysos construct. Winckelmann's influential picture of Greece has now become proverbial: a sunlit place of order and harmony, so harmonious that even in the famous *Laocoön and His Sons* at the Vatican, where writhing figures are engulfed by snakes, the characters are seen as "serene." Winckelmann's Greece is obviously ruled by Apollo, and it represents a Golden Age.

Winckelmann was influential in the development of Nietzsche's classical interests as a schoolboy at Schulpforta, but even more important was the youth's exposure to the *Frühromantiker*.[3] What impressed him most about these men was their earnest effort to *remythologize* the culture after the dry years of the Aufklarung. Friedrich Schlegel, leading theorist of the Jena School, was the closest in spirit to Nietzsche. It was he who called for a "new mythology" to be rooted in Greece. His aphoristic style, his irony, and his willingness to contradict himself—speak in paradox and parataxis, especially in the *Atheneum Fragments*—all remind one of Nietzsche. But Schlegel finally converted to Catholicism, which made it easy for Nietzsche to "overcome" *this* kindred spirit—as would prove to be the case with all his influences, including mentors (see the discussion of Wagner that concludes this chapter).

The topos to which the *Frühromantiker* returned for their revolution in aesthetics, following Winckelmann, was Greece. They set about with demonic zeal to grasp, reassert, and relive the Greek experience, and not insignificantly for our present study, the bacchic god, ignored by Winckelmann, reenters the drama here. Though Nietzsche claimed to be the first to elucidate the *psychology* of Dionysos, his romantic predecessors had already developed a rich vocabulary of that experience. They had also spoken of the polarity of Apollo-Dionysos, which Nietzsche extensively develops.[4] But their context was a Christian one, and their goal a unity of pagan and Greek, of Dionysos and Christ. Novalis's effort to reestablish a theodicy ("Christianity or Europe") in politics and to express a mystical union of Dionysos and Christ in his poetic works is a good example of a deep and widespread phenomenon. However, Nietzsche was more impressed with Hölderlin's immersion in a Greek spirit that moved beyond both Winckelmann's "sunny" Greece and Novalis's Catholic universalism. Nietzsche is in some respects the culmination of the romantic love for the Greeks, but in his drive for going behind (*hinter-fragen*), he deepens the search, relentlessly moving beyond the frame of Christian ethics, "beyond good and evil," finally to the place of eternal becoming in the "Cosmodicy" of Herakleitos.[5]

Nietzsche's Aestheticism

Nietzsche's aestheticism is not a self-contained realm separate from a "real world" of nonaesthetic objects but an attempt to "expand the aesthetic to embrace the whole of reality," as Allan Megill in *Prophets of Extremity* accurately describes his effort.[6] This aestheticism begins within the romantic project, one that includes a whole set of issues as defined by Kant: the beautiful as disinterested pleasure in an object, the idea of the sublime, the concept that art follows *natura naturans*, not *natura naturata*, and the theory of the artist as genius.[7] But Kant consistently subordinates aesthetics to ethics. Following upon the "second aesthetic turn in modern philosophy," whereby "Schopenhauer and his heirs" subordinate Reason to art and play, the rationalist aesthetics of Kant and Schiller are turned upside down.[8]

Benjamin Bennett, in a seminal article on Nietzsche's aesthetics in *The Birth of Tragedy*, argues convincingly for a strong Schillerian influence upon that book. Thus Schiller would appear not only to have mediated Kant for the romantics but also to have moved Kant's aesthetic project closer to Nietzsche's full-blown aestheticism. Nietzsche himself cites Schiller's views on the function of the chorus in *The Birth of Tragedy*, and several critics have pointed to the close resemblance between Schiller's agonistic forces, *Formtrieb* and *Stofftrieb*, and Nietzsche's Apollo and Dionysos.

But Bennett points to Schiller's idea of the "beautiful illusion" as the central influence. In Nietzsche the myth of illusion, the work of Apollo, is a constantly renewed creative act. Bennett cites in particular a striking passage from the *Säkular Ausgabe* as evidence of Schiller's anticipation of this position: "the reality of things is the things' own work; the appearance of things is man's work, and by enjoying appearance, the mind no longer enjoys what it receives, but what it itself does" (*Säkular-Ausgabe*, 12:105).[9] From Nietzsche's perspective, Schiller seems to be a stuffy classicist and a Platonist. Yet Schiller is himself a poet-philospher, and his goal of an "aesthetic State" strongly echoes Plato's *Republic*, with the poet-philospher as king. The proximity of another king, Herakleitos's Zeus as child-tyrant building and destroying worlds, is closer than it might seem—hidden in Schiller's rationalist robes.

Bennett's clearest emphasis in the analysis of Nietzsche's *Birth of Tragedy* emerges in the following: "in conscious art [there] is an intensification, not a modification, of the essentially mythical; in conscious art, myth becomes more fully itself."[10] If this is true, and I think it is, then one can see that the revolution in aesthetics and the remythologization of the *Frühromantiker* unite in Nietzsche's view of art as the intensification of myth; the aesthetic becomes the ground of the phenomenal.

We can see with a "critical backward glance" (Nietzsche's 1886 preface to *The Birth of Tragedy*) that all this was headed toward a regrounding of aesthetic thought in the pre-Socratics, those "pure" philosophical types who drew Nietzsche's relentlessly probing spirit.[11] This chapter's epigraph, taken from *The Birth of Tragedy*, in fact clearly relocates the topos of our inquiry in Anaximander and Herakleitos, rather than in Winckelmann, Kant, and Schiller: "Only as an aesthetic phenomenon can existence and the world be eternally justified."[12] Aestheticism here becomes the new ground, freed from the ethical imperative to which Kant and Schiller still bound it. This is Nietzsche's *archon*, and it provides the foundation for the new temple of aesthetics.

The "justification" of existence is the language of Anaximander, as Nietzsche's citation in *Philosophy in the Tragic Age of the Greeks* (*PTG*) clearly indicates: "Where the source of things is, to that place they must also pass away, according to necessity, for they must pay penance and be judged for their injustices, in accordance with the ordinance of time" (4:45). For Anaximander, coming-into-being must "pay" for its existence through going-out-of-being (the entire cycle for the Hindus is called simply *avanagamana*). Existence is a *moral* phenomenon: "It is not justified, but expiates itself forever through its passing" (*PTG*, 4:45–46). The expiation of becoming is through death. Unlike Anaximander, Herakleitos sees the strife of becoming as justification in itself, not "requiring penance." With Herakleitos, Hesiod's Eris is transformed into the cosmic principle of eternal justice: "Everything which happens, happens in accordance with this strife, and it is just in the strife that eternal justice is revealed" (*PTG*, 4:55). Herakleitos also compares the continual becoming of existence to a child playing at draughts at the seashore. Anaximander's—and Kant's, I might add—*moral* universe is finally replaced by one in which God (*BT* section 4) or "the will" is an aesthetic draughts-man: "tragic myth has convinced us that even the ugly and dis-cordant are merely an esthetic game which the will, in its utter exuberance, plays with itself" (*BT* section 24).

The Birth of Tragedy: The Apollo-Dionysos Contrariety

The Birth of Tragedy is Nietzsche's most important book. Not only about the *birth* of tragedy, it is about its *death* as well. But its subti-tle, "From the Spirit of Music," comes closer to our aims, as we shall examine later in this chapter ("Contemporary Deities of Art"). *The Birth of Tragedy* is a "focussing of all forces on a single point" in order to grasp the essence of the tragic age of the Greeks. Our focus, however, is upon another point, another moment, which we can know only by a certain indirection, not unlike the knowledge that Narcissus (or Mallarmé's heroine of mirrors, Hérodiade [Salomé]) gains by looking into the pool. One way of reading Nietzsche's endlessly fertile work is by look-ing at what it hides or ignores, rather than taking literally his thunderous assertions, being neither entirely closed to Niet-zsche's insights, as was Wilamowitz's positivistic reading, nor vic-tim of the uncritical reading by Wagner or, later, Walter Otto. Another figure hides in the folds (Mallarmé's ubiquitous *pli*) of the veil that hangs of necessity between the brother-gods who are locked in the curious struggle that Nietzsche claims produces art. The figure is Orpheus, who at this juncture of European arts and letters momentarily stands between Apollo and Dionysos.

In *The Birth of Tragedy* Nietzsche personifies Dionysos and Apollo as deities whose dialectic produces tragedy. For him Greek tragedy is the epitome of human existence, a model for the cultural revival that he so fervently desired for the young, Pruss-ian-dominated German state, which had just been galvanized by the defeat of the French in 1870 (upon the eve, in fact, of the publication of Nietzsche's first book). These gods are two funda-mental forces, a *Widerspruch* (contradiction): "artistic energies which burst forth from nature herself, *without the mediation of any human artist.*"[13] Dionysos represents *Rausch* (intoxication); Apollo

Traum (dream). As dream, Apollo is the "veil of illusion" (or "maya"), the *principium individuationis* of Schopenhauer (and undoubtedly Schiller's "beautiful illusion," as well). From this point of view the whole world of form arises, covering the areas of dream, prophecy, and the subtle illusion this principle works in waking life. Aesthetically, Nietzsche associates Apollo with the plastic arts: architecture, sculpture, painting, and epic poetry.

Dionysos, on the other hand, is the equivalent of Schopenhauer's will, the *Urgrund* or *Ur-Eine* who "unselves" into the world of *Schein*, the beautiful illusions of the Apollonian realm. He personifies the creative, form-producing *Genie* of Goethe, Schelling, and Schiller (Goethe's *Bildungstrieb*). Dionysos is the lyric artist par excellence, and, by the Greeks' own assessment, the hero of tragedy, one of whose representations was the mask. The masks were huge, often carved in stone, and therefore not to be worn by actors. To Walter Otto, they were a sign of his uncanny presence.[14] Dionysos is the Stranger, a *deus absconditus* always ready to unselve from the well of Being, causing riot, orgy, mayhem—unless ordered by the rules of tragedy into the complex Apollonian-Dionysian balance that Nietzsche saw governing the "Tragic Age of the Greeks." As opposed to the Apollonian plastic artist, who is "committed to the pure contemplation of images" among which he lives (see Wordsworth, for example), the "Dionysiac musician, himself imageless, is nothing but original pain and reverberation of the image."[15] Whereas the epic poet is shielded by his delight in appearance, "so that this mirror of appearance protects him from complete fusion with his characters—the lyric poet . . . himself becomes his images, (which) are objectified versions of himself." Pointing to the superficial nature of what was called "subjective" poetry ("subjective poetry is merely bad poetry"), Nietzsche weakens the subject-object debate of the early romantics.[16] The creating subject is not the "I" of the waking man, but the "'I' dwelling, truly and eternally, at the basis of things."[17]

The distinction that Nietzsche draws between these giant patrons of art, of dubious accuracy in terms of actual Greek cult, is invaluable as a tool for analyzing the fundamental forces at work in the production and presentation of art. Dionysos and Apollo characterize art as two complementary modes, which are indeed analogous in form (if not content) to Greek *nomoi* (laws of

being).[18] Though he participates in an epochal shift in the aesthetic structure of the West, he does so from a Dionysian perspective, missing a subtle but significant event, namely, the moment in
which Apollo (and all the wondrous and ordered array of forms
with which Western art was built) begins to withdraw and disap-
pear into his contrary, Dionysos.[19] In this moment of reversal,
Nietzsche's "maenadic soul" sings the new dithyramb, turning his
back upon another aspect of the phenomenon—the reappearance
of Orpheus, marking the threshold between the modal forces
represented by Apollo and Dionysos. This is the Orphic moment
of the latter part of the nineteenth century, a moment personified by Stéphane Mallarmé. If Orpheus is a mediator of these two
realms, then the moment to watch for his epiphany is either that
of Dionysos's "unselving"—the "classical" moment when those
fortunate Greeks created our culture—or, alternatively, the "decadent" moment when Apollo's veil lifts for an instant, revealing
the Void behind the blank eye-slits of the tragic mask.

Nietzsche anticipates this second process: "Apollonian consciousness was but a thin veil hiding from him (the Greek) the
whole Dionysiac realm. In order to comprehend this, we must
take down the elaborate edifice of Apollonian culture stone by
stone until we discover its foundations."[20] (The program for the
deconstructionist movement, which owes so much to Nietzsche—
and to Mallarmé—is explicit here.) Nietzsche's metaphor, however, is that of a philologist/archaeologist, and as such is the
wrong modality for catching something that is "in the air," happening swiftly. Nietzsche ignores this evanescent moment, identifying instead with Dionysos/Christ, and becomes Dionysos the
Crucified. More nimble, Mallarmé dances the Orphic moment,
creating an anti-world out of its negative transcendence.

Parallels

Nietzsche (1844–1900) and Mallarmé (1842–98) had much in
common. Each was intensely solitary, visionary, and antibour-
geois.[21] Both were teachers by profession, although Nietzsche
retired early due to his abysmal health, whereas Mallarmé clung
doggedly to his work as English teacher in a series of provincial
lycées (and ultimately Paris). At the end of his life he finally

retired, exhausted, with only a few years' respite from a grinding existence.

Both suffered from mental problems. Nietzsche's are well known; his own writings, especially toward the end, partially document this.[22] Mallarmé experienced a protracted spiritual crisis at Tournon (1864–69), where he underwent a kind of death, an "ego-death," which he recognized as being akin to that sought by Buddhist monks in their disciplines—except that his ascesis was neither Buddhist nor Christian.[23] At the nadir of this experience, he wrote to his friend Henri Cazalis that the only way he could tell he was still alive was to look at his face in a mirror.[24] Even after this crisis was resolved, or rather channeled into the poetry of his mature years, he went through years of acute headaches and, according to one unbelievable account, suffered ten years of total insomnia.[25] Nietzsche acknowledged that pain was his great teacher, giving him the unique occasion to "become himself" by accepting it and creating despite it—thereby becoming his own best example of the stoic concept *amor fati*: love of one's fate. Nietzsche, freed from the laborious life of a pedagogue by debilitating illness, found a tonic in writing philosophy. Mallarmé the insomniac lived the life of a pedagogue, family man, friend and mentor to scores of literary men and women. And he wrote poetry—a process of alchemical transformation wherein he transformed himself into his own inimitable destiny, thereby transforming the manner of writing poetry as well.

Worn Counters

Both Nietzsche and Mallarmé were quick to suspect the ability of language, as ordinarily perceived and used, to convey truth-value. This was at the center of the deepening crisis in Europe which they both recognized, and their articulation of the problem was characteristic, one might say constitutive, of the *Zeitgeist*. Nietzsche discusses this in his "On Truth and Falsehood in an Extra-Moral Sense" (1873):

> What is truth? A movable host of metaphors, metonymies, and anthropomorphisms: in short, a sum of human relations which have been poetically and rhetorically trans-

ferred, and embellished, and which, after long usage,
seem to people to be fixed, canonical, and binding. Truths
are illusions which we have forgotten are illusions: they are
metaphors that have become worn out and have been
drained of all sensuous force, coins which have lost their
embossing and are now considered as metal and no
longer coins.[26]

In a similar vein, Mallarmé, in the preface to the *Traité du
Verbe* of René Ghil (1886), writes:

Narrer, enseigner, même décrire, cela va et encore qu'à
chacun suffirait peut-être, pour échanger la pensée
humaine, de prendre ou de mettre dans la main d'auttrui
en silence une pièce de monnaie, l'emploi elémentaire
du discours dessert l'universel reportage, dont, la littérature exceptée, participe tout entre les genres d'écrits con-
temporains.
   A quoi bon la merveille de transporter un fait de
nature en sa presque disparition vibratoire selon le jeu
de la parole, cependant, si ce n'est pour qu'on émane,
sans la gêne d'un proche ou concret rappel, la notion
pure?[27]

Both men see words as worn counters that have lost their power
to transfer any reality. Nietzsche's response to this situation is sav-
agely to tear apart the illusions that the world keeps serenely toss-
ing back at him, and to create a new man, a new category of
being, the *Ubermensch*, who will reinvest language with sensuous
force through the spilling over of his radical affirmation of life.
This Overman, the hypostasized result of humanity's evolution-
ary fumbling toward authenticity (nonreactive, affirming rather
than negating), is Nietzsche's new myth for a humanity that has
lost connection with the mythic fabric of its life.
   The problem that each of these men address was summarized in Kant. Kant's human language-universe is largely self-ref-
erential, a whole symbolic realm where all truths are human
truths with no necessary or discernible connection either with
the "world out there" or to another, hidden world. Nietzsche's
reply to this situation is to forge ahead into Kant's thicket, slash-
ing through the linguistic deadwood. Mallarmé's response, as

one can see already in the passage above from the Ghil preface, is more delicate, indeed "classic." The French poet clings to the esoteric tradition that affirms that there is a connection, indeed a referent for the "miracle" that language performs, a *metapherein* or transport from a realm that is ordinarily hidden to us. According to this tradition, there are two or perhaps multiple worlds, for which the poet as magician, shaman, or priest is capable of performing a transfer from this hidden realm into quotidian reality. In Mallarmé's case, however, this clinging is masked and undercut by the poet's irony, whereby he makes a continual effort to cover his tracks by a kind of calculus that erases individual images, replacing them by the cumulative "poetic effect."[28]

Though the perception of the realms involved has changed radically, it is through his obedience to this task that I see Mallarmé as an idealist, indeed a kind of Platonist. Except the transfer that is being wrought is of a very different kind. Nietzsche put his finger on it, as have most philosophers of world significance since him, namely by proclaiming the death or the end of metaphysics.[29] Mallarmé affirms this death of metaphysics as we have known it, but he installs in its place the *possibility* of another ontic realm, which is pointed to by critics' assessments of its "negative transcendence." To be faithful to this task is the task of the Orphic poet in our time, and Mallarmé is the first modern Orphic poet.

Both artists are fascinated with the dicethrow, as Gilles Deleuze observes in his *Nietzsche and Philosophy*.[30] But according to him, the resemblance remains superficial, masking a key difference in their respective attitudes toward chance and necessity. For Nietzsche, echoing Herakleitos, they are yoked: "necessity and random play, oppositional tension and harmony, must pair to create a work of art."[31] For Mallarmé, on the other hand, they are unalterably opposed. As Deleuze summarizes, "The dicethrow only succeeds if chance is annulled; it fails because chance continues to exist." Deleuze, I believe, is correct in seeing in Mallarmé something like "the old metaphysical thought of a duality of worlds" where "chance is like existence which must be denied, necessity like the character of the pure idea or the eternal essence."[32] But rather than finding in Mallarmé the affirmation, as the "last hope of the dicethrow," "its intelligible model in the other world," I find the notion of that world, "some vacant, higher surface," a limit or horizon of this one.

For our purposes, however, the most significant comparison of Nietzsche and Mallarmé emerges from their views on music. Life, for each of them, is fundamentally aesthetic. And music has a special status as that art form which has the power to overcome art's merely illusory quality, an *aperçu* Nietzsche took from reading Schopenhauer, though it also clearly fit his own intuition. Mallarmé's reflection on the process of creation in lyric poetry led him to see music and literature as one, both springing from the same hidden source.[33] The figure of Orpheus that emerges from this reflection in the French poet's work is the analogue of Nietzsche's Dionysos, who represents for Nietzsche the common root of music and tragedy. Both Nietzsche and Mallarmé are attempting to return to an "original" music, first conceptualized by the Greeks as *mousike*.[34]

Mousike: "Geist Der Musik"?

Toward the end of the *Phaedo*, Socrates reports a dream in which he is told to "practice the arts" (or "make music," from the root *mousike*). Socrates' response is to compose poetry—something that Nietzsche also attempted.[35] In his retrospective "Critical Backward Glance" to *The Birth of Tragedy* (1886), Nietzsche reproves himself for not having taken his own advice, to be a "music-playing Socrates."[36] The epithet is obviously an echo of the Socrates of the *Phaedo*. Nietzsche, as a classical philologist, is well aware of the meaning of *mousike*: a collective singular expressive of the unity of the arts, represented by the Muses, who embraced all aspects of artistic creation. They are the traditional matrix, daughters of Memory (Mnemosyne), who sanction the transfer of the "Inherited Conglomerate" by bestowing the poetic gift (*mania*) upon the lyric poet. But Nietzsche radically shifts the purport of the phrase in the *Phaedo*, where Socrates concludes that the "supreme music is philosophy." The result is a highly complex paradox, a veil in whose folds are hidden Wagner, Schopenhauer, and Orpheus as well.

The paradox actually begins with Plato, whose use of *mousike* in the context of Socrates' teachings is a foil behind which a profound *metapherein* is taking place. To say that the "supreme music is philosophy" is already to leave the traditional sphere of activity of *mousike* and to substitute *anamnesis*, the soul's recollection of her travels, for the rote learning of *mimesis* as a basis for knowledge (Havelock's thesis). Socrates as the "new Orpheus" is not unlike the Orpheus of Francis Bacon, who sees him as an "easy metaphor for philosophy personified."[37]

Original music, then, refers to:

1. the music (*mousike*) that the Muses first bestowed upon the poet
2. the original music of the soul, the pulse and melody by which it remembers its being; thus the substance of *(a)* the *récit*, as in the great Platonic cosmogonic myths or *(b)* the *lyric*, as in Archilochus (its historical origin) or Orpheus (its mythic/archetypal origin)
3. the authentic voice of the lyric poet who must renew the mythic and linguistic fabric of being in every era (this is what Mallarmé means by a *retrempe*, a reimmersion of that fabric).

Nietzsche identifies this lyric voice sometimes as that of Archilochus, his choice as archetype of the lyricist, but more often as Dionysos. In Dionysos we have made the complete circuit to the place of origin not only of the lyric (in Nietzsche's terms, at least) but also of tragedy, which arose from the ritual worship by means of music, dance, and dramatic action of the god of the mask.[38] The Dionysian *dithyrambos*, whose musical aspects we know very poorly, is for Nietzsche the putative origin of tragic lyric, the *Urgrund* out of which issues the "Geist der Musik."

Finally, to realize fully the complexity of this multitissued figure, "a music-playing Socrates," one must follow the paradox into Nietzsche's own persona. True to the substratum of the myth, there is an unstable tension in the figure between its archetypal resolution as Orpheus or as Dionysos. The statements "a music-playing Socrates" and "this book should have been sung, not spoken" (1885), both driven by a "stammering . . . maenadic soul," jointly suggest that this musical Socrates is Nietzsche. Ultimately Nietzsche becomes a Dionysos, who as the "Anti-Christ" undergoes crucifixion, shattered by the final madness.[39] But in the "music-playing Socrates" one senses the presence of Orpheus hovering just beyond the threshold of his attention. This liminal presence begins to coalesce in the figure of the "other Wagner," to which we shall now turn.

Contemporary Deities of Art

Max Baeumer, in an excellent and thorough article, demonstrates convincingly that Nietzsche's claim to be "the first to comprehend the marvelous phenomenon of the Dionysian," is a gross overstatement. According to Baeumer, Dionysos was reborn in the early Romantic era (Hamann, Herder) and nourished by poets (Hölderlin, Novalis), philosophers (Schelling, Gotthilf Schubert), mythographers (Creuzer, Bachofen), religious historians (Welcker, Preller), and the archaeologist Müller.[40] Comprehensive as Baeumer's summary is, he barely touches upon two Dionysian figures who loom large in *The Birth of Tragedy*. The definitive Nietzschean Dionysos, who manages to supersede all the others, is an amalgam that includes two contemporary "deities," Schopenhauer and Wagner. When Nietzsche entitled his first book *Die Geburt der Trägodie aus dem Geiste der Musik,* the *Geist* to which he referred is perhaps more *their* music than any Greek models. *The Birth of Tragedy* is really about the eclipse of ancient tragedy and its *rebirth* through Wagnerian opera, the *Gesamtkunstwerk*.

Nietzsche never highlighted the Greek sense of *mousike* in the text of *The Birth of Tragedy*, though it might have served as a foil for the protean "spirit of music." What remained important from the Greek milieu was the role of music in tragedy. In Nietzsche's account, Aeschylus was the archetypal tragedian, displaying a tragic "unity" far purer than anything Aristotle ever had in mind. As composer-lyricist, director, and actor, Aeschylus came closest to the putative origins of tragedy in the ritual worship of the god. As attested by the Greeks, Dionysos himself was originally the only actor in the drama, represented by his commanding and ubiquitous presence as a mask. The ultimate unity, Nietzsche intimated, was that of Dionysos and Aeschylus (as it was Dionysos:Archilochus in the sphere of lyric poetry). That his much-admired Wagner identified himself with Aeschylus made Nietzsche's affirmation of the musical origins of tragedy that much easier.[41] And all of the great artists whom Nietzsche admired (each a world-creator in his own right) are, ultimately, Dionysos. Including Nietzsche.

The identification of Dionysos with music is a curious one for a classical philologist to make. Apollo, not Dionysos, was the musical god for the Greeks. In terms of tragedy, music was always clearly subordinate to the word—that is until the late Euripidean tragedy and the era of the new *dithyrambos*, when matters abruptly changed. This reversal, giving music ascendancy over the word, is just the opposite of what Nietzsche would have us believe of Euripides' priorities. And it ironically would align the hated Euripides with Wagner.[42]

The main reason for these distortions is ontological and derives, I believe, from the deepest source of Nietzsche's philosophy, the characterization of the nature of being as Will and Representation in the masterwork of Arthur Schopenhauer, *Die Welt als Wille und Vorstellung*. The development in the German literary-philosophical tradition of Dionysos as the formless, infinite, intoxicated Genius, creator of art and world alike, well qualified the god for Nietzsche's translation from Schopenhauer's Will. And the complementary aspect of a reflective and form-giving *negative*, or limiting power qualified Apollo as Schopenhauer's *principium individuationis*. One might say that Nietzsche combines Schelling's aesthetics with Schopenhauer's metaphysics.[43]

But still another key Schopenhauerean insight fixes the identity of Dionysos as music. For Schopenhauer music is a "copy of an original which can never in itself be directly represented." It is "as immediate an objectification of the whole will as the world is, . . . as the Ideas are. . . . Music is not a copy of the Ideas, but a *copy of the will itself.*"[44] The other arts are *Vorstellungen*, copies of Ideas (which Schopenhauer uses in an enhanced Platonic sense). As such they are illusions. Music, which "gives the innermost kernel preceding all form, or the heart of things," is not.[45]

Though Nietzsche was later to draw away from his near-total embrace of Schopenhauer's philosophy during the writing of *The Birth of Tragedy*, the fundamental terms of his own philosophy were cast here. Of lesser philosophical importance was the intoxication with the musical ideas of Wagner, though Wagner was exceedingly important to him for psychological reasons.[46] Wagner himself felt the influence of Schopenhauer, and his term *absolute music* resulted from that influence.[47] As Wagner grew older, he realized that his own musical ideas and practice were not consonant with Schopenhauer's metaphysics of music, and thus tried belatedly to adjust to this situation, with unconvincing results.[48]

Musical Metaphysics: Wagner in Nietzsche and in Mallarmé

In his *Gesamtkunstwerk*, the total art form where he tried to overcome the false union of music, word, and action in the operatic tradition, Wagner again sought the putative union of the arts under the aegis of music in early Greek tragedy.[49] Initially, both Nietzsche and Mallarmé were strongly drawn to Wagner, seeing in his "music drama" the realization of their deepest hopes for the rejuvenation of European culture. Both ended by repudiating him, since each in turn realized that the supposed "unity" of Wagnerian opera was imposed after the fact and was not, as Schopenhauer argued it must be, a musical unity prior to words. Thus for Schopenhauer, in a musically unified production of mixed modes, for example opera, or Beethoven's choral symphony (which Schopenhauer found immensely successful), the words can in no way impose meaning upon the notes, which exist as an independent modality *necessarily* prior to all other art forms. The notes signify *through* (or despite) the accompanying art forms, which they transcend.

As noted above (note 34), direct influence upon Mallarmé by Schopenhauer seems unlikely. In Wagner's case, direct influence can be maintained. As Nietzsche says in *Nietzsche contra Wagner*, Wagner *belongs* in France, where during his life he was indeed better received than in Germany. In this late collection of reflections published after the composer's death, as well as in the brilliantly acerbic piece *Der Fall Wagner*, Nietzsche analyzes a second Wagner, hidden in the heavy folds of the sorcerer-Wagner's Dionysian illusion.[50] In this corrective to the excesses of his youthful adulation, Nietzsche finds the truly masterful Wagner in the "spinn[er] of details . . . our greatest miniaturist in music who crowds into the smallest space an infinity of sense and sweetness."[51] It is in unlocking the hidden moments of the soul, where "he masters the shy glance of concealed pain, of understanding without comfort, of the farewell without confession" that he shows himself "as the Orpheus of all secret misery."[52] This second Wagner, a figure who is "hidden, hidden from himself," is another *décadent* who joins our oddly matched pair, Nietzsche and Mallarmé. Whereas Nietzsche claims to have overcome his decadence, it is this very decadence that forms the grounds of artistry for Wagner and Mallarmé.

Mallarmé wrote two pieces on Wagner. One is an "Hommage," among the more impenetrable of his sonnets. I will not dwell upon it here, except to note the interpretation of L. J. Austin, who sees the collapse of the main pillar among the "mobilier" in the first quatrain as the implicit end of the French romantic theater in the death of its Samson, Hugo. Here is the quatrain:

> Le silence déja funèbre d'une moire
> Dispose plus d'un pli seul sur le mobilier
> Que doit un tassement du principal pilier
> Précipiter avec le manque de mémoire.[53]

Anthony Hartley, whose Penguin *Mallarmé* is the best introductory collection (in English) of the poet's verse and criticism, finds Austin's interpretation "strained." However, a recognition of the importance to Mallarmé of the monumental, of his consuming passion for the theater, and of the central place Wagner's music-drama would play in a culturally rejuvenated Europe prepares one to see the aspect of succession, even of "consecration" ("Le dieu Richard Wagner irradiant un sacre" [the god Richard Wagner glittering consecration (l.13)]), in the dramatic sequence Hugo-Wagner.[54]

Mallarmé's second piece is from his "Médaillons et Portraits." It is a thick mixture of admiration and ironic criticism that finally resolves into the latter.[55] At the outset, Mallarmé speaks of Wagner in jealous terms. He is a contemporary French poet excluded from the "pompes souveraines de la Poésie," whereas Wagner is lionized in public spectacles (at least in Paris). But after a page describing the wasteland that Wagner might illuminate (Mallarmé repeatedly writes to the brink of deification, then backs off), he ends with the resolute "Singulier défi qu'aux poètes dont il usurpe le devoir avec la plus candide et splendide

bravoure, inflige Richard Wagner!"[56] For Mallarmé, Wagner is a
usurper in the wasteland, like his fellow monument Hugo ("Le
vers, je crois, avec respect attendit que le géant qui l'identifiati a
sa main . . . de forgeron, vint a manquer; pour, lui, se rompre").[57]
Add this to the statement a few lines later of a "concours de tous
les arts suscitant le miracle" (a competition of all the arts creating
a miracle), and one has the scene of a contest. Mallarmé accepts
the challenge, as he did when Debussy told him that he wanted to
set "L'après-midi d'un faune" to music. Mallarmé's response: "I
thought I already had."[58]

Mallarmé welcomes the advent of the music drama to a stage
which has become inert and impersonal. Like Nietzsche, he speaks
of the modern theatergoer who "disdains to imagine" but must be
dragged to the brink of illusion, convinced only by the fireworks
of special effects. But he speaks in religious terms, "sortilège . . .
Initiation . . . solennités," of the expectancy this "stranger" excites
in "la Foule" (the Crowd), and applauds Wagner's "wedding of personal drama and ideal music."[59]

For Mallarmé, unlike Nietzsche, from whom it elicits a deep
repugnance, "the Crowd" represents the hope of a new religion,
an aestheticized creed laid on the old foundations of "la Cité, qui
donna, pour l'expérience sacrée un théâtre" (the City, which gave
[us] the theater for this sacred experience).[60] For the second time
in history a public, first Hellenic, now German, considers "le
secret, représenté, d'origines. Quelque singulier bonheur, neuf et
barbare, l'asseoit: devant le voile mouvant la subtilité de l'orchestration, a une magnificence qui décore sa genèse."[61] But through
the strains of admiration broods a note of irony: "new, barbar-
ian," a "decorative" magnificence.[62]

The image of a moving veil for the ripples of sound from
the Wagnerian orchestra is particularly apposite in a text that
emphasizes the efflux of Wagnerian music. The moving veil
bears a close kinship with the "disturbance of the veil" in the temple of poetry ("with significant folds and a little tearing") at
Hugo's death.[63] In "Crise" however, one has the sense of a veiled
monument: explicitly, Hugo is a monument in the desert, something rigid hidden behind the formal folds. The emphasis in
"Richard Wagner" is upon fluidity, a wavelike quality. The "moving veil" holds a shimmering iridescence that tokens the presence, in *this* Wagner, of Orpheus, who *is* the veil, the boundary

between the Apollonian illusion and the Dionysian ground. The
following passage eloquently evokes the entire range of the interplay of the Dionysian-Apolline-Orphic, speaking of a music that:

> n'a de cet art que l'observance des lois très complexes,
> seulement d'abord le flottant et l'infus, confond les
> couleurs et les lignes du personnage avec les timbres et
> les thèmes en une ambience plus riche de Rêverie que
> tout air d'ici-bas, déité costumée aux invisibles plis d'un
> tissu d'accords; ou va l'enlever de sa vague de Passion, au
> déchaînement trop vaste vers un seul, le précipiter, le tor-
> dre: et le soustraire à sa notion, perdue devant cet afflux
> surhumain pour la lui faire ressaisir quand il domptera
> tout par le chant, jailli dans un déchirement de la pensée
> inspiratrice.[64]

Wagnerian music drama, the poet affirms, is particularly
rich in tone painting, in a synaesthesia that "confounds the colors
and the lines of the character with the (musical) timbres and
themes." The resultant Dream-ambiance is a robe fabricated out
of the invisible folds of a "tissu d'accords" that describes the
weaving of a host of pleasant illusions into one Apolline mantle.
Or, it rides on a Dionysian "wave of Passion," an "immeasurable
unleashing" that precipitates and twists the hero.[65] In the last
four lines from the citation above, the "notion" against which the
hero is protected and screened ("le soustraire") is a wave of passion, the "Musique" at the core of the superhuman "afflux." Here
clearly is a rhythmic ebb and flow of the Dionysian and the
Apolline that resolves into the figure in the last two lines of the
citation: Orpheus, who "tames everything by the song that surges
forth in a tearing of inspired thought."[66]

This subtle passage represents the turn of Mallarmé's mind,
the referential frame in which he received the composer's dramatized tone poems. For he wrote it without ever having *seen* a Wagnerian opera.[67] Like Nietzsche, whose first interest was stirred by
hearing only the Prelude to *Die Meistersinger*, Mallarmé's admiration was based upon hearing the orchestral Wagner at the Con-
certs Lamoureux. These occasions were the specific ritualized
ground for Mallarmé's deeply felt sense of expectancy among "la
Foule" at the concert hall—not the Paris Opera. He therefore

maintains, along with this hope, a certain distance from the phenomenon of the Wagnerian opera. The éclat that he describes in
this piece is experienced from a distance, like the fireworks of the
Franco-Prussian War that accompanied the musical assault upon
French lyric sensibility. Unlike Nietzsche, Mallarmé never became
a Wagnerian, and thus he never set himself up for the tremendous sense of betrayal that Nietzsche experienced as soon as he
set foot in Bayreuth. As Judy Kravis points out in *The Prose of Mallarmé*, the fact that Mallarmé had this distance from the Wagnerian phenomenon freed him to treat his subject in a more
theoretical fashion.[68]

Nevertheless, like the enthusiastic crowds across town at the
Paris Opera, he is excited by the new union of music and the theater—at least by the idea of it. But he is also dubious that all the
arts can be drawn together successfully. Certainly he doubts the
unity of the scheme, audible in such phrases as "harmonious
compromise." Unlike Nietzsche, he is never burdened by conflating Greek tragedy, the Dionysian, and the Wagnerian. While
Wagner "concilia toute une tradition intacte . . . avec ce que de
vierge et d'occulte il devinait sourdre" (conciliated an entire tradition intact . . . with the virginal and the occult he divined
welling up), it is left ambiguous whether this wholesale transfer
involves attic tragedy:

> Une simple adjonction orchestrale change du tout au
> tout, annulant son principe même, l'ancien théâtre, et
> c'est comme strictement allégorique, que l'acte scénique
> maintenant, vide et abstraite en soi, impersonnel, a
> besoin, pour s'ébranler avec vraisemblance, de l'emploi
> du vivifiant effluve qu'épand la Musique.[69]

This "simple orchestral addition," which makes all the difference,
annuls the principle of the ancient theater but at the same time
vivifies the empty scene, so that ancient drama is, as it were,
aufgehoben in the Wagnerian drama ("annulant," "vivifiant").

The pattern throughout (as we find often in Mallarmé) is
one of enthusiastic assertion, followed by ironic undercutting,
many conditionals, qualifiers, fundamental exceptions. For
instance, after praising the "hymen" that Wagner has achieved
between music and drama, in the succeeding paragraph he backs

away, noting that "philosophically," Wagnerian music only "juxta-
poses" itself with the drama (compare "une simple adjonction
orchestrale"). But then, immediately, he adds that music "pénètre
et enveloppe le Drame de par l'éblouissante volonté et s'y allie"
(penetrates, envelops and allies itself with Drama by its dazzling
will), ending however, with the enigmatic "sauf que son principe
même, à la Musique échappe" (except that its very principle
escapes Music). This escaping essence, a "volatilization," to use
Mallarmé's term from "Les dieux antiques," is a necessary given
in Mallarmé's outlook, one of the characteristic qualities of his
Orphic moment. It occurs once again in this piece when, after
hyperbolically "expiring" at the foot of Wagner's "incarnation,"
and making pilgrimage to the "raréfactions" and "sommités"
(summits) of Wagner's music, he ends with an evocation of the
"arrière prolongement vibratoire de tout comme la Vie" (vibratory aftereffect of everything, like Life itself) ("Richard Wagner,"
p. 545). It is this aftereffect, the phenomenon of lingering overtones, that Mallarmé seeks to identify (or produce with respect to
his poetry).

Though the majesty of Wagner's attempt impresses him,
Mallarmé never becomes a Wagnerian, which is inarguably clear
in the final paragraph. Here Mallarmé distinguishes himself
from the true disciples, who, in order to find "le salut définitif,
vont droit à l'édifice de ton Art, pour eux le termin du chemin."[70]
By ironic contrast, he asks to be permitted simply to "goûter,
dans ton Temple, à mi-côté de la montagne sainte" (to taste from
your Temple, halfway up the holy mountain), which is contrasted
with the "voyage fini de l'humanité vers un Idéale" (the finite voyage of humanity toward an Ideal). The implication is that the
Wagnerians (whose lassitude reminds one of Nietzsche's "last
man") have "finished" the "finite" voyage.

At the close of the piece, the "voyage" is characterized in
terms of physical and spatial elevation; "au pieds de l'incarnation" and "ces sommités" (p. 545) lead to scaling "l'édifice de ton
Art," "la montagne sainte" (p. 546). But until then the predomi-
nate metaphor for the journey has been that of a river: "flux de
banalité charrié" (p. 541), "vivifiant efflux qu'épand la Musique"
(p. 542), "le flottant et l'infus" (p. 543). Summing up this movement, which declares the necessity of a return to origins, as in
Nietzsche's return to the "birth" of tragedy, the poet concludes:

"Tout se retrempe au ruisseau primitif." (p. 544). We find this same term, *retrempe* (resoak or retemper), at the center of the retooling of poetics in Mallarmé's "poëmes critiques."[71] Here, though, in the context of Wagner's music drama, it is not quite apposite, merely a gesture in the right direction. For the entire sentence reads: "Tout se retrempe au ruisseau primitif: pas jusqu'à la source."[72]

In section nine of *The Birth of Tragedy*, Nietzsche describes the leveling effect of the Dionysian current:

> the high tide of the Dionysian destroyed from time to time all those little circles in which the one-sidedly Apollinian "will" had sought to confine the Hellenic spirit. The suddenly swelling Dionysian tide then takes the separate little wave-mountains of individuals upon its back, even as Prometheus' brother, the Titan Atlas, does with the earth. This Titanic impulse to become . . . the Atlas of all individuals, carrying them on a broad back, higher and higher, farther and farther, is what the Promethean and Dionysian have in common.[73]

Nietzsche's image owes much to this striking image from Schopenhauer, which indeed carries Nietzsche's wave upon *its* back:

> Just as the boatman sits in his small boat, trusting his frail craft in a stormy sea that is boundless in every direction, rising and falling with the howling, mountainous waves, so in the midst of a world full of suffering and misery the individual man calmly sits, supported by and trusting the *principium individuationis*.[74]

Schopenhauer, in turn, must have somewhere in mind the image of Tristan in his rudderless boat, setting out for Ireland and Isolde.

Compare Nietzsche's remarks on the "Dionysian current" with the passage from "Richard Wagner" that we examined above (p. 69), where the Apolline "Rêverie" is lifted up ("enlever") by the current of Wagnerian music: "sa vague de Passion, au déchaînement trop vaste vers un seul," and "le précipiter, le tordre."[75] To return to the source of the musical stream requires a

certain precision that these passages of Dionysian flooding high-
light by contrast. In *Nietzsche contra Wagner*, Nietzsche compares
Wagner's "infinite melody" to "walk[ing] into the sea, where one
gradually loses one's secure footing, and finally surrenders oneself to the elements without reservation: one must *swim*."[76] Nietzsche goes on to contrast the "swimming, floating" which this sea
of sound required of the listener to the dancing which the older
music inspired. There is a *tension* required in listening to music, a
"measure": "maintenance of certain equally balanced units of
time and force, [that] demanded continual *wariness* of the listener's soul."[77] For this balanced, measured tension, Wagner substitutes "rhythmic paradox and blasphemy," which constitutes a
clear "danger" to music in its "complete degradation of rhythmic
feeling, *chaos* in place of rhythm."[78] Finally, on the Apolline side
of this imbalance, Wagner's dramatic art depends more and
more on "naturalistic" gesture, unconnected to "any law of plasticity," striving for *"effect*, and nothing more."[79]

In his own survey of the realm of this "law of plasticity" (la
figuration plastique), Mallarmé also fixes his attention upon
dance: "La Danse seule capable, par son écriture sommaire, de
traduire le fugace et le soudain jusqu'à l'Idée."[80] He had a particular passion for dance, and many have observed that it was
through this medium that Mallarmé saw most clearly his ideals of
aesthetic unity. Mallarmé used it often as a master metaphor for
verse, one that conveys the rhythm of flowing lines, crescendo-
decrescendo, a figural music that is *seen* as well as *heard*. Dance,
as visual poetry, enacts figures. Here in "Rêverie" though, he
applies the figure to Wagner's own "extraordinary but inachieved
ostentation": it is an all-encompassing vision, seen by an "ama-
teur," of the "Spectacle futur," where Music approaches Theater
"pour en mobiliser le miracle."[81] As our reading of "Richard Wagner" indicates, this "miracle" did not live up to its vast promise.

In the end, both Nietzsche and Mallarmé saw in Wagner
images of themselves. Mallarmé withdrew the projection even as
he wrote "Richard Wagner: Rêverie d'un poete français." Nietzsche, in these late reflections upon the man who had been the
carrier in Nietzsche's youth of the personas of both Aeschylus
and Dionysos, finally withdrew his as well. The Wagnerian personas that remained for the two men were remarkably similar—
much closer to Orpheus than to Dionysos. But it was Mallarmé

who was to enact the figure of the dance in his poetry, an Orphic "translation of the fugacious and the sudden up to the Idea," a process of "volatilization." In his guerrilla tactics against the European philosophical tradition, Nietzsche also thought it necessary to "know how to dance with words": "to dance with the pen," as he showed best in *Zarathustra*.[82] Yet what he *lived*, when none of his contemporaries (especially Wagner) could fill the void, was the identification Nietzsche:Dionysos, the Anti-Christ. On this reef he shipwrecked, in an "immeasurable unleashing toward a sole being . . . ," a "twisted precipitate."[83]

The Orphic Moment of   4
Stéphane Mallarmé

We saw in chapter 3 that one aspect of Mallarmé's Orphic moment is the quality of the *kairos* that he shares with Nietzsche: the crisis of language in Europe during the last decades of the nineteenth century, in which the forms of western art break down, and Apollo with his "veil of maya" disappears back into his contrary, Dionysos. As I have noted, Mallarmé calls this period an "interregnum"; Nietzsche, an "entr'acte." Whereas Nietzsche identifies with Dionysos, Mallarmé takes on the role of Orpheus, who appears as the phosphorescence, the brief shining forth that accompanies this moment, and rides it, continuing to manifest the presence of this threshold god throughout his life and work. The aim of this chapter is to demonstrate how the moment is characterized in that life and work.

LIFE, POETRY, CORRESPONDENCE

Two Critics, Two Pathways, and the Moment Between

To contextualize this particular "Orphic moment," I propose looking first at the work of two critics particularly interested in the phenomenon of modern Orphic poetry. In her fine study *The Orphic Voice* (1960), Elizabeth Sewell examines the post-Renaissance figure of Orpheus in terms of three essential moments of the myth. The first is that of the singer-musician, charming the animals, trees, and minerals through his incantations. This is the moment par excellence of the culture-hero, which she explores through the work of Bacon and Shakespeare, who collaborate in the paradigm shift from the mechanical to the organicist, the "Great Instauration" which she provocatively calls "post-logic."[1] The second moment is the *katabasis-anabasis* theme of the loss and retrieval of Eurydice, which she envisions in terms of the Romantics, chiefly Goethe and Wordsworth. The most fitting example of this second moment for Sewell is *The Prelude*, that unwieldy poem on the "growth of the mind," or the marriage of Wordsworth and Nature.[2]

Sewell sees the final step in Orphic poetry as the singing, prophesying head, floating with the lyre down the Hebrus. This is the unquenchable Orphic Voice, embodied for her in the remarkable outpouring of Rilke's *Sonnete an Orpheus*. The seam which she makes in the line of Orphic poets is between Wordsworth and Rilke, omitting the whole revolution in French poetry that began in Nerval and Baudelaire, came to maturity in Mallarmé, and continued in Rimbaud, Valéry, and a host of twentieth-century poets, many of whom one might appropriately characterize as "Orphic."[3] In giving her genealogy of modern Orphic poetry, Sewell decries the fact that the Orphic challenge is dropped by those who are potential "Orphic minds," in particular Mallarmé and Valéry. Curiously, she finds this task engaged in works of the midcentury by Hugo and Renan: the challenge to trace the "natural history of the mind" through the joint disciplines of biology and poetry. In the end, she rejects Mallarmé as a "failed Orphic poet." To the contrary, I believe that it is Hugo, rather than Mallarmé, who represents a deadend.[4]

A penetrating study of Orpheus in modern continental literature by Walter Strauss, *Descent and Return: The Orphic Theme in Modern Literature* (1971), opens another direction of inquiry. Strauss points to a different Orphic strain that develops after the middle of the nineteenth century, bifurcating the pathway of Orphic poetry. With the exception of Nerval, who is the bridge between the Romantic Orpheus and the new note of Mallarmé, he omits the French Romantics, whom he generally places in the illuminist tradition, rather than with Orphism proper.[5] Commenting upon her choice of accent in the tradition of Orphic poetry, Strauss says succinctly, "Sewell . . . opts for Goethe over Mallarmé."[6]

Against Sewell, Strauss sees a genuinely Orphic pathway leading to the necessity of "negative transcendence" in Mallarmé's
poetry. At the beginning of the century, he finds Hölderlin understanding best the "essential" condition of poetry, which Strauss
describes as "acceptance of a night situated between a departure of
the gods and an awaited epiphany."[7] But by 1870, Sturm und
Drang is a century old, and romantic political hopes have been
dashed twice—first by the aftermath of the French Revolution, then
by the unsuccessful revolt of 1848—and the very possibility of genuine communication through language has come into question.
Under these conditions, it is Mallarmé who sums up the situation
for Strauss: "with Mallarmé divine transcendence is abolished altogether and night accepted as the only reality in which an epiphany
can occur."[8] At this juncture, Prussia is on the verge of forging the
first German nation-state, one that will prove to be the very antithe-
sis of Novalis's mythical medieval kingdom. Now the stern father
Bismarck rules above, the Mothers below, and the questions are, as
Strauss notes: "Is the sacred possible?" and "Can the poet exist in
the modern world?" These questions are exultantly answered in
Rilke's dramatic outpouring of 1923. But they have not yet dawned
on the Promethean Hugo, whose confident "blacksmith's hands"
heroically transform everything they grip.[9] Rather, these are questions that Baudelaire perversely begins to frame and Mallarmé tentatively begins to answer.

Like Sewell, Strauss envisages three "moments" in the evolution of modern Orphism. The first two are the same: (1) enchanting the "natural world," the moment of the culture-hero (the
Ficinian Renaissance), and (2) the descent-return motif, which he
extends across the nineteenth century into French poetry, rather
than effectively limiting it to German-English Romanticism, as
Sewell does. But Strauss sees the third moment differently; it is the
sparagmos, rather than the prophesying head, that represents an
epiphany of the "supra-mundane angel of the inner life" (Jean-
Paul).[10] Strauss's deviation here is crucial, for in terms of the progression of the myth into the era of modernity, it establishes a
dominant tone of fragmentation and defeat: the void of the exis-
tential desert (Sartre's Mallarmé) or the flaccidity of the unstrung
lyre (Ihab Hassan's *The Dismemberment of Orpheus*, 1971).[11] His own
emphasis, explicitly indicated in his title, is upon the second
moment, but the scenario for the future, which his concluding

chapter ("Orpheus, Paradigm or Paradox?") leaves tentative, leans
at best toward paradox. By contrast, Sewell's image of the final
moment, embodied by the Rilke of the *Sonette*, ends with "the affirmation of the unity of all the forms of nature, between the galax-
ies and the mythological lyre," and the singing head, "which is
poetry and thinking, prophetic and unquenchable."[12] This is "the
interpretive myth" of the human mind, which is the middle term
of the unity, "part of the dynamic of the system, . . . united, by its
forms, with whatever in the universe it is inquiring into."[13]

Orpheus as Horizontal Oscillation

Whereas Mallarmé's Orphic quality might well be seen in terms
of the second moment, the nightmare of the "Nuits de Tournon"
and its resolution in poems and letters of the mid eighteen sixties
embodying a descent-return, I experience a different moment,
resonating throughout the poet's work. Though it does not pre-
clude the *katabasis-anabasis* theme, this moment nevertheless
finds a different accent in Mallarmé's Orpheus. It is yet another
reading of the third basic moment of the Orpheus myth, one
between those chosen by Strauss and Sewell—between the *sparagmos* and the triumphant final image of the prophesying head.
Instead of viewing Mallarmé's poetry as a variation upon the
descent-return theme, with its emphasis upon the vertical, or
depth dimension, I propose focussing on the horizontal: the first
stirrings back to life among the scattered bones surviving
Orpheus's *sparagmos*. Viewed in terms of the solar configuration
of the Cox/Mallarmé "Dieux antiques" piece, Apollo occupies
the position of high noon, Dionysos lies directly opposite at the
abysmal pole, and Orpheus defines the zone where these
"extrêmes se touchent." Orpheus, then, is the horizontal axis that
is the *limen* of that touching—the "dawning" or "setting" of the
sun.[14] This may be diagrammed simply as:

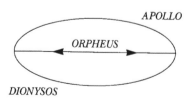

This moment does not involve the heroic (vertical) descent-return, or the shattering *sparagmos*, or the eloquence of the Orphic Voice, singing "high and clear" (Sewell) from the endlessly prophesying shamanic head in the *Sonnete an Orpheus*. It is more a reflexive action, not so much in a mechanical sense as in the sense of an act consequent upon the poetic labor of embracing the nullity, tenaciously holding on until the scythe of time ends its sweep, just beginning to return from the extreme moment of negative horizontal oscillation. In Nietzsche's terms, it might be the moment beginning the Eternal Recurrence, but here, in characteristically Mallarméan fashion, it is a turn infinitessimally small.

With respect to the narrative cycle of Orpheus, then, Mallarmé's Orphic moment occurs when the scattered limbs first begin to stir back to life. It is also an internal event, a psycho-biographical moment perhaps precisely reckonable in the prose poem "Le démon de l'analogie" (1865), to which we shall turn shortly. Expressing both of these aspects of the moment is a characteristic oscillation in Mallarmé's verse, a "volatilization" given by a tensive quality of language that surfaces throughout the poetry, letters, and "poëmes critiques." This oscillation is like a reflex, registering the shudder as Orpheus passes between the gaping void of the Dionyisan *Ur-Eine*, with its immense gravitational pull, and the rigid frame of an Apolline form that has lost its suppleness.

The oscillation or vibratory reflex is key to Mallarmé's Orphic moment, enacting the myth in language. The syntactical and metaphoric operations *perform* the delicate oscillation in the barely perceptible "rising" that is the re-membering of Orpheus's scattered body (for Sewell, "the body of poetry"). Even in the preface to his translation of Cox's pedestrian *Manual of Mythology*, through which Mallarmé brings the latest "scientific" view of myth (Max Mueller's euhemerism) to the French schoolchild, the poet performs this characteristic operation. The gods, "a little superannuated" in his age, must be "delivered" from their appearances as persons and returned to their primitive state of natural phenomena, "comme volatilisées par une chimie intellectuelle."[15] A few lines further, describing the reproductions of the gods used as "fleurons et culs-de-lampes" between chapters of the text, he says they are necessary "pour fixer un instant en l'esprit la figure des dieux avant leur évanouissement."[16] This "volatilization" and "fixing" registers the disintegration of the traditional images of the gods, their "éparpillement en frissons articulés proches de l'instrumentation."[17] But rather than reverting to natural phenomena through this process, as Mallarmé/Cox suggests, they become "fixed" anew in the poet's linguistic operations.

This vibratory tension of the poet's verse functions as "un balbutiement" (mumbling or babbling) underlying the emanation of words, issuing from a "centre de suspens vibratoire..étant ce qui ne se dis pas du discours."[18] Like the gods—whose ambience must be seized before they vanish, registering the *essential* ("la notion pure")—any appearance or fact of nature, "brut, immédiat," requires this priestly devotion, which is the poet's "Orphic duty":[19]

> A quoi bon la merveille de transporter un fait de nature en sa presque disparition vibratoire selon le jeu de la parole, cependant, si ce n'est pour qu'en émane, sans la gêne d'un proche ou concret rappel, la notion pure?[20]

The phenomenon of the barely perceptible beginning, the faint tremor of vibration from the "centre de suspens" of the "unsayable," has as its inverse the "presque disparition vibratoire" (almost vibratory disappearance). The first is analogous to the birth out of the Dionysian Ground; the second, the disappearance, as the *iota* of the *Ur-Eine*, back into it.

It is hard not to hear, to imagine, all this as *sound*, especially since the overall metaphoric context in the Ghil preface is musical: "le Dire . . . rêve et chant";[21] "quelque chose d'autre que les calices sus musicalement se lève."[22] But the place from which the master speaks is *prior to sound*. At the "centre du suspens vibratoire" there is vibration. Not auditory or visual vibration, but vibration, period. The suspension of sense, the checking of the imagination—"le silence au vol du cygne"—grounds one in the silent darkness that reigns before Mallarmé's "singing of mystery" (Hugo Friedrich). "La poésie pure" is like music, because each has no referent. At the core of Mallarmé's poetics is the place where music and verse are indistinguishable. Thus poetry is not a species, a subset, of music. "La poésie pure" is the music before music.

The Prelude of the Cricket

A letter of the Tournon years provides an analogue to the poetic/musical principles laid down in the Ghil preface. The dialectic between "un fait de nature" and "la notion pure" is especially fine, for the poet, in this miniature epiphany, hears that purity in the "fait": the song of a solitary cricket. Here the barely nascent *is* sound:

> Hier seulement parmi les jeunes blés j'ai entendu cette voix sacre de la terre ingénue, moins décomposée déja que celle de l'oiseau, fils des arbres parmi de la nuit solitaire, et qui a quelquechose des étoiles et de la lune, et un peu de la mort; mais combien plus *une* surtout que celle d'une femme, qui marchait et chantait devant moi, et dont la voix semblait transparente de mille mots dans lesquels elle vibriat et penetrée de néant! Tant de bonheur qu'a la terre de ne pas être décomposée en matière et en esprit était dans ce son unique de grillon.[23]

The device of withholding the identity of the "sacred voice of the earth" until the end of the long period, stretching to include the stars, moon, and death within its simple and artless domain, is a brilliant stringing of the fundament, the *monochorda* of the lyre. One is reminded of the Orphic touch in Clement of Alexandria's account cited in the prologue, in which a cicada leaps into the breach when Eunomus breaks a lyre string in midperformance at the annual Delphic poetry contest. But even more à propos than Eunomus's cicada, this cricket, with its sound that is both *une* and "unique," provides the continuo that reveals the thousand cracks in the woman's song—"decomposed" and "penetrated with nothingness." By contrast, the cricket's song is full of the earth's "happiness . . . at not being decomposed into matter and spirit." This cricket's chirp is asymptotic to the beginnings of sound, defining the Orphic moment in the simplest of terms—in contradistinction to the quavering human voice. Between this autochthonous song and the austere plaint in Mallarmé's swan-sonnet (see discussion, pp. 88–90 below), the full range of the Orphic lyre is strung: from simple "fait de nature" to "la notion pure."[24]

The cricket's song is the prelude to the still, small moment when Orpheus begins once again to sing at his lyre. Among the widely scattered remnants of his torn body, something begins to stir, barely perceptible, "presque vibratoire." We do not yet have the remarkable Orpheus of unquenchable song, his severed head singing incantations as it floats down the Hebrus, which Sewell feels is the very incarnation of poetry. This is not yet the time for the completion, the *Vollendung*, of the cycle of the Orphic legend, integrated in the body of Rilke's poetry. But we do have a key moment in the myth's cycle, a moment of deathly stillness, yet pregnant with poetic song, the "voix sacre de la terre." The happy cricket is the prelude, the unassuming harbinger, of the hour when things, "les faits de nature," will burst forth with sympathetic song in response to the lyre of Orpheus.[25] When she labels Mallarmé a "failed Orphic poet," Sewell overlooks the subtle beginnings to the great Orphic outpouring that is Rilke's. There is *necessity* in the moment of pure negation, attended with impeccable ritual by our priest "du Néant." With her organicist reading of the Orpheus myth as the union of "Poetry and Natural History," she overlooks the quiet fruit of Mallarmé's own "natural history," given in the song of his humble cricket.

The Demon in the Dark Center

> For Orpheus's lute was strung with poets' sinews.
> —Shakespeare, *Two Gentlemen of Verona*

"Le démon de l'analogie" is a prose poem written at Tournon, near the beginning of Mallarmé's years of agony. It represents a condensed, painful lyric moment,[26] inexplicable, but for Mallarmé a rich, almost inexhaustible mine, containing a setting and a cast of figures—many of the recurrent images with which he performs his poetry. It records the psycho-biographical aspect of the poet's Orphic moment, where he is indeed "strung." On stepping into the street from his apartment, he has "the definite sensation of a wing gliding . . . on the strings of an instrument," which is replaced by a feminine voice saying, "The Penultimate is dead," a phrase from an unwritten poem that haunts this one. In this voice, "Je . . . reconnus en le son *nul* la corde tendue de l'instrument de musique, qui était oublié et que le glorieux Souvenir certainement venait de visiter de son aile ou d'une palme, le doigt sur l'artifice du mystère."[27] The voice is an aural premonition–as the first sense was tactile ("la sensation propre")–of the vision that awaits him at the window of a lutenist's shop. The sounds of this voice, an anima-voice, emerging independently of the poet ("enfin elle s'articula seule, vivant de sa personnalité")–play with the increasingly distressed man, who tries to control her by a grammatical explication of "Pénultième," and by "reading" the haunting verse in *his* voice, with his own stress. Thus his defensive strategy is to utilize, in turn, the two personas that he harbors: first the "professeur du lycée," then the poet. But when he does this he thinks: "la corde de l'instrument, si tendue en l'oubli sur le son *nul*, cassait sans doute et j'ajoutais en manière d'oraison: 'Est morte'."[28] To ease the tension from the voice ringing in his ears, coupled with the image of the instrument's string, the two joining in the phoneme "nul," he logically projects the snapping of the string: "la corde . . . cassait sans doute." Thus he tidies the verse line ("*'Est morte'* se détacha de la suspension fatidique plus inutilement en le vide de signification"),[29] while at the same time pronouncing the death of the nightmare. But the effort is premature, for he now looks up to find himself at the vitrine of a lutenist's shop:

> Mais où s'installe l'irrécusable intervention du surna-
> turel, et le commencement de l'angoisse sous laquelle
> agonise mon esprit naguère seigneur c'est quand je vis,
> levant les yeux, dans la rue des antiquaires instinctive-
> ment suivie, que j'étais devant la boutique d'un luthier
> vendeur de vieux instruments pendus au mur, et a terre,
> des palmes jaunes et les ailes enfouies en l'ombre,
> d'oiseaux anciens. Je m'enfuis, bizarre, personne con-
> damné a porter problement le deuil de l'inexplicable
> Pénultième. ("Le démon de l'analogie" [1864])[30]

The poet, all his senses full and stretched taut, stands for an instant at the crossroads of an antiquity he no longer grasps and the new moment whose shape he will never fully discern, know-ing in this moment that he must bear "Le démon de l'analogie" on his back. He is the string of the forgotten instrument that pro-duces the sound "nul" of "Pénultième," occupying the place of destruction of an ordered analogical hierarchy reaching back to

Plato and Pythagoras.[31] He is also the vessel (*athenor*) for containing the protracted tension of the birth of the new.

None alone can capture the exquisite pain of Mallarme's
synchronic moment at the shop window, but a whole series of
poems, read as one overlaid image, cumulatively reveals the
poet's dying into the "Penultième"–just before the birth of the
new song, as the scattered limbs of his sacrifice become "presque
vibratoire." The instrument of our modern Orpheus, which lies
suspended in a void of disuse, tantalizingly close, but behind Mallarmé's all-important window, is no longer the lyre but the lute. It
is a simple but rich substitution, amplifying the original vehicle
of Orphic deliverance with overtones of the athenor and of
ironic fullness.

The lute (*mandore*–an antiquarian lute, increasing the
remoteness of the image) of "Une dentelle s'abolit" (1887) suggests the motif of pregnancy, birth, and stillbirth so important in
Mallarmé.[32] This sleeping instrument in the first tercet of "Une
dentelle s'abolit" is the dust-gathering "pauvre poète" of the letter to Cazalis (Jan. 1865[33])–a "hollow void" or potential pregnancy, an image of absence in fullness:

> Mais, chez qui du rêve se dore
> Tristement dort une mandore
> Au creux néant musicien
>
> Telle que vers quelque fenêtre
> Selon nul ventre que le sien,
> Filial on aurait pu naître.[34]

The window is here again as paradoxical opening at the threshold of the creative act, approached through the axial words
"Telle" and "vers." "Tel" designates the wide, but unspecifiable
domain of the "as if"; "vers" is the fulcrum that tilts, leans, or
projects toward the ambiguous limit–the asymptote–of the
poem's arc. "Telle que" is doubled–in both sound and sense–by
the internal rhyme: "Telle que . . . quelque . . ."

"Cantique de Saint Jean" (Tournon/Besançon 1864-67),
with its terse hexasyllabic and even more condensed tetrasyllabic
lines ending each quatrain, executes the Baptist chillingly,
quickly, and efficiently, comparing "ma tête surgie" (the identity

Mallarmé:St. John is explicit) with the precise moment of the sun's setting. Here the poet, as John the Baptist, is "le Penultième"—and in terms of the solar Orpheus in the "Dieux antiques," Orpheus is evoked by the setting sun, "incandescent," with his blood diffusely spread on the horizon. The horizon is yet another variant of the limit, the asymptote, the "penultimate." We have as further instance of our central image, a simultaneous trembling at the moment of sacrifice:

> Je sens comme aux vertèbres
> S'éployer des ténèbres
> Toutes dans un frisson
>   A l'unisson
>
> Et ma tête surgie
> Solitaire vigie
> Dans les vols triumphaux
>   De cette faux.[35]

"A l'unisson" is an inversion of "le son nul," suggesting the anterior musical unity that is accessible through the sacrifice of the "penultimate," just as the surging head is an inversion of the setting sun. The site, the container registering this reaping of the head of the Baptist/Poet, which surges up at the moment of the sun's death like a flower cut by the scythe at the day's end (compare the scythe of time at the moment of transferral from Apollo back to Dionysos, p. 79, above), is the body of the poet, specifically his spine: "I feel as if shadows were spreading in my vertebrae all in a shudder, at once." The entire poem is masterful in its evocation of one sudden, supreme moment, which is consonant with the *sparagmos* of Orpheus. The place of song, though, is not the severed head but the vertebrae, image for the scattered body ("un frisson / à l'unisson"). Instead, the head looks toward the glacial heavens, "En quelque bond hagard / Son pur regard," ending with the anticipation of a reciprocal image, an answering constellation: "Penche un salut."[36]

"Sainte" (1865), one of Mallarmé's most perfect poems, is an extremely delicate reflection of the moment at the lutenist's window. The moment is superimposed upon others, notably a vision of Saint Cecilia in a monstrance pane. We know this from another version of the poem from the same year in the collection of Henri Mondor, entitled "Sainte Cécile jouant sur l'aile d'un chérubin," which seems to be the original.[37] In revision, the image of an angel enclosing (*clore*) a harp in the third quatrain undergoes a brilliant transformation; the Angel's (now in caps) flight *becomes* the harp. Here are the two quatrains:

> Sainte à vitrage d'ostensoir
> Pour clore la harpe par l'ange
> Offerte avec son vol du soir
> A la délicate phalange

becomes:

> A ce vitrage d'ostensoir
> Que frôle une harpe par l'Ange
> Formée avec son vol du soir
> Pour la délicate phalange.

In each case there is enjambement of the "délicate phalange," leading across the chiasm to the saint's finger. And the final quatrains are the same:

> Du doigt que, sans le vieux santal
> Ni le vieux livre, elle balance
> Sur le plumage instrumental,
> Musicienne de silence.[38]

But in the amended version the "phalange" (the tip or end-joint) is shared between the angel's wing and the saint's finger. It is an extraordinary feat, bringing the two phalanges together, one a finger joint, the other the analogous end-joint of the visitant angel's wing—a "plumage instrumental," which her finger barely touches, forming a delicate and fluid axis that is a momentary, microcosmic form of the Spindle of Necessity from the *Republic*, book 10. The "essence" here is on the brink of volatilization, so that the *musicienne* plays a palpable silence: "presque vibratoire."[39] One other brief point about the enjambement. The touching of two flexible joints ("phalanges") across the chiasm gives the effect of a hinge, so that the images on either side become panels of a miniature dyptich. This observation is just another of a whole series of appreciations of the antiquarian aspect of this finely crafted piece, which has been seen as an annunciation and a missal painting, or an old monstrance pane.[40] The small scale of all of these makes them objects appropriate to a devotional study.

The scene could also be that of the antiquarian's shop. Let us compare its imagery with two details from "Démon": (1)"Je sentais que j'avais, ma main réfléchie par un vitrage de boutique y faisant le geste d'une caresse qui descend sur quelque chose, la voix même" (that is, the voice he heard as he stepped into the street) and (2) "la sensation propre d'une aile glissant sur les cordes d'un instrument." In "Sainte," the saint poises (*balance*) her finger on the the wing-as-instrument, which is also the meeting point between the two sides of the monstrance. This is remarkably close to the experience of the poet in "Démon." There, leaning against the glass, the poet places his hand on the medium, giving the visual illusion from a perspective above the objects strewn on the floor that his finger is just poised on the string of the mandore. The cumulative image then brings together the poet's hand, reaching to touch through the glass the "ailes enfouies en l'ombre, d'oiseaux anciens," and the finger of the saint in the monstrance pane, resting upon the angel's wing tip, which has become harp. It is the *crépuscule*, the moment of the death of the sun, the surge of the Baptist's decapitated head, the visitation of the Angel and the pause at the lutenist's window. I do not think it would be too much to suggest that this is a foreshadowing of Rilke's Engel: here a guardian of the negative moment that Mallarmé holds in poetic tension throughout his career. The whole sequence, from "Démon" through these later efforts, bears the powerful imprint of what I can only call Mallarmé's *daimon*.

"Don du poème" (Tournon, Oct. 1865) probes another direction this moment might have taken, and the result is a pitiful stillbirth of the bird who could have been the bearer of the "ailes . . . d'oiseaux anciens" from "Démon":

> Je t'apporte l'enfant d'une nuit d'Idumée!
> Noire, a l'aile saignante et pâle, déplumée,
> Par le verre brûlé d'aromates et d'or,
> Par les carreaux glacés, hélas! mornes encor,

> L'aurore se jeta sur la lampe angélique.
> Palmes! et quand elle a montré cette relique
> A ce père essayant un sourire ennemi,
> La solitude bleue et stérile a frémi.[41]

All the elements are here again: the glass, the feathers (joined in this instance by the palm-branch), and later in the poem, old instruments—the viol and clavichord. The bird of the stillbirth is black, recalling the oracular crow of Apollo (also Poe's Raven) and the important figure from the Orphic theogonies, Nyx (Night), a large black-winged bird who may be seen as the depositor of the Orphic egg whence Eros/Phanes emerged. The father is, in one inflection, the poet as father-creator, in another, "l'azur," identified in line eight.[42] The distant heaven itself echoes with the shock of the monstrous birth: "sourire ennemi . . . stérile a frémi." The shudder is not one of just awakening but rather more like the anticipatory shudder of the Baptist at his beheading. It is not time for flight/birth; the moment must be held in suspension, as in the exquisite image from "Sainte": ". . . elle balance / Sur le plumage instrumental."

Finally, in the sonnet "Le vierge, le vivace, et le bel aujourd'hui" (1885), we again witness the moment, but now, twenty years after his experience at the shop window, Mallarmé is its master:

> Le vierge, le vivace et le bel aujourd'hui
> Va-t-il nous déchirer avec un coup d'aile ivre
> Ce lac dur oublié que hante sous le givre
> Le transparent glacier des vols qui n'ont pas fui!
>
> Un cygne d'autrefois se souvient que c'est lui
> Magnifique mais qui sans espoir se délivre
> Pour n'avoir pas chanté la région ou vivre
> Quand du stérile hiver a resplendi l'ennui
>
> Tout son col secouera cette blanche agonie
> Par l'espace infligé a l'oiseau qui le nie,
> Mais non l'horreur du sol ou le plumage est pris . . . [43]

This poem, as does "Sainte" in a quieter, less dramatic way, retains the tension that the poet had not been able to bear in "Démon," running from the shop window, "bizarre, personne condamné," descending into the hell whose necessity he recognized in that instant. Now, in the poet's maturity, he has built in deliberate, impersonal fashion a vessel suitable to contain what had been thrust upon him in "Démon," and shattered in the "verre brûlé" of his premature effort in "Don." Here the poet is again a bird, but now a swan, caught in the ice. As such, he is implicitly a reincarnation of Orpheus.[44] I see this poem as a second take of "Don," whose mangled, self-engendered bird presents a complex Orphic image, with overtones of homo and autoeroticism in the yearning for milk directed to the masculine sky. But this time, the swan, though caught in the ice, denies and thus endures his fate: "des vols qui n'ont pas fui . . . Pour n'avoir pas chanté la région ou vivre."

The poem is held throughout in a state of enormous tension, both in terms of the potential energy of the swan ("Va-t-il nous déchirer avec un coup d'aile ivre?" "Tout son col secouera cette blanche agonie") and in terms of an irony that represents a balance of opposing forces: "Par l'espace infligée a l'oiseau qui le nie." Instead of an explosion through the vertical "iced panes" of "Don," shattering iced glass and bird-child of Night, the swan denies the firmament that bounds it. Its majestic shiver also asserts a kind of equilibrium with the horizon of ice, an unusual conflation of Orphic images: swan and horizon. The remarkable thing about the poem is that it states with such force the theme of the poet's impotence, which had been humiliating in "Don du poème," but is now perpetually on the brink of vibration, poised between *potentia* and action.

In the end, Mallarmé triumphs by enduring the ontological moment to which he is condemned at the lutenist's window, patiently reworking it throughout his life. By working the cold, sterile field of his labors, he advances the cause of poetry, enduring *sparagmos*, with only faint hints that he might gain the incantatory head of Orpheus. Only in the last tercet, with consummate irony, does he get stellar consolation:

> Fantôme qu'à ce lieu son pur éclat assigne,
> Il s'immobilise au songe froid de mépris
> Que vêt parmi l'exil inutile le Cygne.

For as Walter Strauss has brilliantly pointed out, the perspective is now that of the constellation Cygnus, "le cygne d'autrefois" having become "le Cygne."[45] Though our poet is not to have a singing head, he does gain an intimation of the second part of the mytheme, being constellated in the bright night sky like Orpheus's lyre.

Poëmes Critiques: The Orphic Moment
in Mallarmé's Criticism

> Oublions la vieille distinction, entre la Musique
> et les Lettres.
> [Let us forget the old distinction between Music
> and Literature].
> —Mallarmé, "La Musique et les lettres"

Mallarmé's discussion of poetics spreads throughout his work—from his letters to his art and theater criticism—but the central texts are the "poëmes critiques": "La musique et les lettres," "Crise de vers," and "Le mystère dan les lettres." The term *poëmes critiques* immediately indicates how far we have come from the Platonic idea of the poet. Plato's poet, the *rhapsode* of the *Ion*, who rode the winds of the divine afflatus, was incapable of critical thinking or dialectic. Plotinus had altered the Platonic view of the artist, making him a creator, a maker (from the root, *poein*, or *poiesis*). This key neoplatonic alteration is the foundation for the new aesthetics, which the romantics began, Nietzsche and the aestheticists of the "l'art-pour-l'art" extended, and the deconstructionists claim to have completed. Mallarmé is a fulcrum in this developing progression: the moment of balancing, "presque vibratoire."

To "forget the old distinction between music and letters," a striking proposal at the dénouement of Mallarmé's most knotty exposition of his poetics, brings us by *epistrophe* (reversion to the source) to the place where we began, the invention of philosophy. Or, to the moment *just before* it—the "Pénultième," to borrow a heavily valenced word from the poet's lexicon. Or, placing it squarely in the tradition which concerns us, to his response to the question: "Avant Homère, quoi? . . . Orphée." For Mallarmé, accomplishing this is neither a matter of intuitively projecting oneself back to the moment of origins, like Vico's Orpheus who is "a den of a thousand monsters," nor one of remythologizing one's tradition, like Novalis or Wagner. Nor is it a matter of proclaiming oneself the new bard, a "Voyant" who destroys such antique distinctions through the sheer violence of the poetic voice, like Rimbaud (whom Mallarmé deeply distrusted).[46] It is rather the adoption of a subtle dialectical process, where the *operations*—not just the sound, cadence, and rhythms—are musical, unifying "music and letters" from the outset.[47] The lecture "La musique et les lettres" presents this subtle dialectic in exquisite detail.

The discussion that follows—primarily of "Musique," but with "Crise de vers" and "Le mystère dans les lettres" in supporting roles—will be conducted around the source where "la poésie pure" jets out (*jaillir*, an extremely frequent term in the poet's lexicon), the place of the music before music. This source is a place that the poet may approach and watch: the place of the gatekeeper, like Plato's shaman Er. But it is not a place he can ever reach. One of Mallarmé's greatest talents, I believe, is to describe the comings and goings near this source, which is no longer the place of the Muses near the mouth of the Helicon, on the slopes of Olympus (or Parnassus), but a junction in the coordinates of the "omnipresent Line"[48] that inscribes imaginative space.[49] Earlier, in a letter to Aubanel (1866), he had envisioned himself as a sacred spider, spinning out threads from his mind that form at their points of connection a "marvelous lacework . . . which already exist in the heart of Beauty."[50] Here, in keeping with the increasing movement toward impersonality, it is the "omnipresent Line" that inscribes the patterns laid down in the heart of Beauty. And Stéphane has become an "aptitude of the spiritual Universe," a site for its development.[51]

"La musique et les lettres"

"La musique et les lettres" is the title of an invited lecture that Mallarmé gave to the Taylor Society, London, in March 1894. The distinguished foreign guest of the Society is at the height of his career, and the text exudes his pride and confidence upon the occasion. Much of Mallarmé's verse, especially in the post-Tournon period, is "occasional"; this includes, for example, the

various "Tombeaux" with which he eulogized his fallen com-
rades. Here in London he seizes the opportunity to create an
"occasion," a kind of literary nova in which he gives a definitive
statement of his poetics.

In the beginning, with characteristic irony, he brings news:
"des nouvelles . . . [l]es plus surprenantes. . . . On a touché au
vers."[52] This is the touchstone of the entire evening's difficult lecture, and it is doubtful whether many present understood its
meaning, since the revolution in verse structure in Britain had
been underway for quite some time. The breakdown of the classical alexandrine, on the other hand, was a contemporary and
indeed shocking event in France, an event that Mallarmé, an
impeccable classicist himself, realized was epochal.[53] In terms of
our present framework, this singularly simple statement, "On a
touché au vers" (We have landed at poetry),[54] emblemizes the
process of disappearance of the Apollonian world.

For Mallarmé, the two modes—music and letters—parted
only for an "ulterior meeting" of an earlier state, one that was
"évocatoire de prestiges situés à ce point de l'ouïe et presque de la
vision abstrait."[55] The analogous thought in "Crise de vers" is:
"Ouïr l'indiscutable rayon—comme des traits dorent et déchirent
un méandre de mélodies: où la Musique rejoint le Vers pour former, depuis Wagner, la Poésie."[56] In unmistakably Orphic language, the poet brings us back again to the Orphic (*Ur*) moment,
on the verge of hearing and seeing, but presensory: "to hear the
unquestionable ray . . . adorning and tearing apart a meander of
melodies." The "meander" evokes the Hebrus, carrying its
melodic source with it.[57] What we normally call "music" and "letters" are the "face alternative ici élargie vers l'obscur; scintillante
là..d'un phénomène, le seul, je l'appelai, l'Idée."[58] This Idea, to
which our arts can only point, is that which is sandwiched
between, as it were, the two alternate faces; just as Orpheus is the
evanescent moment between Apollonian form ("scintillante")
and Dionysian *Ursprung* ("élargie vers l'obscur").[59]

Indeed, this analogy is one that Mallarmé might find appropriate, for in the next paragraph he says, "L'un de ses modes
incline à l'autre et y disparaissent, ressort avec emprunts: deux
fois, se parachève, oscillant, un genre entier."[60] Disappearing into
one another, then reappearing, borrowing substance from one
another, thereby creating an entire "oscillating" genre, is pre-

cisely the way in which Being appears through the mediation of the realms of the Delphic brothers. The oscillation is a sign of Orpheus's presence, like the flickering shadows on the walls of Plato's Cave.

To reinstate the unity of music and literature, "moyens réciproques du Mystère," is to submit to the prior jurisdiction of the "Idée," remembering that the Idea, the source of the reciprocation (or oscillation), can nowhere be found except by its effects and relations.[61] To trace it requires entering into the den of the "sacred spider" in an attempt to follow the "co-ordinates of analogy," which Walter Strauss points out elude him in "Démon."[62] Here they do not, and he is so confident of his grasp of the gestalt that he calls these central remarks a "proof" of the "postulate" that "Literature exists . . . alone, to the exception of everything else."[63] In a sense, this "proof" is a defense of his frequently quoted remark that "Toute chose au monde existe pour aboutir dans un beau Livre" (Everything in the world exists to end up in a beautiful Book). This Book, a "spiritual instrument," is Mallarmé's version of Coleridge's oft-projected life-poem and Novalis's encyclopedia containing all things.[64] Only his was to be condensed, modeled after the alchemists' "grimoire."[65] "Un coup de dès" was perhaps its first installment. "La musique et les lettres" constitutes notes toward its defense.

As with Shelley's claims for poetry, "la Littérature" and "le Livre" both encompass the wide realm of human vocation.[66] Mallarmé's strategy in this defense is twofold: (1) to claim for literature the entire spiritual repertoire of the race, such that its emanations return in an *epistrophe* of renewal—"tout ce qui émane de l'esprit, se réintègre"[67]—and (2) to broaden the understanding of what constitutes "music," so that the common basis of "La musique et les lettres" may be discerned again in "the verbal orchestration" ("Crise de vers") that resounds underneath texts.[68]

In "Le mystère dans les lettres" he describes this music as "l'air ou chant sous le texte, conduisant la divination d'ici là, y applique son motif en fleuron et cul-de-lampe invisibles."[69] The "fleurons et cul-de-lampes," wherein we encountered the vanishing gods as mnemonic topoi between chapters in "Les dieux antiques," now invisibly mark the return of what was "torn"—a "meander of melodies." This "air" *conducts* through the architectonic structuring principle of the cul-de-lampe (the flanged, "floral" portion of a column that braces the joint between the column and the horizontal sill above it: a kind of flying lintel or pro-toarch). It is this kind of structuring principle—unlike the architectural support, invisible—which constitutes through "div-ination" the hidden musicality, the modal support for the text.

Mallarmé's "proof" that "only literature exists" (note the postmodernists' debt to this postulate) opens with a key statement which gives the other side of the fundamental dialectic enacted in Mallarméan verse: "La Nature a lieu; on n'y ajoutera pas" (Nature exists; we cannot add anything to her).[70] Seemingly contradicting the assertion about literature, it is conveniently ignored by the poststructuralists among Mallarmistes. But the two statements constitute a genuine contrariety, and the "réciprocité de preuves" that they exchange is the driving engine of Mallarmé's thought and poetry. This is a shift from the position of Poe and Baude-laire, who emphasize the artificial over the natural, reacting to the overly sentimental, gushy treatment of nature in the roman-tics. Mallarmé, who was even more a poet of artifice than Baude-laire, asserts that all of this is within the domain of nature; the poem, consciously achieved, is the place of asserting the simulta-neous dominion of "literature" and "nature."[71]

We shall now look at the core of the "proof" in "Musique," remembering that with Mallarmé the verbal precision is not dis-cursive (in the middle, he says in fact the opposite) but neverthe-less leads, by exceedingly evocative effects, to a clear notion of what literature does and to what the "Idea" in the Mallarméan sense might be:

> La Nature a lieu, on n'y ajoutera pas; que des cités, les voies ferrées et plusieurs inventions formant notre matèriel.
>
> Tout l'acte disponible, à jamais et seulement, reste de saisir les rapports, entre temps, rares ou multipliés; d'après quelque état intérieur et que l'on veuille à son gré étendre, simplifier le monde.
>
> A l'égal de créer: la notion d'un objet, échappant, qui fait défaut.
>
> Semblable occupation suffit, comparer les aspects et leur nombre tel qu'il frôle notre négligence: y éveillant, pour décor, l'ambiguité de quelques figures belles, aux intersections. La totale arabesque, qui les relie, a de ver-

tigineuses sautes en un effroi que reconnue; et d'anxieux accords. Avertissant par tel écart, au lieu de déconcerter, ou que sa similitude avec elle-même, la soustraie en la confondant. Chiffration mélodique tue, de ces motifs qui composent une logique, avec nos fibres. Quelle agonie, aussi, qu'agite la Chimère versant par ses blessures d'or l'évidence de tout l'être pareil, nulle torsion vaincue ne fausse ni ne transgresse l'omniprésent Ligne espacée de tout point à tout autre pour instituer l'idée; sinon sous le visage humain, mystérieuse, en tant qu'une Harmonie est pure.

Surprendre habituellement cela, le marquer, me frappe comme une obligation de qui déchaîna l'Infini; dont le rhythme, parmi les touches du clavier verbal se rend, comme sous l'interrogation d'un doigté, à l'emploi des mots, aptes, quotidiens.

Avec véracité, qu'est-ce, les Lettres, que cette mentale poursuite, menée, en tant que le discours, afin de définir ou de faire, à l'égard de soi-même, preuve que le spectacle répond à une imaginative compréhension, il est vrai, dans l'espoir de s'y mirer.[72]

Briefly, four general themes are under discussion First, the practice of literature involves seizing the relationships among events and objects according to an (author's) interior pattern, a simplification of the world according to his "taste." The statement about the "état intérieur" recalls Schiller's remark about the "musical mood" (*Stimmung*) that preceded his writing verse, which is part of Nietzsche's argument for the musical source of lyricism. Likewise, Baudelaire remarked that a poem started with a "mood," not its sense.[73] Second, this pattern is an entire network or web of relations where the events take place (or the objects appear) fleetingly, so that what one perceives is always escaping or disappearing. The events are self-effacing. As one critic, James Lawler, puts it succinctly, "beauty [in Mallarmé] is created out of the interplay and mutual destruction of a system of images."[74] Likewise, Rémy de Gourmont says that our poet "dissociates" rather than associates. As Mallarmé insists, his aim is to "paint not the thing but the effect it produces." The effect, traceable as an after-resonance in the web of relations, remains after first the object, then the image "dissociates." This remnant is a

"notion" of the object and the momentary evanescence of the
"Idea." Third, working against the use of the language of reporting, the poet "habitually surprises [the ideal]." Ordinary language (*quotidien*) is stretched in order to "unleash Infinity"[75]
according to a new rhythm, a new fingering (*doigté*) of the "verbal
keyboard." Mallarmé continues to develop the theme from the
preceding paragraph of the "melodic encoding" that "quietens
with our very fibers the motifs that compose [the soul's] logic."
We will return to amplify this theme—the poet as instrument—in
the discussion of "Crise de vers" at the chapter's end. Fourth, literature is a stretching, yearning, or hope: a curve ("totale
arabesque") asymptotic to the proof that the "spectacle" outside
is a mirroring of one's "imaginative comprehension." The
"omnipresent Line" inscribing space from "every point to every
other for the purpose of instituting the idea" defines the ultimate
limit, the apogee of the Platonic curve in his work. It is the two-
dimensional "Divided Line" of Plato's theory of forms reinscribed in Mallarmé's more spatially oriented universe. As such,
it idealizes the coordinates of space itself as the ultimate grid
upon which the "ideas" are hung.[76]

"Crise de vers"

"Crise de vers" (1885) was published several years before "La
musique et les lettres." It employs the same ironizing journalistic
tone as the opening of "Musique," proclaiming the "exquisite,
fundamental crisis" of literature, which "even the press"
announces daily, mostly to the disfavor of Mallarmé and "le Symbolisme." He speaks of witnessing "a disturbance of the veil in the
temple, with significant folds and a little tearing."[77] With exquisite irony, Mallarmé states that the veil would have been rent
sooner if it were not for the presence of Victor Hugo, the "father"
with "the hand of a blacksmith" standing behind it.[78] Thus the
Orphic moment, if you will, delayed its birth until this tenacious
blacksmith's hand had loosened its grip. [79]

Whatever the role of Hugo, and the slights here in "Crise"
of Baudelaire's crucial position in the "rénovation de rites et de
rimes,"[80] Mallarmé is on hand for an Orphic purification: "par la
retrempe et l'essor purifiants du chant" (by the retempering and
the purifying flight of the song).[81] This is a "libre disjonction aux

mille éléments simples" (a free disjunction into the thousand simple elements), a "recovery of [the] vital divisions" (ses coupes
vitales) of language. These "thousand *simple* elements" form a
contrast with the "thousand" impurities of the complex voice of
the young woman in the poet's account of the cricket in the
Lefébure letter. They are like "la multiplicité de cris d'une orchestration, qui reste verbale"–or the thousand cries of a flock of
birds, or of crickets. The disjunction into these simple elements
represents a kind of atomism, as in Leucippus and Democritus,
where the elements, like the torn limbs of poetry, each move
from a "centre vibratoire," liberated by "une brisure des grands
rythmes littéraires . . . et leur éparpillement en frissons articulés
proches de l'instrumentation."[82]

The Orphic language, "dispersion in articulated shudders,"
is particularly thick here, and the presence of Orpheus: torn, but
bearing potential song in every morsel, is palpable. It is, to Mallarmé, a great and historic opportunity to be on the scene of this
breaking, at the precise moment (the Orphic moment) of rend-
ing the veil, in position to "rechercher . . . la transposition, au
Livre, de la symphonie" (research . . . the transposition of the
symphony into the Book).[83] As in "La musique et les lettres," this
transposition is due not to the "sonorities" of orchestral instruments but to "l'intellectuelle parole à son apogée que doit avec
plénitude et évidence, résulter, en tant que l'ensemble des rap-
ports existant dans tout, la Musique." At its apogee, the word
establishes the ensemble of relations that permeates all things.
This apogee corresponds with the moment at the negative end of
the oscillation whose arc defines the forms of Western art. The
ensemble is "la Musique," what was once called *"mousike"*: the
unsundered plurality of all the human arts.

That this apogee or moment of plenitude corresponds to a
moment of disjunction, marking an abyss over which the coordinates of the "omnipresent Line" are laid, is suggested by an analogous statement, but working the other way, from "Musique," in
which the poet affirms that literature is a "spell" (*sortilège*) whose
purpose is to liberate, "hors d'une poignée de poussière ou réal-
ité sans l'enclore, au livre, même comme texte, la dispersion
volatile soit l'esprit, qui n'a que faire de rien outre la musicalité
de tout."[84] Reading these two passages against one another, one
may see that the plenitude of the word in the first corresponds to

the "dispersion volatile" of the spirit in the second (compare the volatilization of the gods in "Dieux antiques"). In the latter, Mallarmé names this process of volatilization a "spell" (*sortilège*). In both texts the conclusion of the operation is music as the ensemble of relations among all things.

The Poet as Instrument

> Toute âme est une mélodie, qu'il s'agit de
> renouer; et pour cela, sont la flute ou la viole de
> chacun.
> [Every soul is a melody which must be renewed;
> everyone's flute and violin exist for that.]
>   —Stéphane Mallarmé, "Crise de vers"

> Toute âme est un noeud rhythmique.
> [Every soul is a rhythmic knot.]
>   —Stéphane Mallarmé, "La musique et les lettres"

Earlier I suggested that the setting for "Démon"—the antique lutenist's shop—was a "knot of necessities" that provided an endlessly fertile ground for Mallarmé's versification. The theme that emerged strongly from examining a series of poems in this light was that of the poet as instrument. Shakespeare's astonishing remark—that "Orpheus' lute was strung with poets' sinews"—was offered as *leitmotif* for this identification. Since the original lyre of Orpheus was the one that he inherited from the northern Apolline shaman, an instrument framed by the carapace of the turtle and strung with animal sinews, the remark places the lyric poet directly in the line of inheritance of the "animal-master." This tradition is more direct, and therefore truer to the original archetype, than is the more widely spread motif of Orpheus/ Christ as shepherd of sheep. The custodial role, with the god as a glorified herdsman, is yet another example of neolithic influence upon the figure, and is thus evidence for Mallarmé's striking observation about "la grande déviation homérique" in poetry. I agree with both the Hellenic tradition and with Mallarmé in seeing Orpheus as representative of an earlier stratum, where the identification with the (hunted) animal and the spiritual leader of the hunt, the shaman, was implicit.[85] This is the point of the *sparagmos*, and his connection to Dionysos, who enacts even more explicitly the identification of hunted and hunter. This older tradition persisted obliquely in the Middle Ages,[86] and returned toward the center in the Renaissance, where a most striking example is provided in the hell-panel of Bosch's famous triptych. Here Orpheus is depicted both as "strung" or crucified on the lyre, and pilloried about the neck of the lute.[87]

The identification of poet and instrument performed by the poetry proper is further elaborated in these critical pieces, where Mallarmé extends the figure to cover the "rénovation de rites et rimes," which occurs throughout the body of poetry. The key verbs are *renouer* ("renew" or "retie") and *retremper* ("resoak," also "retemper"). The "traditional instrument" is the alexandrine, subject to a "deliberate mutiny" in the experiments of Jules Laforgue, opening the way for others. The inherited fabric is "worn to the threads"—necessitating the "retrempe." But the image of retempering is also apropos to the restringing of the poet's lyre (or lute, or mandore). The workshop for this "renovation" is the soul of Everyman, which is both "une mélodie, qu'il s'agit de renouer," and "un noeud rhythmique." French prosody undergoes a "modulation . . . individuelle," revealing the necessary ties between the soul's rhythm and the rhythm of prosody. Mallarmé testifies in "Crise" to a democratization of poetry, which is at the basis of this epochal shift: "quiconque avec son jeu et son ouie se peut composer un instrument, dès qu'il souffle, le frôle ou frappe avec science; en user à part et le dédier aussi à la langue."[88] An aristocratic poet himself, he is ambivalent about the swarming of "la Foule" into the halls of the Muses, thus the ironic tone that creeps into this remark. Though he accepts the necessity of the "retrempe," he asserts that the classical forms, and the alexandrine, will still be utilized for the "formal occasions" that he loved so well. But the existence of the "vers libre" and the experiments in form associated with it (his own "Un coup de dès" demarcating, temporarily, its limits) bring a tension to the craft which Mallarmé welcomes.

I spoke above of the destruction of the object in Mallarmé's verse, a salient quality that several critics have noted, most eloquently Richard. This destruction, which opens a space for the evanescent Orphic image—a suggestion, mood, or evocation (all summarized in Mallarmé's "notion") occurs in the breast of the poet as well. He must not only learn to see the objects of the physical world in novel ways but also listen to a different inner melody. The knotty phrase from "Musique," "Chiffration mélodique tue, de ces motifs qui composent une logique, avec nos fibres," bears directly on this process. In another context, replying during an interview in *L'Echo de Paris* to Jules Huret's request that he define "le Symbolisme," he said, "C'est le parfait usage de ce mystère qui constitue le symbole: évoquer petit à petit un objet pour montrer un état d'âme, ou inversement, choisir un objet et en dégager un état d'âme, par une série de déchiffrements."[89] This latter remark constitutes an application of the Cartesian calculus to the poetic interdiscipline between states of the soul and the soul of objects. In either case, in mathematics or in soulwork, the result depends upon dealing with the smallest possible increments of the subject in question. What Mallarmé seems to be saying in the "Musique" *koan* is that the "melodic encoding" that the poet performs "with his fibers" establishes new grounds by quieting—or "killing"—the accepted "motifs" that formed the habitual bases for the action of logic. The encoding in effect "decodes" and replaces the "topics"—to use the term from classical rhetoric—upon whose prior establishment all logical operations depend.

Finally, consonant with a new melodic encoding and a retying (*renouer*) of the rhythmic knot, the fingering (*doigté*) of the "clavier verbale" must be reworked, so that ordinary words (*aptes, quotidiens*) may be utilized to produce the poet-alchemist's magical transpositions. The stakes in this "jeu suprême" are high: "afin de qui déchaina l'Infini." The poet is making a religious gamble, risking his being and substance against the stacked deck of "le hasard." In addition to the science required to make oneself an instrument, the poet must be willing to serve himself as the experimental ground. Sometimes he feels the cords being stretched to the breaking point ("Démon"); at others, they slacken, and he feels like an antiquarian instrument, moldering in some attic or alleyway ("le pauvre poète," Letter to Cazalis, Jan. 1865). What is strung, what is unstrung, what is restrung: all of these involve the fiber, the sinews of the poet. The workplace in which the "Crise de vers" is enacted is the soul of the poet, precisely and exquisitely attuned to the passion play of "le Verbe."[90]

Tombs, Fans, Cosmologies: A View from the Prison House

5

Mallarmé's recognition of the necessity for retempering springs from the Platonic basis of experience; namely, that our lived truths are the resonances of the soul. These re-soundings emerge as *récits*, recitals of the soul's stories. But because soul reposes in the "musicalité de tout," these stories or myths are emitted as melody and rhythm, a melody and rhythm that are her own cadence.[1] As I argued in chapter 2, the great eschatological myths of Plato have the quality of *récits*, deriving their authority from the impression they give that here, indeed, is the recollective speech of the soul. The speaker *has been there*. This is the key to the Platonic *anamnesis*, which is the basis of all knowledge for him and for the figure Socrates. It is my conviction that this quality of a *récit* is fundamental to the mode of activity of the Orphic poet.

The context for our brief analysis of Plato's myths in chapter 2 was that he was a cosmologist, producing protestant versions of original myths emphasizing the continuous life of the soul, circulating through a tripartite cosmos. They were part of the "Orphic protest," roughly contemporaneous with other revised cosmologies, whose broad themes were analogous.[2] Like Empedocles, Plato envisages the vault of heaven as the roof of a cave, and earthly life takes place, metaphorically, within a cave. Movement within the various realms is portrayed as the reciprocal motion of fluids, either as *aer* or as water. Thus in the *Phaedo*, the greater Greek world (*oikoumene*) is shown to be part of a vast interlocking hydrostatic system. In the *Phaedrus*, Plato gives a complex image: the ebb and flood of eros as the action of a reciprocal tide, which is fire and water and passion, all at once. Combining these two settings, the tripartite cosmos becomes a kind of grotto. As we shall presently see, this is also a key image for Mallarmé, operating with the same kind of energics as those in the *Phaedrus*.

Tombeaux

As Plato's master metaphor for the nature of human existence enfolded within Gaia was the Cave (and its many analogues), Mallarmé's was the tomb: *tombeau* or *sépulture*. For Socrates, philosophy was preparation for death. For Mallarmé, death was the precondition of poetry. His personal ego-death, recorded in several letters of the Tournon period, established the conditions for writing his mature poetry. As dialectic cleared the soul of the dense mists rising from the lakes of *oikoumene*, enabling its eye to rise to receive the brilliant rays of the sun dawning upon the "true earth," so the perspective from beyond the life of *bios*, that of the tombstone, frees the Mallarméan poet-hero into self-fulfillment: "Tel qu'en Lui-même . . . l'éternité le change" (So that eternity changes him into himself ["Tombeau de Poe"]).

As many critics have argued, the objects of these elegies—Gautier, Baudelaire, Poe, Wagner, De Banville, Verlaine—all serve in the memorialization of poetry as reconstituted in their work. Each poet becomes in death a monument, a fragment of some obscure disaster, a meteorite ("calme bloc ici-bas, chu") quietly evoking the fiery trails of original comet-souls.[3] In death they become receptacles, like the "nooks" of Pherecydes into which Phanes deposited his seed. Collectively, they are the site ("à travers ce que fut [nous]") for the continued "development" and "mirroring" of the spiritual universe. As Mallarmé says, "Fragile comme est mon apparition terrestre, je ne puis subir que les développements absolument nécessaires pour que l'univers retrouve en ce moi son identité."[4] Thus for Mallarmé the old Orphic equation, *soma = sema*, would be thrown back upon itself, a statement about an "aptitude" (roughly the equivalent of the Greek *daimon*) of the universe for realization. The body is an opportunity for building a tomb adequate to memorialize the yearnings and migrations of spirit, or as D. H. Lawrence put it, to build the "ship of death."

The tomb, or "naufrage" (the shipwreck of "Un coup de dés"; "quel sépulcrale naufrage" of "À la nue accablante tue"), is a fragment "des affres nécessaires" (equally, "des *astres* nécessaires"), one that nevertheless contains the pattern of the whole. Thus it is like the echoes from the "shell" to which Rodenbach compares the master of *les mardis*, which "simplify the universe."[5] Unlike Plato's image in the *Phaedrus* of human beings as oysters trapped in their shells, the shell that our modern Orpheus inhabits is empty, so that the echoes (*rumeurs*) of the universe may sound therein.[6] The tomb, on the other hand, is a lasting testimonial to the flight of this shadow, a memorial to the "locutionary disappearance of the poet." Mallarmé's efforts in the "Tombeaux" are to perform a double act of disappearance: (1) the volatilization of the dead poets and (2) the removal of his own authorial voice from the elegy. In the "Tombeau de Poe," the effect is that the block of granite is both source and site. In the "Tombeau" to Verlaine, the dead poet's *daimon* is hiding in the grass, much like the solitary cricket, the atom of joy that will once again emit the Earth's song.

Both the cave and the tomb are varieties of prison, a motif that Plato develops in the *Republic*, through manacling the human inmates so that they cannot see the sun, and in the *Phaedrus*, via the oyster-prison image and the intricate damming and releasing of the waters of eros across the barred entrances to the wing follicles of the souls of lover and beloved. The prison motif is equally strong in Mallarmé, especially in the many images in his early poetry of ice and glass and in the futile efforts of his avian heros to break through the medium or veil. I am thinking now particularly of the swan in the sonnet, "Le vierge . . . ," and the miscarriage of the bird in "Don du poème." But against this attitude of futile striving, or vain mirroring, as in the tortuous Hegelian self-observation of Hérodiade, the later "Tombeaux" and thematically related sonnets have an atmosphere of calm, as in the "calme bloc" of Poe's tombstone.

The struggles that preoccupied or engulfed each of the poets in these *hommages* reverberate in these final settings, but the "*tombeaux*," as cosmic monuments, describe an arc (like the "tête de Saint Jean"), setting limits and containing the echoes of

their thunder. This is particularly effective in the Baudelaire sonnet, where Mallarmé employs the dead poet's idiom, which he
had successfully imitated in youth, to create a setting that is both
squalid and sublime. The opening lines fittingly evoke the "eye of
the soul" sunk in the mire and muck of earthly life:

> Le temple enseveli divulgue par la bouche
> Sépulcrale d'égout bavant boue et rubis[7]

The buried temple is the tomb of the poet, who still "slobbers"
forth his verse, at once mud and jewels, the mixed products of
the "sewer" where Baudelaire chose to dwell poetically. And in a
masterful stroke, one of a number of brilliant resolutions to the
necessities of rhyme (here: rubis/Anubis; subis/pubis), Mallarmé
invents as the shade of the dead poet an "immortel pubis," a flying pelvic bone that "reverbérates": echoing in its solidity the
erotic transports of life, but fixing the act as a shell by its skeletal
rigidity. Like Plato, who, to extend the domain of the eldest god,
whimsically but unerringly created the "gods'" version of Eros,
Pteros the flying phallus, Mallarmé illustrates in this shrewd gesture his own Orphic pedigree, creating a feminine analogue to
Pteros.[8] Yet this pelvic muse rests outside the sealed crypt that is
Baudelaire's legacy as a member of the order of Stéphane's
"Tombeaux," seating herself "Contre le marbre vainement de
Baudelaire." And, with echoes of the "inquiétude . . . et un peu sa
déchirure" of the "voile de la Déesse," she is "Au voile qui la ceint
absente avec frissons." She is "shudderingly absent" from the "veil
that girdles her": a hole, an aporia, hieroglyph of le Néant, ghost
of the ancient mother of all, Nyx.[9] While the marble vault guards
the "buried temple" of Baudelaire's poetic legacy, she, his Shade
and "tutelary poison," surrounds the tomb with the *Néant*, whose
aer we must breathe, and die of it. The pairing of contraries in
this superb sonnet: tomb and bird, slime and jewels—is a sure sign
of its Orphic kinship with Plato's daimonic cosmos, from the
mud of hell to the brilliant colors of the stones of True Earth. All
is held in reciprocal tension: the (scavenger) jackal Anubis of the
first stanza, its "muzzle ablaze like a wild howl," is nevertheless
preserver, as Egyptian god of embalming, of the monumental
body of the poet; the pubis is "absente," but "avec frissons"; the
boundary stone (herm) of marble is in turn bounded by the "tute-

lary poison," guardian shade of the death that we necessarily breathe in approaching the dead poet's achievement.

Eventails

The density of the *"Tombeaux"* is balanced in Mallarmé's work by the whimsically erotic fan ("Eventail") poems. Many critics have remarked upon the peculiar appropriateness of Mallarmé's inscribing fans with poems, creating emblems of the subtle and evocative power of words, which "'speak' the movement of the fan," as Judy Kravis notes.[10] To me, they are kin to the "prayer flags" still widely used in Tibet, Bhutan, and Sikkim. Closer still to our topos, they evoke the Orphic relics, the engraved bone-plates from Olbia and gold-plates of southern Italy, whose bold message—"Son of earth and starry heaven"—percolates up from the tombs, the spiritual principle acting as the subtle "vowel" that lets these delicate materials sing.[11]

Mallarmé's wisps, inscribed upon the fans belonging to the ladies to whom they are addressed, are flecked with the glancing light from the rustle of Phoenix wings—the principle that emerges from the chthonic depths of the tomb. In "Eventail" ("de Madame Mallarmé"), the fan emblemizes the angelic power of words, messengers ("Aile tout bas la courrière") that descend into verse as the lady's fan flutters into the salon: "Rien qu'un batte-ment aux cieux / Le futur vers se dégage / Du logis très pré-cieux."[12] The fan is "limpide," letting through the light from "quelque miroir," but it has at the same time "Pourchassé en chaque grain / Un peu d'invisible cendre." Translucent mirror of a suggested Beyond, it is nevertheless invisibly tainted by the old titanic nature, present as ash, which purchases/pursues the limpid, seemingly pure image into every grain.[13]

In "Autre Eventail" ("de Mademoiselle Mallarmé"—his daughter Geneviève), the poet hides himself, a "subtle lie" of an enfolded bird in her hand ("Garder mon aile dans ta main"). The folding and unfolding of the fan evokes her quiet metamor-phoses as she undergoes the awakening of puberty, as each "cap-tive stroke delicately pushes back the horizon." This "battement" is the beginning pulsation of desire, within whose opening wing-folds the poet-father also resides, as the young girl's secret. Then, in the third stanza, this subtle and quiet little drama suddenly opens to reveal the cosmic reach of the operation:

> Vertige! voici que frisonne
> L'espace comme un grand baiser
> Qui, fou de naître pour personne,
> Ne peut jaillir ni s'apaiser.

Desire, held in check, "folded" into the fan, yields to the vertigo of space, quivering like a giant kiss with no object, space charged with a kind of virgin birth having nowhere to be born. The poet asks if she feels this "savage paradise" within her:

> Sens-tu le paradis farouche
> Ainsi qu'un rire enseveli
> Se couler du coin de ta bouche
> Au fond de l'unanime pli!"[14]

Again, the "buried laughter" is their secret: that she, too, is desire folded into a fan, from the corner of her mouth to the "unanimous fold" underneath. In the final quatrain, all is again calm—even "stagnant"—as the "blanc vol fermé" of the closed fan reposes. Yet the vast energies hidden within this emblem of awakening passion are again suggested in the final image of its repose: "Contre le feu d'un bracelet": a contained fire that mirrors both the setting sun and the closed fan, a retracted flight with the capacity to burn.

In another "Eventail" addressed to his lady friend Méry Laurent, the poet's "battement" delivers a bunch of frigid roses, which melt into a laugh of drunken blossoming. Again, though, in the third stanza this stroke reaches far beyond the seemingly closed confines of a fan in a parlor, reverberating "A jeter le ciel en détail" (To cast heaven in detail).[15] Finally, in the love-poem, "Si tu veux nous nous aimerons," Mallarmé places his work squarely at the center of the master metaphor of the *Phaedrus:* "Un baiser flambant se déchire / Jusqu'aux pointes des ailerons" (A flaming kiss tears itself apart right to the wing tips).[16]

The Folded Wing

The poet's wing has the capacity to storm heaven, as when, in this last "Éventail," its "battement" serves "À jeter le ciel en détail." It also can perform the inverse operation, penetrating the under-world, as in Mallarmé's characterization of poetry as "un sylphe suprême" fulcrumed upon the "pointes d'aile autochthone" (autochthonous wing tips) of bats in "Théodore de Banville."[17] But at other times, as with the abandoned, unstrung instruments, it is only a potential power. In the sonnet "Quand l'ombre menaça de la fatale loi," the "vieux Rêve" folds its "indubitable" wing into the poet. Here is the first quatrain:

> Quand l'ombre menaça de la fatale loi
> Tel vieux Rêve, désir et mal de mes vertèbres,
> Affligé de périr sous les plafonds funèbres
> Il a ployé son aile indubitable en moi.[18]

The shadow, threatening the old Dream with its fatal law, evokes "le hasard" and its ubiquitous menacing position vis-à-vis the human Dream: that out there awaits a Presence, that the poet can defeat inertia and burst through the container, be it ice or glass or here, the oppressive ceilings, creating the effect of the tomb. Characterizing the Dream as "desire and sickness of my verte-brae" evokes the turtle-lyre, the ectoskeletal instrument of the shaman becoming here a more elusive endoskeletal yearning from the center of the poet's being. The Dream's folded wing reaching into this bodily sanctuary evokes the action in the *Phae-drus* of cogenerative eros; though here it is more like an invest-ment, which will be redeemed in the tercets:

> Oui, je sais qu'au lointain de cette nuit, la Terre
> Jette d'un grand éclat l'insolite mystère,
> Sous les siècles hideux qui l'obscurissent moins.
>
> L'espace à soi pareil qu'il s'accroisse ou se nie
> Roule dans cet ennui des feux vils pour témoins
> Que s'est d'un astre en fête allumée le génie.
> [translated in note 18]

There are three parts to a single topos here: the poet's body in the first quatrain, the ebony room of the second, and the earth seen from the depths of space in the tercets. Each of the first two stanzas has an element linking it to the following stanza. The "plafonds funèbres" of the first quatrain unite it with the "ebony room" of the second. This ebony room contains in turn "guirlands célèbres" that "Se tordent dans leur mort." The midnight room of "Igitur," with its writhing furniture, is quite close here: the dark room under the eerie glow of insomnia takes on the aspect of the night sky. The garlands, of a family with the wreaths, lace curtains, and tinseled borders of mirrors, are the analogue of star clusters: constellations, the Milky Way, and so on. So the second stanza looks forward to the splendid imagery of the tercets, where the old Earth, despite "hideous centuries," is a "festive star," shining forth the mystery of its "grand éclat." Mallarmé's sense of poetry as celebration, a "fête," breaks through here, as does the poet's heightened perception as a wager in the Pascalian sense. It is as if the depths of space from its own "vile fires" mirrored back the shining gem hidden underneath the mire of *oikoumene*. The undertone of menace and foreboding remains throughout the poem as a challenge for the festive spirit, which announces itself despite the necessity of this contrary element (thus, "l'ombre menaça" [1.1], "siècles hideux," [1.11], and "Roule dans cet ennui des feux vils," [1.13]). The final tercet shows the topos that contains the action as balanced, with the matter-of-fact line, "L'espace à soi pareil qu'il s'accroisse ou se nie" (Space ever like itself [even] if it grow or deny itself). Genius is the factor that tips this balance, though appropriately retaining the metaphysical tension, since the fires that bear witness to the "éclat" are "base," "vile."[19]

Reciprocal Fires: Constellations and Earthly Effulgences

"Quand l'ombre menaça" is the first of a group of four sonnets published together at the end of the Tournon descent.[20] We have already discussed the next sonnet of the group, "Le vierge, le vivace" in the previous chapter. Here I only want to point out the continuation of the theme of the folded or encased wing as an image of vast potential energy. For as I indicated in that previous discussion, though the wing is frozen into the ice, seemingly useless, the swan-poet's dignified scorn enables it to transcend its earthly prison—indeed to the extent that he is constellated in the night sky.

Passing over "Victorieusement fui le suicide beau" to the last of this sonnet group, "Ses purs ongles," we again encounter the Mallarméan/Platonic theme of the reciprocal mirroring of heaven and earth, once more mediated by the room or dwelling. The figure that bridges the *metaxy* this time is "L'Angoisse, ce minuit," which as Richard points out, is a variant of Night, who reaches into the heavens with "Ses purs ongles . . . dédiant leur onyx," forming a stunning variation of the stars-on-black ground motif.[21] She carries "Maint rêve vespéral brûlé par le Phénix / Que ne recueille pas de cinéraire amphore."[22] Once again we have the midnight anguish of the sleepless poet, reaching hungrily into the heavens with precious stones that are mirrors of the stars, the onyx of its fingernails. These are, at the same time "the host of evening dreams burned by the Phoenix that are not received in a cinerary urn." In the first two sonnets of the group, the poetic vessels contained their material; in "Vierge," almost perfectly, in "Quand l'ombre . . ." more enigmatically. In the second two sonnets, however, a gap opens between the poems as vessels and their mercurial material. In "Victorieusement fui.." the sprung suicide (usually interpreted as consummated in "Igitur"–an artistic suicide usurping its author's) is a *revenant*, leaving the poet's tomb "absent." And "Ses purs ongles" presents a whole series of unfilled vessels. In the first stanza, it is the "cinéraire amphore," echoing the absent tomb. The second stanza is one of Mallarmé's most "empty":

> Sur les crédences, au salon vide: nul ptyx,
> Aboli bibelot d'inanité sonore,
> (Car le Mâitre est allé puiser des pleurs au Styx
> Avec ce seul objet dont le Néant s'honore).

The stanza in effect doubles the unfilled vessel: "nul *ptyx*" in a "salon vide." This *ptyx*, is a shell, folded upon itself, thus a kind of conch, with which the "Master" has gone to gather tears from the Styx. This image is very close to that at the end of "Igitur," where Igitur swallows the drop of Nothingness absent from all the oceans.[23] In the tercets, the theme continues with an empty north window that opens upon a mirror–doubling the metaphor of the medium (glass, mirror, ice)–an enigmatic openness that then appears, at this dying moment, to fill:

> Mais proche la croisée au nord vacante, un or
> Agonise selon peut-être le décor
> Des licornes ruant du feu contre une nixe,
>
> Elle, défunte en le miroir, encor
> Que, dans l'oubli fermé par le cadre, se fixe
> De scintillations sitôt le septuor.

Though it is night, this moment preserves in passing the dying fire of the sunset. Probably the "gold" of the unicorns is the gilt swirl of a baroque mirror frame, as the unicorns rush toward the watery nymph who appears momentarily in the fluid medium of the mirror. Though dead, like the now vanished sunset, the image of the nixie is kept alive, "scintillating," as her image is returned by the Great Bear (*le septuor*).[24]

In all of these sonnets there is a mirroring, a reciprocity of vision, which is so characteristic of Mallarmé's poetic universe, as Richard demonstrates with penetrating sensitivity. The poet, though on his way to "elocutionary disappearance," is focally present in "Le vierge." In fact, as Lloyd Austin demonstrates, he is linked by this image to a whole tradition in Latin and French poetry.[25] But in "Quand l'ombre," which Richard calls the "most Mallarméan" of them all, and in "Ses purs ongles," it is the *site* of the poet's labor that becomes paramount: the empty drawing room at midnight, with the omnipresent constellations as returning figures of man's shaping intelligence (even when man is absent). The perspective in these two poems follows "quelque équilibre supérieur," whereby two midnight moments are mirrored.[26] In "Ses purs ongles" it is the moment seen from earth. In "Quand l'ombre menaça" the perspective reverses, and the mocking indifferent black screen of space, "rolling tediously" upon itself, for a moment shows the earth's "grand éclat," by the light of "feux vils."

As in Plato, Mallarmé's universe is daimonically charged, fired by a reciprocating action like that given in the *Phaedrus*'s model. The images depicting this activity are often the same: the flight of wings, birth as an escape from a vault or prison, sexuality as tying together the most disparate of elements. However, Mallarmé's version does not give the *source* of the movement. The poet has disappeared, replaced by words, a network of knots at the interstices of the encompassing web he left behind. These wink and glimmer, like stars seen through the atmosphere, a lace-work (*dentelle*) of wreaths and garlands, so that at times one doubts their existence, as in "Une dentelle s'abolit / Dans le doute du Jeu suprême." But though this vast web is a dubious winking of points in space, demarcating the *Néant* as would a net thrown into the heavens, it nevertheless remains a *net-work*, prod-uct of an artisan whose images the poet can only hope to grasp fleetingly, at the moment of their disappearance.

The Book, the Grotto, and Self-Initiating Words

Using a splendid image that is a kind of *Aufhebung* of the tomb and the fan, Mallarmé writes that "le Livre" is a "minuscule tombeau . . . de l'âme" (a miniscule tomb of the soul).[27] Like the fan, the "Book" hides its meaning in its folds. But, in contrast to the fan, and consonant with the tomb, "le Livre" is a building up, a "tassement" of pages, which create the density of a tombstone in their "épaisseur." Instead of being the peaceful wreckage strewn through the cosmos by a process of fragmentation, the inverse operation holds here, building soul page by page, as soil is built through the decay of vegetable matter, leaf by leaf.[28] The effect of "le Livre" as density is reinforced further when the poet calls it a "bloc pur," with reverberations of the "calme bloc" of the tombstone. Moreover, "the Book," this "miniscule tombeau de l'âme," is a grotto: "tout de pages à l'état subtil, qui sont là comme un fond de grotte précieuse demeurée le beau sépulture pour y vivre avec une enchanteuse idée."[29] Here the paradox of "le Livre" and of writing comes home, for though as tomb it has monumental overtones, it is *au fond* "à l'état subtil," revealing its precious contents only when the medium is active; the word is a *jaillissment* upon the air, either as the music of tone and breath or as the flight of wings rustling from the silently read page.[30] To Richard, Mallarmé's grotto is a vibrant, fluid open space, ready to expend itself as the rising up of poetry. Indeed, following Roden-bach (who is our chief source for what the poet said at his "mardis," the Tuesday evening salons at his apartment on the rue de Rome), he goes on to say that Mallarmé saw himself as grotto.[31]

But there is something more here which is tremendously important for the emergent modern theory of poetics. Instead of using "sépulcre," which is the synonym of tomb, Mallarmé says "sépulture," which is the (place or) *act* of burying.[32] He is reaching for the same connotative sense as in the epigraph to this chapter: the poet must sculpt his own tombstone. Against the monumental solidity of the *bloc* and the *tombeau*, he emphasizes the *act* of digging (*creuser*), sculpting, divining. The paradox of "le Livre" as legacy achieved and yet as a life lived remains richly alive in these words. It is the *act* of creating poetry, which draws upon and uses up all of the poet's energy and substance, a "desperate expenditure of energy" as Peter Dayan calls it, which is paramount to Mallarmé.[33] As Milton wrote, the end of life is "to be a true poem."

In an exceedingly dense and truly remarkable image of the grotto, Mallarmé speaks of it as an *activity of words*. The passage is from "Le Mystère dans les lettres":

> Les mots, d'eux-mêmes, s'exaltent de mainte facette reconnue la plus rare ou valant pour l'esprit, centre de suspens vibratoire; qui les perçoit indépendamment de la suite ordinaire, projetés, en parois de grotte, tant que dure leur mobilité ou principe, étant ce qui ne se dit pas du discours: prompts tous, avant extinction, à une réciprocité de feux distante ou présentée de biais comme contingence.[34]

Words act on their own, but they arise from the "vibratory center of suspense," the spirit (or mind) dwelling at the center of the operation. This spirit is that which does not "speak itself," the "unsayable" out of which poetic discourse projects itself—what I called in chapter 4 "the music before music." The effectiveness of words depends upon their being intimately linked to the "unsayable part of discourse."[35] The "many facets" of the words are the "walls of the grotto" through which words "exalt" and "project" themselves. As in the case of the "belle sépulture" above, it is the act of projection or construction that matters.

Though my first efforts at interpretation of this dense remark had to do with shadows projected upon the walls of the Cave (i.e., "*sur* parois de grotte")—this is clearly *not* what Mallarmé has in mind but a classically biased Platonic reading. Anthony Hartley translates "projetés, en parois de grotte" as "projected like the walls of a cavern" (see note 34). But even this is slightly off the mark. I suggest instead "projected into grotto walls." As I have continued to wrestle with it, I have come to see it as a statement about *the process of building* the cave walls. In the physical analogy, slow dripping of water over vast stretches of time *creates* the walls, seemingly solid entities that are indeed built up by progressive deposition of the minerals around which the water droplets had formed. So is a body of language built up by slow accretion. But if one pays attention not to the projected structure, the "language wall," but to the process by which it is created, one encounters a reciprocating action in dynamic motion, analogous to the properties of charged molecules of mineral water. This is a more subtle form of the Platonic process, the motion engendered by the *ionic* play of fire within water.

Mallarmé is clearly pointing to *process* and its careful and momentary distinction from the solidity of forms that veil the events they purport to present, and it is congruent with the indirect, evocative function of language that Mallarmé highlights at every possible turn in his work.[36] The mirroring that goes on in "les abrupts, hauts jeux d'aile, se mireront . . ." is the mirroring of the play of language itself, not of higher realms to lower realms. But this play "s'enlève en quelque équilibre supérieur, à balancement prévu d'inversions."[37] Again, it is the process that is all-important, not the goal or end state (which is the *limit*, and thus not reachable for Mallarmé, as I have affirmed several times). Rising to a higher equilibrium is, put plainly, the process of physical change, where higher means lighter, airier, less dense. At its most extreme it is *volatilization*: the movement from solid to gaseous form.[38] Kravis grasps this well when she observes that, in Mallarmé, "the sacred is not the invisible, but the distillation . . . into invisibility, of the physical."[39]

In one of his most famous remarks, Mallarmé asserts that:

> L'oeuvre pure implique la disparition élocutoire du
> poète, qui cède l'initiative au mots, par le heurt de leur
> inégalité mobilisés, ils s'allument de reflets réciproques
> comme une virtuelle traîné de feux sur les pierreries,
> remplaçant la respiration perceptible en l'ancien souffle

lyrique ou la direction personnelle enthousiaste de la
phrase.[40]

This is quite close to the process whereby words build a mutifac-
etted "grotto," lighting "before extinction" "a reciprocity of distant
fires." Here we have a *virtual* operation, which keys the interactive,
reciprocal "interilluminating" action of words, an indirect process
of obtaining meaning that begins from a slight imbalance ("le
heurt de leur inégalité mobilisés"), like the formation of a water
droplet around an ionized molecule or the irritant that forms the
nucleus of the pearl. Mallarmé contrasts this, in my interpretation,
with both classical *poiesis* ("la respiration perceptible en l'ancien
souffle lyrique"), and romantic versification ("la direction personnelle enthousiaste de la phrase"). The reciprocal "lighting . . . of
distant fires" and the "interillumination of reciprocal reflections,
like a virtual trail of fire on precious stones" are examples of the
"possession lointaine" that characterizes "l'érotique mallar-
ménne."[41] In this erotics, it is neither the "moi" nor the divine
afflatus who lights the fire, but "la poésie pure," which arises spontaneously and "musically, like the calyxes of absent flowers"—once
the poet achieves the discipline to stand alertly aside.

Notice that throughout all of these passages, *words* behave
like *dice*. In the citation from "Mystère," they exalt themselves "in
many a recognized facet." In this passage from "Crise," their
mobilization proceeds from the "shock of their inequality" (the
permutations of number as the word-dice strike one another).
Again, the trail of fire on the precious stones is dependent upon
their property of being "facetted." Finally, in a passage from
"Musique" that we have already examined, "l'esprit" attempts the
"repatriation of it all": "chocs, glissements, les trajectoires illim-
itées et sûres" (shocks, slides, unlimited and sure trajectories).
Negotiating the syntactical minefield for the referent of "de tout,"
one finds that it is "le verbe" for which Mallarmé "reclaims the
restitution."[42] Words, self-casting, display a differentiated pattern
whose meaning can be read, giving them a "shape"—as does the
mind when reading the dicethrow in the heavens.

It is characteristically modern that the operations performed by the soul in Plato, its motions waxing and waning like
moon-tides, are here performed by the words themselves. Words
are self-propelling, *but dependent upon the priority of the unsaid.* For

Mallarmé, language is at its most expressive when it works obliquely, so that something is created between the words and the "things themselves." What he wants to evoke is the in-between quality, the "reciprocating" movement of "distant fires" (the best example of which is the mutual mirroring of earthly and stellar constellations). The movement, as we have seen, is evanescent, caught "before extinction," as the words "s'enlève en quelque équilibre supérieure" (rise up in some superior equilibrium).[43]

The First Dice-toss: Igitur as Iota of the Ur-Eine

"Igitur" (1867–69) is one of those pieces at the margins of litera-ture: a work that the poet wished to be excised from his papers. As the poet's son-in-law Edmond Bonniot clearly points out, Mal-larmé had marked the manuscript "Déchet": failed (or shelved).[44] Nevertheless, as in most similar cases, the poet's request was not heeded, and the little monologue was admitted into the poet's corpus. It is also a boundary-piece marking the end of an era: the resolution of the Tournon crisis in a kind of "philosophical sui-cide."[45] Before it, Mallarmé is an emulator of Baudelaire, still struggling for his own style—as well as for his very life, as the let-ters of the period demonstrate. After it, the poet has a new confi-dence, as if he, like Igitur, has had the courage to "swallow" the *Néant*, so that it becomes the very ground of his work, rather than the exteriorized "azur" of the earlier period.[46] It belongs in the present discussion because it gives a background for the later "Tombeaux," which are among the most successful of his works, adroitly combining form and content to create, building on Baudelaire, a new vehicle for the elegy. Finally, it gives a rich back-ground for "Un coup de dès," showing the "education," as it were, of the stripling who becomes in the later cosmological poem the old man who reperforms the enigmatic dice-toss. In "Un coup de dès" the topos undergoes an inversion, replacing the descending stair into the well-tomb with the Mallarméan cosmos stretched to its fullest in the distiche of foam-capped sea and constellated night sky. What we see in "Igitur" is the event in embryo.

As a companion for negotiating the text, I have relied chiefly upon R. G. Cohn's *Mallarmé: Igitur*.[47] The first full-length study of the work, it fills an important gap in the field of Mal-

larmé studies. Cohn essentially sees "Igitur" as a variation in the
hero's "Night Sea Journey" (Joseph Campbell, Carl Jung), a
dialectic between the male idea and the female unconscious, figured as light-dark and up-down polarities, the rhythmic pulse of
diastole-systole, wave peak and wave trough. While the attempt at
a mythic setting is somewhat heavyhanded, many of Cohn's
analyses pinpointing the theme are on the mark. He joins many
critics in attempting a symbology of the title.[48] Drawing upon
Mallarmé's orthographic alchemy, he views the *i* of Igitur's name
as the masculine, assertive phallic principle, whereas the trough-
shaped *u* is the feminine, a receptive container. The *i* is tonally
bright, trim, upright, and phallic. Cohn associates it with the *iod*
of the Hebrew alphabet, "the mystic letter par excellence" (the *J*
as in *Jhvh*), as well as with Ixion, who fascinated Mallarmé. I will
discuss its kinship with the "sonnet en yx," "Ses purs ongles"
(which Cohn also notes), in the conclusion of this section.

For Cohn, the title initiates a dialectic of its dominate elements, as well as encoding, like a hieroglyph (a "Cratylism"), the
essential meaning of the poem.[49] He reviews comments that
would make *igitur* an allusion to a particular instance, as in
Roland de Renéville"s "igitur perfecti sunt coeli," from the Vul-
gate, or to Descartes's *donc*—though the latter is actually an *ergo*.[50]
But I think Cohn comes nearest the mark when he moves beyond
the narrower sense of the word: "the word *igitur* has an air of
metaphysical nudity about it, expressing nothing but a pure relationship; it is close to mere silence or a punctuation mark or a
term like *ecce* (as in *ecce homo*)."[51] He goes on to make a highly
provocative suggestion, which moves us fully into the "ontological" realm that I want to explore in what follows, namely this:
"One muses that Mallarmé might have called his hero *Point*,
recalling the 'point dernier qui sacre' of "Un coup de dés." And
more: "Musing further, we recall that he associated a *point d'exclamation* with one of his key symbols, the feather."[52] Cohn makes
much of Igitur's feather, which reminds me of the scene at our
primary biographical topos, the lutenist's shop in Tournon. But it
is the *point* that primarily interests me, including its variant in "!"
This is Igitur as the iota of the Ur-Eine, yet another inflection of
Mallarmé's Orphic moment.

Almost all of the commentators agree that the inspiration
for "Igitur" is *Hamlet*, wherein Mallarmé follows Hugo and

Baudelaire in seeing "the drama of Man."[53] It is a sketch for a
"metaphysical" play, a spare *récit*, a monological drama that takes
place in a severe, reduced landscape: a room, empty but full of
creeping furniture, with a spiral staircase leading down into a
well that culminates in a sepulchre with double doors. It is cast in
black and white: the white stars against the black sky, answered,
as in "Un coup de dès," by the white foam-caps of the sea; black
letters against white page; black holes like gunshots in the pure
white surfaces of the dice. As Cohn points out, Igitur, like Hamlet, is dressed in black velvet capped by a fringe, "une dentelle"
(white collar), and a feathered cap.

"Igitur" also seems to echo, for an attenuated moment,
some key features of the Orphic theogonies. The first is the scene
of the Orphic anthropogeny: the ambush, deceit, and ritual
sparagmos performed upon the infant Dionysos in his birth-cave
by the *kouretes*-turned-Titans. The second is the key role played by
Nyx: "la Nuit" in the notes following the first assay of the drama,
but represented as well by her variants: Néant and Minuit. In Mallarmé's intuitive fumbling, he picks up these ancient materials
and begins to grope towards the modern morality play of Beck-
ett. "Igitur" represents the whimper at the end of a second dramatic circle, initiated by the Theogonies (among which we find
this story of the infant Dionysos), a circle that has been inscribed
within the first: the emergence, in the Attic tragedy, of Dionysos
as hero and only actor. The original satyr-chorus, exuberantly
reflecting the epiphany of its god in the clamorous round-dance,
now gives way to the ghostly presence of the *ancêtres*, the Phrygian din replaced by their thin echo, the odd *chuchotements* (whisperings). As I suggested earlier of Orpheus, Igitur is the dot, the
iota of the *Ur-Eine*, punctuating the moment of disappearance of
Western art into its source for a *retrempe*.

Igitur and the Infant Dionysos

How is this scene like that of the infant Dionysos and his tormen-
tors? Obviously, there are differences. Dionysos is an infant, Igitur an adolescent.[54] Dionysos is murdered, Igitur a suicide. The
scene of Dionysos's death is clamorous, that of Igitur's so quiet
that he is terror stricken hearing the beating of his own heart.

Dionysos is brought back to life by his father Zeus (who, in the Orphic version, is his mother as well). And Igitur? We do not know his fate after his action, though there are several hints in the poet's subsequent work that some kind of rebirth occurs. If so, it is more paradoxical than life giving. In a sense, we still live in the attenuated moment of the death of Igitur. If there are oscillatory shudders, they may well be death tremors, though even these give rise to curious effulgences in the midnight glow of Igitur's chamber.

But there are curious similarities between the two figures. Though there is (perhaps) a difference in age, they are both figures *in potentia*: the seed of possibility, not its accomplishment. The scene of action is the same: our familiar topos of the cave/tomb (the well in "Igitur" hints at the potential for water, and it is thus an analogue of the grotto). Dionysos has his toys, Igitur his accoutrements. The dice have their analogue of sorts in the *konos*, a spinning top (symbol of the pine cone on the *thyrsus* of Dionysos). Also common to the two is the mirror. In the Orphic story of Dionysos's death, the child is chiefly diverted by his fascination with his image in the glass. The Neoplatonists interpreted the myth to depict the dispersion of his substance in the "traps of matter"; thus portions of the divine were left deposited in the simulacra of the lower world. With "Igitur," the mirrors seem to be the two doors of the awaiting tomb (which Mallarmé identifies with Night, reminding me of the Egyptian crypts that contained images of Isis, her arms outstretched to receive the corpse), reflecting an infinite regress of the hero's specular moment descending the staircase to his death. More than a diversion, the mirrored images invite Igitur into his inevitable fate.

The heart has a significant role in each narrative. Igitur keeps hearing whisperings (the pronouncements of the ancestors), then the beating of wings (supposing them to be bats), but finally the sound comes down to the two-stroke *battement* of his own heart. He is distressed by hearing this sign of his continuing existence ("cette perfection de ma cértitude me gêne") and curses "la nécessité, d'habiter le coeur de cette race."[55] In the earlier narrative, the heart of Dionysos is spirited away by Athena, who delivers it to Zeus, enabling him to resuscitate his heir (we shall return to this aspect shortly for further adumbration). Igi-

tur's "ancestors" bear a resemblance to the Titans in the Orphic
tale, their heart beating in his breast the sign and carrier of his
impending destiny. Instead of performing the sacrifice by overwhelming the victim from without, the *ancêtres* move even more
cunningly, as whispering heartbeats inexorably leading him in
the downward spiral to his waiting tomb, like a conch retreating
into its shell.

The deaths of the two figures are both overdetermined.
Dionysos is torn apart, boiled, roasted, then eaten. This unusual
sequence, which has received voluminous analysis over the centuries, is no more curious than Igitur's death by candle, book,
and poison.[56] Dionysos's murder and *sparagmos* are an explosion;
Igitur's suicide is an implosion, as befits a narrative that is an
inversion of the first one. The key point upon which this implosion hangs is drinking the drop of the Néant. In a way in which
she has not heretofore appeared, the original of Igitur's
Néant/Nuit/Minuit, the Hesiodic goddess Nyx, is ripe for swallowing. Thus the whole extraordinary series of swallowing, regur-
gitation, and rebirth that we witnessed from the Rhapsodic
Theogony (chapter 1) finally concludes. Let us examine it.[57]

The Return of Nyx

Igitur responds to the first demand to "blow out the candle"
(thereby snuffing out the characters of the *grimoire* who lived by
its grace) with the words "Pas encore." This sonorous echo recalls
Poe's raven, another black bird whose apparition arrives at midnight, the Orphic moment of "Igitur."[58] This sound-apparition
thus establishes the presence of Night even before her arrival as
Minuit in the subsequent scolia..[59] In these *ébauches,* the "Scolies"
or "Touches" that follow the *récit* proper in the *Oeuvres complètes,*
the poet experimented at length with having *la Nuit* play the role
of narrator.[60]

This extensive experimentation with *la Nuit* as heroine of
the text inspires Maurice Blanchot (whose further elaboration of
Mallarmé's Orphic moment we will examine in the conclusion) to
equate Night and Igitur, "theater and hero."[61] Whether or not
one accepts this interpretation, Night figures in a continual
dialectic that progresses through the *récit.* Certainly, the figures

la Nuit and Igitur are congruent in the Midnight Instant, which is both the doubling of the vertical phallic vector (as the two congruent hands of the clock [Cohn]) and the blackest part of night.[62] It is the appointed hour of Igitur's suicide, when he will go lie down in the tomb on the bed of his ancestors' ashes, blow out the candle, close the Book (*le grimoire*), and drink from a vial the drop of the *Néant*.

Drinking this drop is the telling act through which Igitur fits into the overall pattern of masculine protest, attempting a kind of male parthenogenesis. Like Zeus, he is beholden to Night. And like Zeus, he is determinedly self-sufficient, *virginal* in the Greek sense of the word, taking his fate into his own hands. He is a combination of Zeus as omophagist and Dionysos as seed or "heart," with a key difference. Instead of swallowing creation, as Zeus does by swallowing Eros/Phanes/Erekpaios, or the phallus of Uranos, or any of the variants concerning the resuscitation of Dionysos, Igitur swallows *anti-creation* in the form of "the drop of the *Néant* absent from the ocean."[63] (As Mallarmé notes in a marginal comment, this is the "absorption" of the dice as chance (*le hasard*). This "goutte de néant" is the essence and seed of Nyx, secreted as the "coup de dés" at the moment (*minuit*) when Igitur and *la Nuit* are congruent.

Igitur's position as an unlikely ontological hero in a renewed age of "negative theology" comes chiefly from the drop of Nothing that he now contains. This is the germ of another creation, whose fruits will be negative. As the end of his line, fulfilling the fate decreed by his ancestors (and disobeying his "Mother," as the author comments in the "Scolies").[64] Igitur is indeed the iota of the *Ur-Eine*, last vestige of the "vieux rêve," the dream of Maya projected by the creator-Dionysos, who succeeds Zeus as last in the line of demiurges. He is also the last drop of will, the *point* of the exclamation of an exhausted race.[65] As the "point" of the exclamation (!) and as the dot of the *i* he is an ejaculation of his ancestors. Taken together, these characters, ! and *i*, mutually cancel to reclaim the *origin*, the "microcosmic zero core" of "pure Negation."[66] They thus form another permutation of the overdetermined moment, the *Néant* appearing at midnight. In the person of Igitur, these figures perform a nocturnal emission of the Tantric type, retreating back into essence to join the drop of the *Néant* that Igitur swallows. After marching steadfastly and bravely to his sacrificial death, the poet becomes the new demiurge, bearing the paradoxical seed of a new creation, which is both ovum of Nyx and sperm of Zeus/Dionysos/Igitur.

Igitur, conjunct with Night in the instant of midnight, swallowing the "goutte de néant qui manque à la mer," is thus another image for Mallarmé's Orphic moment. Igitur is closer tonally to the "presque disparition vibratoire" than to the "centre de suspens vibratoire" and represents the moment when the "Pénultième" (of "Démon de l'analogie") shades over into the ultimate. In the space where Hölderlin had religiously awaited an epiphany of the vanished gods, the night of the romantics, Mallarmé/Igitur performs another vanishing act, this time absconding with the gods' very ground: Night as the ontological principle out of which all the gods and visible creation had issued. The poet accompanies this nullifying act, drinking the drop of nothingness, by lying down on the bed of ashes. In the numerous rehearsals of this moment, these were called the "ashes of the ancestors," but in act 5, "Il se couche au tombeau," the ashes become those of the stars. This reinforces Igitur's kinship with the Orphic Dionysos, who was the "soul of stars." All of the players—the ancestors, the stars, and the gods (summed up in Dionysos)—join in this reduction to ash with the death of our homunculus.

Atomic Ash and Teardrops

Ash and powder or dust are atoms of Mallarmé's poetic universe, the traces of matter that remain even when all the forms disperse. In this he is much like the Greek atomists, as I have already noted. This is true as well of the Mallarméan "drops": the drop of nothingness, here in "Igitur," and the tears that appear in at least two places, in the "Ouverture ancienne d'Hérodiade" and in the sonnet "Ses purs ongles." These tears or nothing-drops are the nuclei, the material beginnings of an anti-universe, whose shadows we see as the constellations that mark the boundaries of the holes they tear in the fabric (*dentelles*, wreaths, garlands) of Night.

In "Ouverture ancienne" (1866), the princess Hérodiade (Salomé) in her abandoned tower ("cinéraire et sacrificatrice") recalls Axël in his castle (or "El Desidichado"). A blood-red dawn breaks, lighting as a black-winged bird, dragging its wing in the stagnant moat of tears. The drag of this heavily burdened dawn of the "last day," which already feels like the final sunset, is further emphasized in the image of a waterclock whose counterweight is Lucifer:

> Le croissant, oui le seul est au cadran de fer
> De l'horloge, pour poids suspendant Lucifer,
> Toujours blessé, toujours une nouvelle heurée,
> Par la clepsydre à la goutte obscure pleurée.[67]

As the dawn paradoxically plays the part of sunset, so Lucifer performs a reversal with Christ, the "man of sorrows"; Lucifer is the man of tears whose constant wounding is the unending knelling of the hour. The image one gets is a mill wheel driven by Lucifer's tears. Instead of the suspended instant of midnight of both "Igitur" and "Ses purs ongles," the present emphasis is upon the passing of time as a continual wounding (and thus never the final blessing of death). The ever-rising dawn and the ever-renewed hour are doublings of wounds that will not close, quartering Lucifer on the rack of the pendulum, making him a new Ixion. Thus "Ouverture ancienne" is not only an overture in the musical sense, as the initial movement of "Herodiade," but also as an ever-opened wound. In the third and final movement of "Hérodiade," the "Cantique de Saint Jean," the long-awaited setting of the sun is conjunct with the upspringing of the severed head, the "return" movement in the Mallarméan cosmos that is missing from the leaden stillness of the dawn in "Ouverture."

"Ses purs ongles" was written when Mallarmé was in the midst of sketching "Igitur" (1868). Though we have already discussed this sonnet, I return to it now with a deepened sense of its import. Mallarmé had already begun preparing the scene for "Un coup de dés," the master poem that would culminate decades of probing the Orphic moment. "Ses purs ongles" is the closest and most unified thematically of this long series of predecessors, and it is the condensed poetic trial of the spiraling dialectic in "Igitur," abbreviating the whole process in the magnificently crafted lines of a single sonnet. The dark tears of Lucifer now become the tears that fill the Styx, and the unending mill of wounded and wounding time is fixed at the hour of time's harvest, midnight. As I mentioned in the previous discussion of the sonnet, midnight is a variant of night, the darkest point of the darkness, the "heart" of night. This is the point where, in "Igitur," the "goutte de néant" is secreted.

When read in the context of "Igitur," the unfilled vessels of "Ses purs ongles" approach fulfillment. "Maint rêve vespéral brûlé par le Phénix / Que ne recueille pas de cinéraire amphore" now have their resting place in the cinerary urn that Igitur has embraced. "Nul ptyx," the shell that is a superb condensation of the image of the grotto, travels with "le Maître" to the Styx to "gather tears," "giving local habitation and a name" to the rather austere "drop of nothingness that is missing from the sea" (as well as providing a sepulchre for Lucifer's tears).

Cohn has commented brilliantly upon the line in the first tercet, "Des licornes ruant du feu contre une nixe," and its echo from "Igitur": "Corne de licorne," which he sees as a complex relation of virginal but potent male spirituality and the miniature cornucopia of the female dice-horn.[68] But no one, to my knowledge, has remarked upon the other transformation wrought upon this line in the transposition from *récit* to sonnet: the miniaturization of the goddess Nyx (la Nuit) into the *nixe* towards whom the eager unicorns are "bucking" (*ruant*). Following my interpretation, the "defunct naked girl" in the mirror is the poet's reduced, virtualized image of "la Nuit," whom he personnified in the first quatrain (as I suggested in my earlier analysis) as "L'Angoisse, ce minuit."[69] The "purs ongles très haut dédiant leur onyx," the glittering fingernails of Night etching their bejeweled light against her mantle of pitch, come round in the sonnet's conclusion to the scintillating image of the constellation Ursa Major reflected in the mirror, fixing the image of the dying Nyx/*nixe*.

One last image from the poem, emphasizing again the close relation between the Platonic and Mallarméan universes, is the *ptyx*. The critical consensus of Mallarmistes, probably based upon a conversation that Renée Ghil reports having with Mallarmé, is that the word is a neologism. In Ghil's account, Mallarmé told him that he invented the word to create a crucial rhyme for the series "en yx." According to Ghil, Mallarmé designated its meaning as a vase or urn (continuing the sense of amphora from the first tercet).[70] This "neologism," however, is wholly Greek, a combination of *pt* (wing, feather) and *yx* (fold). Among the many meanings listed in Liddell and Scott are: the folds in plates of armor, of entrails, of the countryside, or of a writing tablet (shades of "Le Livre"). Pindar used it for the "folds of song." Many critics, perhaps intuitively following the sense of the Greek, have seen it as a kind of shell: a tiny conch or "folded" amphora.[71]

Intended or not, though, the word carries a much more subtle and basic meaning: a wing folded back upon itself. It thus defines the *potentia* of the "simplest container of reality (or nothing) a sort of womb developed from the merest bend or concave shape, the fundamental female Rhythm." It is "an ultimate or borderline entity, disappearing into and half merging with the original chaos."[72] As an *absent container,* "nul ptyx" is a negative analogue of the original Orphic egg—one that will be recharged with the tears of the Styx. But more than that, it is the inverse of Plato's Pteros, the gods' winged phallus, the essentialized Eros. Pteros, as William Arrowsmith maintains, "defies gravity" in its upward springing. The *ptyx* has a contrary, supergravitational pull into the deepest pit of all, the Styx as grotto of the underworld. The tears that it will contain are the seed of the anti-universe that will culminate in the "Un coup de dés." As container for the tears of the Styx, the *ptyx* is a perfect contrary for Plato's Pteros; each epitomizes in one perfectly balanced image their respective works, the *Phaedrus* and "Ses purs ongles." Finally, in "Ses purs ongles," the analogue of Pteros is the Phoenix, creating the ungathered ash-drops (the seeds of anti-creation, or death) from the "vesperal dreams" it incinerates. And the analogue for *ptyx* in the *Phaedrus* is Plato's image for *soma* = *sema,* the soul surrounded by the body "as an oyster in its shell" (*Phaedrus* 250c).

With this excursion into "Igitur" and the related images of "Ses purs ongles," I hope to have indicated that the previous mining of the Mallarméan topos is not only "Platonic" but also Orphic in a broader sense. Orphism is a form of "masculine protest," as we saw in chapter 1 (Marcuse).[73] The theme of male "parthenogenesis" in "Igitur" connects with many other parts of the poet's *oeuvre,* including "Don du Poëme" and "Le vierge." In these poems our poet and demiurge, both father and mother, is most often a bird, a swan, or other winged creature. In "Igitur," the marvelous bats of "Banville" return, joined by the enigmatic feather in the hat of a bust. But the dominant image of wings, which the suggested presence of bats ("le ventre velu d'un hôte inférieur de moi") reinforces, is one of a mad downward tumble into an underworld, which the poet hears as "le battement d'ailes absurdes de quelque hôte effrayé de la nuit" (the beating of the absurd wings of some host terrified of the night).[74] The beating of wings and the beating of the hero's heart merge until they are indistinguishable. This, in the Mallarméan sense, is what autochthony is about.

The gamut (*la gamme*) of this process is given in "Musique," where the poem has an "aile tendue . . . avec des serres enracinées à vous."[75] "A dipped wing with taloned roots in man" is a union of the two images with which we began our discussion of "The Folded Wing" above: that of the wing folded into the vertebrae from "Quand l'ombre menaça" coupled with the remarkable image of poetry as bats flying up suddenly from the "site" (line of verse) as the "ventilation of gravity," their fulcrum "autochthonous wing tips."[76] In the end, Mallarmé proves to be reworking, in a highly original fashion and within an entirely different fantasy of creation, the Platonic topos of the cave and the phenomenon at the core of his daimonism: the fundamentally basic process of rerooting the soul's wing in the *Phaedrus*.[77] Focussing upon the operative principles, rather than the terms (the apparent world and the world of Forms), we remain with Mallarmé in a universe of Platonic images and reciprocal operations.

Localizing the Rumor: **6**
Homeopaths and
Allopaths

> L'univers est simplifié puisqu'il le résume, dans un coquillage,
> à une rumeur.
>
> —Rodenbach, "L'Elite"

Conclusion

The mirroring of the *septuor* and the image in the mirror, of Nyx
and *"nixe,"* is the kind of reciprocal action from a distance at
which Mallarmé excels, as is the delicate tension between the
absent *ptyx* of the room and the *ptyx*/amphora—its *eidos* in the Platonic sense—at the banks of the Styx.[1] This second metaphor presents another sort of operation. Finding an appropriate home in
a conch-like shell for a tear from the Styx is an extreme condensation of the ebb and flow of the Mallarméan cosmos. In an
account of Mallarmé's performance at the "mardis," his admirer
George Rodenbach concludes: "The universe is simplified since
he summarizes it as a rumor in an empty shell."[2]

This process of *miniaturization* to which Nietzsche finally
reduced Wagner's genius is characteristic of Mallarmé's poetic
staging of the Orphic theater. The image of the master as a shell
containing a "rumor" is particularly effective because it plays on
the paradox of a simultaneous condensation (summary of the
universe into the microcosm of the shell) and vaporization (the
"rumor").[3] Its basic import amplifies a key remark of Mallarmé's,
one we have already discussed from "Musique," namely, "Tout
l'acte disponible, à jamais et seulement, reste de saisir les rap-
ports, entre temps, rares ou multipliés; d'après quelque état
intérieur et que l'on veuille à son gré étendre, simplifier le

monde."[4] Rodenbach's observation is a disciple's-eye view of the master as *operator* in the magical sense of the term, and it is indeed a superb image for the modern Orphic poet as shaman or magus. The basic principle is that of sympathetic magic, whose effectiveness depends upon the operator's ability to insinuate himself into the pattern of the inner working of the universe. The term for this type of operation is *homeopathy*, but it would perhaps be better termed *cosmopathy*.[5]

Beginning with Rodenbach's remark at one end of the spectrum, one might say that there are two basic critical orientations to Mallarmé's poetry. The first is homeopathic (or sympathetic); the second, allopathic. The homeopathic mode is represented by the "Geneva" school of critics, who generally follow a phenomenological approach; their method is showcased in Richard's splendid work on Mallarmé. The allopathic mode is represented in the works of the deconstructionists, principally Jacques Derrida, whose *Dissemination* is pertinent if only because it makes a seam between Plato and Mallarmé, though knitting the threads differently than I have. We will look briefly at examples of both of these critical orientations as a prelude to examining in somewhat more detail the work of an Orphic critic who continues the labor of Mallarmé's Orphic moment in his own critical and fictional work: the novelist-critic Maurice Blanchot.

The Master as Grotto

First, the homeopath. Richard confirms Rodenbach's homeopathic fantasy of Mallarmé, "dream[ing] the dream on," as Jung would put it: "Mais c'est que Mallarmé se rêve lui-même grotte, c'est qu'il s'imagine kiosque, voûte, coquille, 'ramenant,' comme l'écrit fort bien George Rodenbach, 'tout à soi-même et à l'unité, parce qu'il vivait au centre de la nature."[6] Consistently, Richard uses the verb *rêver* to describe Mallarmé's poetic method, building on the critical stance of Gaston Bachelard: both upon his "material imagination" and upon dreaming or musing as a legitimate way of thinking—including thinking about another's work, as the critic must.[7] So Richard is attempting to perform a double act of dreaming: first, explicitly, via the act of placing himself sympathetically in the poet's shoes, and second, implicitly, in the

act of performing this dream with a second dreaming consciousness, his own. For instance, in the last citation it is difficult to
apprehend where Richard stops and Rodenbach begins. This
illustrates a problem with the homeopathic method of criticism.
Such critics as Derrida, Kristeva, and Genette fault him precisely
upon this point: that one loses the distinction between Mallarmé
and Richard; therefore, *L'univers imaginaire de Mallarmé* is a collaboration rather than a work of criticism.

The lines leading up to Rodenbach's essentialist summary
provide a case in point, as Richard rhapsodizes on the theme of
the Master as grotto:

> Image parfaite d'une beauté "tournée au dedans," sorte
> de diamant creux, qui, tout en respectant l'infini papil-
> lotage des choses, réussit à utiliser cette dispersion même
> comme un moyen d'avivement individuel et d'harmonisa-
> tion globale. Heureuse clôture de l'oeuf, brio du diamant,
> plaisir de l'incisivité prismatique, joie de l'autoallumage
> réflexif, la grotte Mallarméenne réunit tous ces bonheurs
> en une seule forme bénéfique.[8]

The image of the grotto is a favorite of Mallarmé: Rodenbach and
Richard use it as a master-metaphor for the poet himself. Richard
takes it as touchstone for a whole treasure-house stuffed with the
now-infamous Mallarméan *bonheur*, substituting his own images
synthesized from the poet's themes. Thus Mallarmé is a "hollow
diamond," a "happy enclosed egg." Mallarmé's own adumbra-
tions of the theme of the poet as center of the universe included
the sacred spider at the center of his cosmic web, "myself
absolutely projected" of "Igitur," and perhaps best of all, the *ptyx*,
which is the tiniest of grottoes, appropriately miniaturized.

Richard sees this position, the hollow diamond with a
"beauty turned within," as singular joyous. The Richardian
terms of *bonheur*, which Genette finds both presumptuous and
excessive, are particularly thick here: (*avivement, harmonisation,
heureuse, brio, plaisir, joie,* and the summary *tous ces bonheurs*). But
life at the center need not be so; as Nietzsche insisted, the "contradiction [*Widerspruch*] at the heart of the world" spontaneously
emits the contrariety Dionysos/Apollo, a contradiction that is
joy and angst at once.[9] Rather than characterizing the Mallar-

méan élan under the sign of *bonheur*, it would probably be more appropriate to talk about an *energizing* quality that emanates from the vibratory center of poetry (as Richard himself demonstrates beautifully).

Perhaps even more telling than the emphasis upon *bonheur* is the fact that Richard grandly entitles the chapter from which this remark is taken, "Vers une dialectitique de la totalité."[10] There is certainly an imperious quality to Mallarmé's poetic thrust, but Richard's Hegelian reading overreaches the mark. The emphasis, however, need not be placed upon "dialectique de la totalité," but taking a subtle cue from Mallarmé, upon the humble pivot of the phrase "vers." Richard's critics certainly have evidence in this passage to substantiate the charge that he overstates his case for the poet as a beneficent, totalizing projector of an imaginal world. The Orphic "rumor" about which Linforth alerted us is reinstalled here, though now, fittingly, in Rodenbach's terms: as the sound (*rumeur*) one hears breathed back by a conch, the condensed earthly echo of the music of the spheres.

Aphilia and the Blinkered Allopath

Now, the allopath. Richard, in all of his dialectical richness, gives the deconstructionists material in this same passage for their preferred reading of the world. Rather than harmonizing the whole, they would remain "respecting the infinite blinking of things" seen through a "prismatic incisiveness." The infinite "blinking" or "flickering" of things is a superb image for a world that is contingent, continually shifting, and binary, as in semiotic codes (e.g., the on-off blinking of the papillas). The second image is also apt: prismatic incisiveness—an image that retains the sense of cutting, as in the sword of logos, but appropriately modified as a refractory operation.[11] Together, they help define the second basic critical stance, which I have called "allopathic." Its point is to isolate that which is foreign within the host that is being pathologized and to incise it. The emphasis is not upon a mode of knowing through likeness (*epistrophe*), becoming that which one seeks to know, but upon always being alert to difference.[12]

Jacques Derrida's *Dissemination* is an allopathic reading of the *Phaedrus*, which he interprets as a commentary on the *phar-*

makon, a doctor-patient relationship where truth is a drug against ignorance, rather than as a text on the phenomenology of *eros*. To this he appends a study of Mallarmé's brief sketch "Mimique," in which a harlequin-mime tickles his wife to death. The latter is presented—replete with reproductions of the parallel texts given on the blackboard—in the context of the "Double Session," a two-part seminar conducted in Paris in 1969. By choosing two pieces of such hugely varying weights, he sets into play an oscillation, designed to reveal the "play" in the mechanism, both the heretofore relatively unexplored function of the *pharmakon* in the *Phaedrus* and the anti-mimetic freeplay of all Mallarméan texts seen via "Mimique." But the oscillation becomes wild, orgiastic hilarity (that part of "Mimique" that obsesses Derrida, a continuing gloss on *pli*), a grotesque rather than an arabesque. In the process, he illustrates his own considerable capacity and brio for play: an unrestrainable urge to expose the aporia that yawns underneath the text.[13] These logical holes are to him both empty (rather than mystical or numinous) and arbitrary. He also ironically demonstrates, in this critique of one of the fundamental texts on love, "an all-dissolving nightmare of aphilia [lovelessness]," as Christopher Middleton describes Derrida's dominant working humor.[14]

That there is a characteristic oscillation in Mallarmé is undeniable (what else have we been talking about?). But it is much more delicate and dignified than Derrida's caricature of it. Derrida is, as both his admirers and some detractors will admit, subtle, but this subtlety is more a product of wit, what Coleridge would call "fancy," than of imagination. Derrida is a vast machine, swallowing any text that comes before it with agility, subjecting it to the reductive distortions of its digestive acids—in a word, bile. If Richard represents a kind of extreme of homeopathic criticism with respect to Mallarmé, then Derrida surely represents the extreme of the allopathic mode. Each might be said to represent an extreme of love: an excess of sympathy in Richard, the kind of love that the carnivore demonstrates toward its prey in Derrida.

Maurice Blanchot, an Orphic Critic

In chapter 3, I spoke of Elizabeth Sewell as an "Orphic critic" (as opposed to a critic of Orphism). My point was that she advances an original inquiry into the underlying unity of science and poetry that the "Orphic voices" of her study pursued. Appending "working poems" for each of her chapters, she performs as an Orphic poet, as well. The Orphic critic sets for herself a task of synthethis, not only analysis, which manifests in her work as poetry born out of the themes she engages in her critical text. As I noted at that stage of the argument, Sewell is working in another line of "Orphic poets," one that might be called "Goethean" (after the last person to approach a working synthesis of poetry and scientific thought). Her connection between poetry and thinking, however, is a firm one for any poet whom we would characterize as Orphic, and Mallarmé is as much thinker as poet (though he is poet first, and that makes all the difference).

In closing this study, I want to touch upon another Orphic critic, Maurice Blanchot, whose work is eloquent testimony to the fact that Mallarmé's Orphism did not constitute a dead end, as Sewell has asserted.[15] I turn to him now not only because he has an uncanny grasp of Mallarmé's Orphism but also because he continues to develop the poet's Orphic moment in his own work. His continuation of the *agon* of the Orphic poet clearly and decisively distinguishes him from Derrida, who gives no evidence that he has undergone the experience of "being strung"; Derrida's is a labor of the intellect and, as such, is full of "esprit." But it is not a labor of a soul who has undergone tempering, or drenching, in the vats of sweat and blood: a *retrempe* of the sort that the Orphic poet/critic must undergo. Blanchot has undergone such a passion, and it shows in the authenticity of his *récits*, which have the momentous density of black holes.

Though a "sympathetic" critic of Mallarmé's poetic enterprise, Blanchot does not attempt to adumbrate an entire imaginal universe, as does Richard, with the latter's considerable gift for analogy. Rather than multiplying and saturating the imaginal space, Blanchot works continually in the opposite direction, intensifying and essentializing until he has created the maximum possible density in the literary moments that he chooses to inhabit. Like Nietzsche's Dionysian lyric poet, he dwells essentially in one painfully reverberating lyric moment: only Blanchot is even more dispassionate in his presentation of that moment than is Mallarmé.

Blanchot is a novelist-critic, though his fiction has the quality of the *récit* rather than the narrative structure of a novel. And his criticism has a similar quality. Writing on a particular author (Kafka, Hölderlin, Mallarmé, Rilke) is always an opportunity for Blanchot to further explore the central question: How is literature possible? In *L'espace littéraire*, his magnum opus, he explicitly casts this inquiry in terms of the myth of Orpheus.[16] In a brief prologue to the book, he points to its center:

> A book, even a fragmentary one, has a center which attracts it. This center is not fixed, yet it is also a fixed center which, if it is genuine displaces itself while remaining the same and becoming always more hidden, more uncertain and more imperious. He who writes the book writes it out of desire for this center and out of ignorance.[17]

This center, he goes on to say, is that section of *L'espace littérarie* entitled "Orpheus's Gaze," which begins with the following: "When Orpheus descends toward Eurydice, art is the power by which night opens." Orpheus is the artist; Eurydice the "night": a closed, hidden, interiority that harbors the dark center of inspiration, which "art" (the artist) descends toward and, possessing sufficient power, opens.[18]

Orpheus, as seen here by Blanchot, bears considerable resemblance to Igitur. Even more, Eurydice, as the "instant when the essence of night approaches as the *other* night," is the moment when Nyx secretes the "goutte de néant," the Midnight of "Igitur." What Mallarmé groped towards in a series of *ébauches* for "Igitur," Blanchot accepts as fundamental. Night has undergone meiosis, splitting into two nights. Within the night of Novalis, a welcoming night, a place of intimacy, rest, and sleep, appears the "other" night, the ontological night in which "one is still outside." This night, Eurydice, is an "apparition" at the heart of night, namely: 'Everything has disappeared.'"[19]

This profound nothingness at the dead center of night is the center towards which Orpheus, the lyric poet as type of the artist, is drawn with an overwhelming force. Blanchot says that "Orpheus is capable of looking at everything, except of looking

this point in the face." He cannot look at Eurydice ("point," "centre") directly, else he loses her. But Blanchot says that he *must*
look out of his overwhelming desire for her, the very soul of his
work. He "forgets ... necessarily" the injunction, because the
"ultimate demand" that he makes "is not that there be a work, but
that someone face this point, grasp its essence, grasp it where it
appears ... at the heart of night."[20] This paradoxical moment is
the quintessential Orphic moment for Blanchot: not the descent
towards Eurydice, nor the charming of the denizens of hell (who
do not appear in Blanchot's sparse setting), but the gaze full of
longing for a vision of this dark, veiled center, which he can never
possess. What Schiller represented as the veiled statue of the goddess Isis ("The Veiled Statue at Saïs"), the English and German
romantics as Night, and Mallarmé as an unsettling dark flutter of
wings and yawning tomb in "Igitur," becomes in Blanchot the
pure dark center of being, the "sacred night."[21]

Igitur possesses Night by accepting her terms. He becomes
one with her in the act of lying down in the crypt at Midnight,
joining his doubled phallic vector (the vertical hands of the clock
at the tolling of the hour) with her echoing chamber.[22] She is the
inevitable roll of the dice which he accepts. But he also swallows
her "medicine"—the "goutte de néant"—thus becoming himself a
vessel for *her*. He is contained by Night as the tomb or crypt; she
is contained in him as the drop of nothingness that he swallows.
He does not try to *see* her, as the unfortunate hero of Schiller's
poem does. Orpheus is more mature than the novice in Schiller's
poem, but as a demi-god (or shaman) he is human enough, in his
impatience and insousciance, to transgress the strict boundaries
of his art, dooming him to lose that which he desired most.

In Blanchot's eyes, Orpheus has a very restricted relationship with Eurydice: "He is Orpheus only in the song: he cannot
have any relation to Eurydice except within the hymn," and he is
"sovereign only in the Orphic space, according to Orphic measure."[23] Their union occurs only within this song. "But in the
song, too," Blanchot says, "Eurydice is already lost, and Orpheus
himself is the dispersed Orpheus; the song makes him immediately infinitely dead."[24] Orpheus "loses Eurydice because he
desires her beyond the measured limits of the song, and he loses
himself, but this desire, and Eurydice lost, and Orpheus dis-

persed are necessary to the song, just as the ordeal of eternal inertia is necessary to the work."[25] Both Orpheus and Eurydice are lost in the fluid *epodé* of the song, and in this shared loss is their brief mutual joining. This dispersal, this loss of identity in the ritual of the magic song, is the evanescent moment, "presque vibratoire": the moment of volatilization when the substance of art just begins to take flight with her master.

So when Orpheus tries to possess this secret center of the night of art in the manner of day, the light of vision banishes her.[26] As long as he remains within the song, night is the "sacred night" that "encloses Eurydice," and "encloses within the song what surpasses the song." Night is itself enclosed by Orpheus's song: "It is bound, it follows, it is the sacred mastered by the force of rites, which is to say order, rectitude, law, the way of the Tao, and the axis of the Dharma." Orpheus's gaze breaks this binding, freeing Eurydice, the paradoxical blessing of the loss. He also loses himself in this moment. In Blanchot's terms, "His gaze is thus the extreme moment of liberty, freeing himself from himself and, still more important, frees the work from his concern." There is a necessity for impatience in this moment, but it must be joined to "the insouciant, weightless gaze of Orpheus."[27]

But how can Orpheus, as a shaman who knows the rules of the game, be so foolish as to forget the injunction? Blanchot's answer issues from that center where he, following Mallarmé, has transposed the question, to the only center he knows: that contradictory space where literature appears in the writer's leap toward inspiration. This is the nuclear moment at the core of the question that they both addressed incessantly: "Qu'est-ce que c'est que la littérature?" Blanchot's answer, though springing from his own ground, is peculiarly Mallarméan, indeed echoing *Un coup de dés*, which remains the limit of our own work, the unreached "Gloire du long désir": "That is why impatience must be the core of profound patience, the pure flash of infinite waiting, which the silence and reserve of this attention cause to spring from its center not only as the spark which extreme tension ignites, but as the brilliant point which has escaped this mindful wait—the glad accident, insouciance."[28]

The Poise, the Medium

> [L]anguage does not, at its most expressive,
> transmit an "Ideal" or "Idée," . . . it is in the
> creation of the poise which *is* language, situated
> between reality and our perception of it, that we
> sense the quality to which poets give the name of
> ultimate.
> —Judy Kravis, *The Prose of Mallarmé*

> Les mots, d'eux-mêmes, s'exaltent à mainte
> facette . . . centre de suspens vibratoire; qui les
> perçoit indépendemment de la suite ordinaire,
> projétés, en parois de grotte, tant que dure leur
> mobilité ou principe, étant ce qui ne se dit pas
> du discours: prompts tous, avant extinction, a
> une réciprocité de feu présentée de biais comme
> contingence.
> —Mallarmé, "Le mystère dans les lettres"

Language as poise. Mallarmé's love of the dance comes to mind; he describes it in the same kind of terms as the creation of literature in the "poëmes critiques." Indeed, in the second extract from "Mystère" he describes the underlying principle of language as poise, where "self-exalting" words, "projected as the walls of a grotto" move on their own but are perceived by the spirit/mind, "center of vibratory suspense," "as long as their mobility or principle lasts, being that which is unsaid in the speech." There is a remarkable homeostasis here between the independent words and the equally independent perceiving spirit/mind, which is characteristic of his remarks on poetics in the inimitable "poëmes critiques." Like the song in which Orpheus and Eurydice fleetingly join, the arousal of the words and the perception by the center are coeval; neither *causes* the other. And this synchronous moment is evanescent. The astonishing action of the words is a pulse, remaining only so long as the "mobility or principle lasts." The "unsayable" is not the eternal *logos* but is itself contingent, appearing only with the motion of words.

Blanchot, in an extended meditation on "Le livre à venir," speaks of this "unsayable" as the:

> preliminary exploration of the totally vacant region
> where language, before it is a set of given words, is a

silent process of correspondences, or a rhythmic scan-
sion of life. Words exist only to signify the area of correspondence, the space onto which they are projected and
which, no sooner signified, furls and unfurls, never being
where it is. Poetic space and 'outcome' of language never
exists like an object but is always spaced out and scattered.[29]

The image of furling and unfurling is amplified in a footnote to
this remark; there Blanchot describes language as "that into
which words have already disappeared and the process of oscillation from appearance to disappearance."[30] The scattering of
poetic space echoes Mallarmé's "éparpillement en frissons": the
dispersion of language ("Crise") as the dismemberment of
Orpheus. But the process of oscillation that Blanchot mentions is
our familiar flickering movement back, the "disparition presque
vibratoire."

Blanchot writes that Orpheus is Orpheus only in song.
Words signify only in the moment of their disappearance:
"Nature is transposed by language into the rhythmic process
which causes its incessant, infinite disappearance," is Blanchot's
summary of Mallarmé's paradoxical statements in "Musique,"
asserting that both nature and literature are sole existents.[31] All
of these statements have to do with the idea of the medium,
which functions only at the moment of mediation. Before and
after the moment in which it is filled it is pregnant or abandoned
space. Words, in all the richness with which Mallarmé evokes
them, are mediums. And the poet himself, the poet as instrument, is a medium: one who bears the shamanic contradiction.
He is not a medium in the archaic sense of being a vessel through
which the "ancient lyric blast" of the muse blows but the spontaneous, synchronous quickening of the "verse-writing intelligence"
(Hugo Friedrich) who is the modern lyric poet after his "elocutionary disappearance" in Mallarmé. Poetry in the Mallarméan
sense is thus much more akin to dance, to drama, to a reading or
a "happening." The poet disappears into the language of the
poem; this is when the poet is truly instrument, and, in Blanchot's
appropriation of Rilke, "ever dead in Eurydice."

In a fine commentary upon one of Rilke's Orpheus-sonnets,
Blanchot emphasizes the simple phrase, "He comes and he goes."

Rather than being the "eternal poet," filled with the *thumos* of the god, he ebbs and flows, like the waves of passion entering the tiny chambers of wing follicles in the *Phaedrus*. At one point, Mallarmé said that, for him, poetry took the place of love, and appropriately his poetry follows the dynamic of the *Phaedrus* rather than that of the *Ion*. It is not a divine afflatus that has swept our poet up, but a reciprocal movement of passion that remains on the phenomenal level of filling and venting microcosmic chambers: a midnight chamber, a shell, a water clock. This movement, always in flux, gone once perceived, is the *va-et-vient* of Orpheus, the Orpheus who appears as a phosphorescence all through Mallarmé's verse, prose, and letters. He is a flickering shadow on the wall of Plato's cave, a rumor whispering within a shell, the balance of a finger on the string of the mandola, the point of a bat's wing as the fulcrum between biosphere and underworld. Blanchot says that Orpheus is the "identity of presence and absence." Through the verse and criticism of Mallarmé, I see him rather as an instantaneous movement, a "momentary god" between absence and presence: an oscillation that is a "disparition presque vibratoire."

Notes

Introduction

1. Though heralded by Schelling and other Germans earlier in the century. See chapter 3.

2. We shall see in the latter chapters that Mallarmé's Orpheus does indeed operate in the fashion of rumor.

3. Plato's *empsychon*, the many-headed beast, is marvelously amplified in Vico's image of Orpheus as a den of monsters (see "Orphic Theorems," p. xix), which Vico may well have found in Plato, one of his three favorite philosophers.

4. Friedrich Nietzsche, *The Birth of Tragedy* and *The Genealogy of Morals*, tr. Francis Golffing (New York: Doubleday, 1956), Sect. 2, p. 24.

5. Mallarmé, discussing the "tragedy of nature" in "Les dieux antiques," says Orpheus occurs on the horizon at sunset or sunrise, thus at the boundary of the realms of Apollo and Dionysos (the latter as guardian of Hesiod's "Brood of Night").

6. Peter Dayan (*Mallarmé's Divine Transposition*) has written a very helpful book both clarifying Derrida's contribution and "saving" Mallarmé from its potential reductionism. Dayan's book will be further considered in chapter 4.

7. Friedrich Nietzsche, *Beyond Good and Evil*, tr. Marianne Cowan (Chicago: Henry Regnery and Co., 1955), p. 85 (aphorism 146).

Prologue

1. Clement of Alexandria, "Exhortation to the Greeks," in *Clement of Alexandria*, tr. G. W. Butterworth, Loeb Classical Library Ser., 1919, p. 5.

Chapter 1. Orpheus as Gap, Border, and Bridge

1. For example, the tension across "discharge in the word of the mythical image" and "resolved into the objective form of myth or of speech." Ernst Cassirer, *Language and Myth* (New York: Harper, 1946; New York: Dover, 1953), p. 36. Cf. also *An Essay on Man* (New Haven: Yale University Press, 1944; Toronto: Bantam, 1979), chapter 2.

2. Essentially following Saussure, not the myth-and-ritual tradition of the Cambridge School.

3. This is the *leitmotif* for Sewell's excellent book on Orpheus as the union of science and poetry, Elizabeth Sewell, *The Orphic Voice* (New York: Oxford University Press, 1960), p. 47, to which I shall return in chapter 4.

4. Cassirer, p. 36.

5. Those acquainted with the philosophy of Giambattista Vico will recognize his "imaginative universals" in Cassirer's contention that "before man thinks in terms of logical concepts, he holds his experiences by means of clear, separate mythical images" (Cassirer, p. 37). The intimate relation between myth and language upon which Cassirer insists is epitomized in Vico's statement: "every metaphor . . . is a fable in brief." *The New Science of Giambattista Vico,* tr. Thomas G. Bergin and Max H. Fisch (Ithaca: Cornell University Press, 1984), p. 129.

6. At the Staatliche Museen, Berlin, there is a lovely red-figured vase showing leopardskin-clad Thracians gathered round Orpheus, who is ecstatically playing at the lyre. The homoerotic overtones that many see in the post-Eurydice Orpheus are clearly demonstrated in this figure. Orpheus's hand has grown together with the plectrum, and the combined gestalt looks like a phallus.

7. Vico was among the first to argue that Homer was such a collective name. Ivan A. Linforth argues that Orpheus and his Athenian priest Onomacritus are also eponymns.

8. E. R. Dodds, *The Greeks and the Irrational* (Berkeley and Los Angeles: University of California Press, 1951); Mircea Eliade, *Shamanism* (London: Routledge, 1972); Mircea Eliade, *Zalmoxis* (Chicago: University of Chicago Press, 1972); Jack Lindsay, *The Clashing Rocks* (London: Chapman and Hall, 1965); Karl Meuli, "Scythia," *Hermes* 70 (1953), pp. 153–64.

9. Eliade points in particular to the skull of Mimir as an analogue of Orpheus (Eliade, *Shamanism,* p. 391).

10. Walter Burkert, *Greek Religion,* tr. John Raffan (Cambridge: Harvard University Press, 1985), p. 180.

11. Ake Hultkrantz's work, *The North American Indian Orphic Tradition* (Stockholm, 1957), provides ample evidence to the effect that the

Orpheus motif of the shaman descending into the underworld to retrieve lost souls (usually a husband or his representative going after a dead wife) is quite ancient and of wide diffusion, chiefly in the North American continent, but also with clear analogues in Europe (though Hultkrantz does not find any direct evidence for European influence upon the North American examples [pp. 184–85]). This particular motif is a variation of the shaman or animal-master's intercession to assure the return of the souls of the animals of the hunt who provided sustenance to Paleolithic man. If one accepts the arguments for an early and wide diffusion of the Orpheus motif, then it clearly antecedes the fertility-cult aspect of the Mediterranean Mother goddess and her dying/rising son, which was the cultic model for agriculturally based Neolithic society. Hultkrantz points out that whereas the shamanistic (Paleolithic) society focussed upon an individual as the carrier of the spiritual energy necessary to contact and move the spirits of the dead, the agrarian society was more collectivistic in outlook. Macchioro's assertion that Orphism was a "collective vision" of the same sort as the "Ghost Dance" religion, which broke out among the Sioux and other western and midwestern tribes at the end of the nineteenth century, seems clearly off the mark, as Hultkrantz's analysis would indicate. He is correct in seeing Orphism as older than the state religion, but not as a collective vision. The latter would not need brokering by the itenerant Orphic priests, the *Orpheotelestai* (Vittorio Macchioro, *From Orpheus to Paul* [New York: Henry Holt, 1930]), chapter 3.

12. If one accepts Hultkrantz's arguments for an early and wide diffusion of the Orpheus motif, then it clearly antedates the fertility-cult aspect of the Great Mother and her dying/rising son, which was the cultic model for agriculturally based Neolithic society.

13. W. K. C. Guthrie, *Orpheus and Greek Religion*, 2d ed. (London: Methuen, 1952), chapter 2. This work has just been reissued (Princeton: Princeton University Press, 1993).

14. Eliade, *Shamanism*, p. 38.

15. Dodds, p. 145.

16. A figure called "Pythagoras" is also documented, but Eliade inclines to think that he is not the same person as the Greek mathematician/priest/cultic leader. The dates don't quite fit, and this Pythagoras is a slave of the Getai, the elite Phrygian warrior cult, which doesn't tally with what we know of Pythagoras of Elia, either (Eliade, *Zalmoxis*, ch 1). Aristeas becomes associated with the Orpheus legend in Virgil's *Fourth Eclogue*, where he represents Orpheus in his role as culture hero, bearing the arts of small farming. In the detail where he chases Eurydice to her death by snakebite, we have what may be read as a Freudian disguise for her "death" by intercourse with Aristeas(/Orpheus). But there is an

ancient and fascinating parallel with the Cherokee Orphic myth. There the rattlesnake is instructed by the gods to bite the sun, who has diverged from its course and burned human beings (compare the myth of Phaeton and Helios). Instead, he bites the sun's daughter by mistake, after which the sun shuts herself up in the daughter's house, and the world lies in darkness (Hultkrantz, *North American Orpheus,* p. 270).

17. Also relevant to this identification is the frequent use of *epoidos* (incantation), which grew out of the archaic Odyssean word *oima,* as descriptive of Orpheus' magical activity. Lindsay reads it as "song as way."

18. Lindsay, pp. 378–79. This is most clearly seen in Aristophanes' incomparable comedy, *The Birds,* where the birds are the dispossessed tribal shamans of a culture far earlier than the Athenian polis. See William Arrowsmith, "Aristophanes' Birds: The Fantasy Politics of Eros," *Arion,* n.s. 1, no. 1 (1973), pp. 119–67.

19. Lindsay, p. 257.

20. Lindsay, p. 317.

21. Lindsay, p. 335.

22. Lindsay, p. 338.

23. Lindsay, p. 317.

24. Homer, *Odyssey,* book 22, cited in Lindsay, p. 347.

25. Lindsay, pp. 378–89.

26. Lindsay, p. 324.

27. Walter Strauss speaks of Orpheus's presence on the *Argo* as "apocryphal." (Walter Strauss, *Descent and Return: The Orphic Theme in Modern Literature* [Cambridge: Harvard University Press, 1971]), p. 5. However, one of his earliest representations is on a *metope* of the sixth century as a male figure, standing between two others on the deck of a sailing vessel, holding a lyre (Guthrie, *Orpheus,* plate 2, Delphi, sixth cent.).

Robert Böhme, *Orpheus: Der Sänger und seine Zeit* (Bern: Francke, 1970) argues for a Mycenaean origin for Orpheus, suggesting that he is the common source for certain passages in Hesiod, Homer, and Parmenides:

1. "the place where Night and Day / Approach and greet each other as they cross / The great bronze threshold" (Hesiod *Theogony,* tr. Dorothea Wender (Harmondsworth: Penquin, 1973, lines 748–50).

2. "[G]ates of iron and a brazen doorstone" before the entrance to Tartarus (Homer *Iliad* 8.13); the place the Laestrygonians live, where "the courses of Night and Day lie close together" (Homer *Odyssey* 9.92–93).

3. Parmenides' voyage from the House of Night into the presence of a truth-revealing goddess, a way that lies through "the gates of Night and Day" (Parmenides frag. B 1.11 Diels = Kranz).

Böhme suggests that Orpheus, as the figure of the threshhold between the worlds, is the common source for all of these. Though most scholars are guarded in their response to Böhme, Guthrie finds the similarities in these passages convincing. (Source for Böhme section of this note: Vernon Robbins, "Famous Orpheus," in *Orpheus: The Metamorphosis of a Myth*, ed. John Warden [Toronto: University of Toronto Press, 1982], p. 10 and notes following).

28. Francis M. Cornford, *From Religion to Philosphy*, (London: Edward Arnold, 1912), p. 195. For Burkert's contribution to the Berkeley colloquy from which I have taken his schema for Orphism as one of three overlapping circles, see note 69.

29. Here, briefly, is the earliest historical evidence of his appearance, culled from Emmet Robbins, "Famous Orpheus," in Warden et al., pp. 5–16. References to plates and figures are in Guthrie, *Orpheus*, with the plates appended at the rear.

1. The words of the poet Ibycus, the fragment: "famous Orpheus" (ca. 600 B.C.).
2. A *metope* from Sicyon, in the northwest Peloponnese (462 B.C.), shows two horsemen, with the profile of a ship between them. On the ship are two men holding lyres. Behind one of them is written, "Orpheus." The two horsemen are conjectured to be Castor and Pollux, and the ship the Argo (see Guthrie, plate 2).
3. Fifth-century vase-paintings, show a) Orpheus, in Greek attire, singing at his lyre, his head thrown back, surrounded by leopardskin-clad warriors (Thracians), who appear to be mesmerized or sleeping (Guthrie, plate 6); b) Orpheus being attacked by hostile women, clad as *maenads*, throwing stones, spears, and agricultural implements at him (Guthrie, plate 4, fig. 4, p. 33).
4. In Euripides' *Alcestis* (438 B.C.), Admetus says, "Had I the lips of Orpheus and his melody / to charm the maiden daughter of Demeter and / her lord, and by my singing win you back from death." This reference seems to refer to a story in which Orpheus is successful in his attempt to bring back his beloved, presumably the same Persephone whom he charms. The name "Eurydice" does not appear in literature before the first century B.C. "Lament for Bion." Before that, she had been Agriope, "Savage Watcher" (Hermesianax, third century)—roughly equivalent to "Wide-Ruler," or Eurydice.

5. A late fifth-century Attic relief showing a man and woman following Hermes. The man is turning towards the woman, touching her left wrist with his right hand, apparently lifting her veil.
In the other hand, he holds a lyre. The names "Hermes, Eurydice, Orpheus" are clearly written above the figures. It is not
likely that the names were on the original, though the identity
of the figures is clear (Guthrie, plate 3). Interpretation of this
frieze is varied, but its close similarity with another *metope* of
the same era at the National Museum in Palermo (showing the
marriage of Zeus and Hera, in which Zeus shows precisely the
same gesture) seems to indicate a scene of union rather than
separation.

30. The best known of these theogonic poems is the Rhapsodic
Theogony of the first century B.C. See the discussion of the Orphic
theogonies at the end of this chapter. See also Guthrie's translation of
Kern's fragments: Guthrie, *Orpheus*, pp. 137–42 (Otto Kern, *Orphicorum
Fragmenta* [Berlin 1922]).

31. Ficino liked to dress as the figure of Orpheus when adminis-
tering musical cures, singing at his lyre. Whether he took this act seri-
ously is a subject of debate. See Frances Yates, *Giordano Bruno and the
Hermetic Tradition* (Chicago: University of Chicago Press, 1964), pp. 62ff.

32. William Arrowsmith, "A Greek Theater of Ideas," *Arion* 2, no.
3, p. 33. In the article to which I have already referred, Arrowsmith
describes this genocide in the ruthless destruction by the Athenians
under Pericles of the male citizenry of the island of Melos, followed by
its sytematic colonization by *cleruchs* sent to administer the needs of the
burgeoning Athenian empire. Arrowsmith, "Aristophanes' Birds," p.
119.

33. Some of the major figures involved in this revolution were
Xenophanes, Herakleitos, and Parmenides, all of whom had their ideas
(*logoi*) in vigorous circulation.

34. For Schelling's views, see discussion of the history of the
Dionysian tradition in Germany, chapter 3.

35. Walter F. Otto, *Dionysus: Myth and Cult*, tr. Robert B. Palmer
(Bloomington: Indiana University Press, 1973), pp. 203–4.

36. William K. C. Guthrie, *The Greeks and Their Gods* (Boston: Beacon Press, 1955), p. 202.

37. Burkert, *Greek Religion*, p. 144.

38. Burkert, *Greek Religion*, pp. 144–45.

39. Burkert, *Greek Religion*, p. 146. Herakleitos captures this sense
well in his *palintropos harmonia*, which I shall examine in the upcoming
chapter as particulary fitting the Orphic poet.

40. Otto, *Dionysus*, chapter 5.

41. Guthrie, *Greeks and Their Gods*, p. 189.

42. Burkert, *Greek Religion*, p. 144.

43. It is interesting to note the ritual parallel with Hera, another of the goddesses who preceded Apollo in the Greek world. Hera retreats annually to renew her virginity.

44. Walter Otto, *The Homeric Gods*, tr. Moses Hadas (Boston: Beacon, 1954), p. 66.

45. Otto, *Homeric Gods*, p. 80. His sources are: *Orphic Hymns* 34.16ff.; Skythinnus frag. 14; Neustadt, *Hermes* (1931), p. 389. (He gives no further bibliographic details.)

46. Burkert, *Greek Religion*, p. 162.

47. Burkert adds that the fact that women are perennially dispossessed helps explain why they are so strongly attracted to a god whose rites remove them for some charmed hours and days from the control of their men and the *polis*. Burkert, *Greek Religion*, pp. 163–64.

48. Guthrie, *Greeks and Their Gods*, p. 165. Rohde had also made the point several decades earlier (Erwin Rohde, *Psyche* [New York: Harcourt, Brace, 1925], p. 283).

49. Jane E. Harrison, *Prolegomena to the Study of Greek Religion* (Cambridge: Cambridge University Press, 1922), pp. 518–34.

50. Here the king's gift of his queen to the god mimicks Theseus's gift of Ariadne to Dionysos (Burkert, *Greek Religion*, p. 164).

51. Carl Kerenyi, *Dionysos: Archetypal Image of Indesructible Life*, tr. Ralph Mannheim, Bollingen series, 65 (Princeton: Princeton University Press, 1976), p. 261.

52. This legend is given in Homer; it is one of his few references to Dionysos.

53. Zeus fathers him of Semele, but when he incinerates her with a thunderbolt, he saves the child, who finishes his gestation and then is born of Zeus's thigh.

54. *Tragodeia* (goat-song) is the favored choice for the etymological source of *tragedy* as well.

55. Kerenyi, *Dionysos*, p. 118.

56. Otto, *Dionysus*, pp. 160–71. Plutarch was the first explicitly to make this connection (Guthrie, *Greeks and Their Gods*, p. 156).

57. Compare Attis, Osiris, Kumarbi (Hittite).

58. Burkert, *Greek Religion*, p. 165.

59. "Cult document" is Guthrie's term (*Greeks and Their Gods*, p. 146).

60. Given its definitive modern definition in Schopenhauer as the *principium individuationis*, which Nietzsche explicitly identifies with the Apolline. Cf. the discussion in chapter 3, below.

61. Otto Kern, *Orphicorum Fragmenta*, p. 33. Cited in Guthrie, *Greeks and Their Gods*, p. 315.

62. In most accounts, the motivation is their own anger, but in some versions it is at the instigation of Dionysus, angered over Orpheus's refusal to honor his cult. This is Aeschylus's interpretation in the fragment *The Bassarides*.

63. A structuralist study of this series of mediations would show Orpheus as the operator, through inversions of each of the pairs: male-female, wild-tame, Phrygian-Greek, Apollo-Dionysos, etc.

64. The *aulos* was a reeded instrument, played like an oboe, incorrectly called a "flute" (M.S. Silk and J. P. Stern, *Nietzsche on Tragedy*, [Cambridge: Cambridge University Press, 1984], pp. 137–38). This Phrygian music enacts the spontaneous eruption of Dionysos amidst the human as *din*. This acccords with Walter Otto's discussion of noise and silence in the sudden appearances and disappearances of Dionysos. Here the Phrygian is binary: the *Maenads'* din is followed by silence—not that of Orpheus, but their own, as trees.

65. Jane Harrison, *Prolegomena*, p. 455.

66. Herbert Marcuse, *Eros and Civilization* (Boston: Beacon, 1955), pp. 162, 171. Cited in Strauss, *Descent and Return*, p. 11.

67. Orpheus displays similarities with Apollo as well, particularly in his role as musician and patron of the arts. Alcaeus speaks of his arrival at Delphi, as "nightingales, swallows, and cicadas sang." Callimachus spoke of the laurel trembling and the swans singing in the air at his approach. In Claudian, when Apollo draws near, the voices of the forests and grottoes are awakened (Otto, *Homeric Gods*, p. 73).

68. Brian Juden, *Traditions Orphiques et Tendances Mystiques dans le Romantisme Français (1800–1855)* (Paris: Kliencksieck, 1971), p. 442.

69. My own view is closest to Guthrie's, but I find Walter Burkert's colloquium paper sketching a domain for Orphism by drawing overlapping circles of Eleusis, Dionysian mysteries, and Pythagoreanism very helpful. Orphism here is less a "movement" than a common denominator, but there is no doubt for Burkert that it existed in some form. Walter Burkert, "Orphism and Bacchic Mysteries," a colloquy at Center for Hermeneutical Studies in Hellenistic and Modern Culture, Berkeley, March 1977. Henceforth cited as the Berkeley Colloquy. Larry Alderink provides a helpful Venn diagram of these overlapping circles in his comprehensive survey of scholarship on Orphism. Larry Alderink, *Creation and Salvation in Ancient Orphism* (University Park, Pa.: American Philogical Assoc., 1981).

70. Burkert presents a compelling argument against seeing the *Orpheotelestai* as part of a sect, but rather as individual and independent craft-priests (*Winkelpriester*). The Pythagoreans, on the other hand,

came as close to being a sect as any religious group in a society that orga-
nized itself around the *polis*, not the "church." Walter Burkert, "Craft
Versus Sect: The Problem of Orphics and Pythagoreans," in *Jewish and
Christian Self-Definition*, vol 3, *Self-Definition in the Greco-Roman World*, ed.
Ben F. Meyer and E.P. Sanders (Philadelphia: Fortress, 1982), pp. 1–22.

71. Cf. Dodds, *Greeks and the Irrational*, chapter 5, "The Greek
Shamans and the Origins of Puritanism," pp. 135–56.

72. Martin L. West, *The Orphic Poems* (Oxford: Oxford University
Press, 1983), p. 264. West, who generally follows in the Wilamowitz-Lin-
forth tradition, urging extreme caution with respect to "Orphism" in
the fifth century, nevertheless writes a cogent case for the existence of a
whole series of theogonies that wrought significant changes upon the
Hesiodic scheme of things long before the versions of late antiquity; this
series ended in the Rhapsodies. Apparently, according to Burkert, the
Derweni cosmogony was read and cited by Plato and Aristotle.

73. The large black-winged bird laying the luminous silver egg in
"the lap of darkness"–her own principle–is another instance of the
black-white dialectic enacted throughout Mallarmé's *oeuvre*. The image
produced, that of a black anti-cosmos surrounding a silver-white gleam,
is the reverse of the die with the impression "one." It is thus a double
inversion of the "twelve," congruent with midnight, that Igitur throws
(see discussion near the end of chapter 4).

74. Guthrie gives a handy reference and translation of Otto
Kern's *Orphicorum Fragmenta* in *Orpheus and Greek Religion* (pp. 137–42).
My summary of the Orphic creation myth and the Orphic anthro-
pogony is taken from Guthrie.

75. The Titans are reminiscent of many a male initiation rite
recorded in the annals of nineteenth- and twentieth-century anthroplo-
gists. The boys' elders appear out of the night, their bodies smeared
with white paint, replete with bull-roarers, one of the types of "toys" with
which the infant is enticed.

76. This is a variation on Vico's theme of the titanic within the
human: here it is first extroverted, then introverted. Though most of the
scholars I have read pass this legend along uncritically, Linforth and
West, following Wilamovitz, object to founding a whole tradition upon
the sole testimony of Pausanius.

There was another story, according to which the goddess Athena
saved the "heart" of Dionysos; this she took to her father, who used it to
resuscitate his son (this was also the subject of a *dromenon* in which the
Thyiades "awakened" the infant by lifting the linen cover of the *liknon*
(basket) in which the child's remains were carried in procession and
revived him by performing an "unutterable act"). Carl Kerenyi suggests
that the object carried in the *liknon*, called "Kradiaios Dionysos," can be

etymologically derived from both heart (*kardia*) and fig tree (*krade*). The ritual phalloi used in various processions were carved from fig wood. Thus the term *heart* in both of these cases could be seen as a euphemism for *phallus* (Kerenyi, p. 261).

77. G. S. Kirk, J. E. Raven, M. Schofield, *The Pre-Socratic Philosophers* (Cambridge: The University Press, 1983), pp. 31–32. The whole pattern is one of swallowing and rebirth, whereby the male demiurge acquires sole authority over creation. Throughout the Greek theogonies what enables this pattern to take place is that something is always held aside, often in a cave, and bears the seeds of the renewable creation. Thus Kronos is hid by his mother until the propitious moment to unsex his father, and Zeus is kept hidden in his Cretan birth-cave until it is time for him to cause Kronos to regurgitate his siblings. During all these movements of reservation, swallowing, and rebirth, the Mother of it all, Night (Nyx), remains outside the action. Focussing upon the power of demiurgy vested in the male leaves her out of the picture. Yet Zeus depends upon her heavily; she is his counselor and his *ground*. At the conclusion of chapter 4, I shall return to this pattern for the delayed inclusion of Nyx in the *récit* of the tiny Hamlet-like Mallarméan hero, Igitur.

78. Herman K. Usener, *Götternamen* (Bonn, 1896). Cited in Cassirer, *Language and Myth*, p. 15.

79. Cassirer, *Language and Myth*, pp. 17–18.

80. Regarding *keres*, see Harrison, pp. 163–217; on *erotes*, see esp. pp. 631–35 of her work.

81. Mallarmé's own fondness for the occasional poem is an excellent example of a decadent awareness of the inherent power of such moments.

82. Cassirer, *Language and Myth*, pp. 19–20.

83. Cassirer, *Language and Myth*, p. 21.

84. An examination of the relation of the words *mode* and *mood* reveals a subtle but important relation, quite close to that between the Sanskrit words *raga* and *rasa*. A *raga*, in modern musicology, is a mode, a strict organization of tone patterns that admits no modulation, no change via "accidentals." Ragas are closely tied to time of day and thus to *rasa*, mood or emotional tone that emanates from the quality of that time. The Greeks, too, paid close attention to time of day; the Hours were considered deities. To speak of tone, mood, or style being important to the gods as modes is to draw on the implicit connection between these two forms of ancient music.

MODES: So the Greek gods and goddesses of the classical age operate in the Greek consciousness as modes. Each god is a whole "world" (Walter Otto): its style and rules for operation. Thus when

Actaeon wanders within view of Artemis bathing and sees her
unclothed, she turns him into a stag who is pursued and torn apart by
his own hounds as a matter of necessity, rather than one of personal ani-
mosity. Nor is guilt, implying intent, at question. It is like the operation
of a law of nature, a nature called "Artemis," whose realm is quite specific, including the law of identity of hunter and hunted (i.e., Actaeon).
Within the *polis*, Artemis belongs in only two circumstances: at childbirth, where the essential event is as wild and primal as its counterpart
in the forest, and when the young adolescents of her "bear clan" invade
the city, acting as clumsy and unladylike as possible to ward off potential
suitors, for whom they are not yet ready. Artemis's twin brother, Apollo
(whom she helped deliver in her role as midwife), is similar to her in
some respects. They are both archers; they both have to do with the initiation of youths of their proper sex. But whereas Artemis teaches the arts
of self-sufficiency in wild nature to young Amazons, Apollo's rites have
more to do with competition in the poetic arts and athletics. She rules
outside the walls of the *polis*, he within. Though these spheres may overlap, as with Artemis's presiding over childbirth, there is an inner logic to
this modal functioning. Once a mode is operative, it must fulfill its law.
And just as there are no "accidentals" in the classical modes of Greek
music, so is there no capriciousness in the operation of the modal force
fields we know as the "anthropomorphized" gods.

   My use of "modes" with respect to the gods is one particular
instance of a general argument that William Arrowsmith, in the introduction to his translation of the *Alcestis* (New York: Oxford University
Press, 1974), makes for all of Greek society, from the gods down to the
lowest member of society (pp. 3–29). His analysis, however, is put in
terms of a *hierarchy* of modalities, which is best demonstrated through
the masking conventions of Greek tragedy; whereas mine is restricted to
the gods. I should also add that my definition of the *daimonic* as a "way
between modes" is in the same general spirit of his analysis.

   85. Joseph Campbell speaks provocatively, in the language of cog-
nitive psychology ca. 1968, of "innate releasing mechanisms" (IRM's),
which contrast with a more open version of the same thing in human
beings, the results being the psychic imprinting of what Jung called the
"archetypes of the collective unconscious" (Joseph Campbell, *Primitive
Mythology*: vol. 1 of *The Masks of God* [New York: Viking, 1972], pp. 31–49).

   86. Harrison, *Prolegomena*, p. 657.

   87. In contrast with Freud's infamous Oedipus complex, David
Miller, following the line of argument in William Lynch's *Christ and
Apollo* (New York: Sheed and Ward, 1960), has argued that Orestes, driven by the desire to murder the mother, is the quintessential type for
modern man (David Miller, "Orestes: Myth and Dream as Catharsis," in

Myths, Dreams, and Religion, Joseph Campbell, ed. [New York: Dutton, 1970], pp. 26–47). Miller heralds the rebirth of the gods in *The New Polytheism* (Dallas: Spring Publications, 1981), but his tentative efforts there are eclipsed by James Hillman, who effectively outlines a "polytheistic psychology" in his remarkable *Re-Visioning Psychology* (New York: Harper and Row, 1975). (Miller gives as an appendix to *The New Polytheism* a shorter version of Hillman's thesis: "Psychology: Monotheistic or Polytheistic?") Hillman, an apostate Jungian, has renamed Jung's "analytic" psychology "archetypal." In a recent issue of *Spring,* the journal of archetypal psychology that Hillman edits, Noel Cobb contributes an article (which I find somewhat unconvincing) naming Orpheus as the figure "behind" archetypal psychology, harborer of images of all the gods (like Plato's *Symposium* image of Socrates as Marsyas the satyr, containing gods within gods behind the rude exterior).

88. In Mallarmé's case, the "momentary god" appears especially in the Tournon experience described in "Le démon de l'analogie," which I will examine in chapter 4.

89. The broad terms in which I characterize the *daimon* obscure somewhat the history of the term. With Hesiod, in a completely different context, *daimones* meant the souls of the dead, especially heroes. The idea of *daimones* as an intermediate class of beings is post-Homeric. In the fifth century the popular belief in the *daimon* as a guardian spirit came into prominence, but it was still seen as separate from the soul (*psyche*). As a separate entity, one could hold a conversation with it, as Socrates did with his *daimonion.* It was a kind of life-partner. With the age of the tragedians Herakleitos' notion of the *daimon* as one's personal fate gained currency. Plato sees the *daimon* as a soul-guide in *Phaedrus* 107d; in *Republic* 617e (which we shall examine in chapter 2), it is both *nous* and condition of life. The Stoics used the term mainly as a figure of speech, but for them it came to mean the ideal personality as contrasted with the empirical personality. This implies that it is distinct from *psyche* but also potentially identifiable with it. Finally, Poseidonios identified the *daimon* with the theological idea that it and the soul were one, one of many individual entities that persist throughout time in the *aither* and enter man at birth (Rohde, *Psyche,* especially note 44, pp. 514–15. See also Burkert, *Greek Religion,* pp. 179–84). The brief summary of the shift in the meaning of *pysche* during the fifth century in the opening section of the next chapter needs to be read with this evolution of *daimon* in mind—which of course renders the whole situation more complex.

90. My reading of the daimonic in this paragraph is indebted to William Arrowsmith, especially his introduction to Nietzsche's *Unmodern Observations,* pp. xi–xiii.

91. Plato, *Politicus* 271 a–b.

Chapter 2. Plato's Orphic Universe

1. A primary example is the description in the *Timaeus* (43–44) of the extreme disorder which the soul suffers when "dropped" into the river of earthly life. (Plato, *The Collected Dialogues of Plato*, ed. Edith Hamilton and Huntington Cairns, Bollingen Series, 71 [New York: Random House (Pantheon), 1963], pp. 1169–70. Unless otherwise noted, all references to the dialogues are to this edition. Translators of dialogues cited: *Republic*, Paul Shorey; *Phaedrus*, R. Hackforth; *Phaedo*, Hugh Tredennick; *Laws*, A. E. Taylor.

2. Rohde, p. 377.

3. Rohde, p. 373.

4. Compare this statement from the Irish bards: "I have been an eagle, a sea coral, I have been a sword in the hand, a shield in battle, I have been a string in a harp" (Walter Burkert, *Lore and Science in Ancient Pythagoreanism*, tr. Edwin L. Minor, Jr. [Cambridge: Harvard University Press, 1972], pp. 162–63).

5. Rohde, p. 382.

6. Plato gives a similar description of the soul dropping into the tumultuous river of life in the *Timaeus* 43–44a.

7. Rohde, pp. 382–83.

8. Dodds, p. 209.

9. Dodds, p. 210.

10. "How deeply impressed upon the Greeks mind such conceptions, derived eventually from Homer, actually were, can be measured by the fact that a conception of the twofold origin of psychic activity, its twofold nature and sphere of action, closely related to that of Empedocles, is continually recurring in more advanced stages of philosophy" (Rohde, p. 383).

11. Burkert, *Greek Religion*, p. 300.

12. This beast is also called the "brutish part of our nature" (*Republic* 589e), "the snake in us" and the "moblike beast" (590b), and the "brood of beasts" (590c).

13. It is interesting to note that the famous quarrel of book 10 follows right on the heels of the metaphor with which Plato ends book 9: that of the farmer who must distinguish between the cultivated and wild plants in the inner bestiary of the soul. Using those terms, it would seem that the cultivated plants ("heads") were the products of acculturation, thus produced mimetically, and that the "wild" ones were the originals, more like what one would find through the process of *anamnesis*.

14. Eric Havelock, *Preface to Plato* (Cambridge: Harvard University Press, 1963).

15. Cornford argues, however, that *mimesis*, which meant "repre-

senting" to Pythagoras, meant "participation" to Plato. We are coming out of the shadows, as it were. (Cornford, *From Religion to Philosophy*, p. 254).

16. Dodds argues plausibly that in the middle dialogues he is focussing not so much upon the ordinary citizen as upon the extraordinary one, stretching the achievable limits of the human. The example that he gives of the Guardians in the *Republic* is an excellent case in point. They are, he says, "rationalized *shamans*" (Dodds, p. 210).

17. Dodds speaks of Plato's efforts in the *Laws* as a "counterreformation" to restore some of the "Inherited Conglomerate" (Dodds, p. 207).

18. Pierre Boyancé, *Le culte des Muses chez les philosophes grècs* (Paris: Editions de Boccard, 1972). He summarizes the orphicized Dionysos well on p. 146.

19. Boyancé, *Culte*, pp. 167–84, esp. p. 184.

20. See also Emile Bréhier, *The Hellenic Age*, tr. Joseph Thomas (Chicago: University of Chicago Press, 1965), p. 89.

21. Lindsay, p. 337.

22. Havelock, p. 276.

23. Nietzsche, on the other hand, calls Plato the "first mixed type [of philosopher] on a grand scale," combining Socratic, Pythagorean, and Heraclitic elements in his doctrine of Ideas (*Philosophy in the Tragic Age of the Greeks*, tr. Marianne Cowan (Chicago: Henry Regnery and Co., 1937). For Nietzsche the "pre-Socratics" were the pure philosophers: poetic characters and visionaries who could not help but utter their original thought in the elemental forms that it took. Plato was a collector, sifter, and synthesizer of these thoughts, which it was his *sophos*, his art, to represent.

24. Plato, *Ion* 536c, cited in Lindsay, p. 337.

25. Havelock disagrees. For him, *sophos* is also the skill of reading the signs of the Muses.

26. Eliade, *Shamanism*, p. 391.

27. And their forms of rebirth, most notably Orpheus's rebirth as a swan, choosing this life in order to avoid being "conceived and born of a woman" (Plato, *Republic* 620a). The swan is also an emblem for Plato (Socrates supposedly had a vision of a swan on the eve of meeting Plato). In chapter 4 we shall examine Mallarmé's sonnet about an exiled swan, frozen in ice.

28. Lindsay, p. 324. Lindsay points out that Aeschylus uses the masculine form, *oimos*, to describe an underworld journey.

29. Gilbert Rouget, *Music and Trance: A Theory of the Relations between Music and Possession*, tr. Brunhilde Biebuyck (in collaboration with the author) (Chicago: University of Chicago Press, 1985), is a very important study that exhaustively reviews classical, Renaissance and

twentieth-century views of the relation of music to trance, possession, and magic. Rouget differentiates between trance (*epoidos*) and possession (*mania*), arguing that the Renaissance notion of "furore poétique" has led astray almost everyone since the first decade of the seventeenth century. In Rouget's analysis, "Poetic furor" refers simultaneously to the following: Plato's theory of enthusiasm (the four *manias* of the *Phaedrus*), Aristotle's theory of the ethos of musical modes, Pythagoras's theory of the harmony of the spheres, and Orpheus as model of the magical art of incantation (*epoidos*) (see Rouget, p. 238 for a summary). He argues that Pythagoras's harmony of the spheres is "pure bokum" (as contrasted with the laws of [musical] consonance, which are scientifically valid). If he is right, then I too am guilty of an overreading, led by the Poetic Furies into a theory of Orpheus and the Orphic poet as a conflation of what he says are clearly separate: trance and possession (and the previous sentence in my text brings in the Pythagorean music of the spheres as well). Following his analysis, Orpheus would merely be a trumped-up magician/shaman, having nothing to do with the *mania* sent by the Muses. He disagrees with Boyancé, saying that the latter substitutes his own reading of *epodé* where Plato consistently uses the Greek for rhythm and harmony. If *epodé* or *epoidos* is indeed restricted to the magical trances worked by the *Orpheotelestai*, then I and many others have a misplaced sense of who the emergent type Orpheus is, as well as making a false judgment that Plato was an unwitting Orphic poet. But the issue is not so simple, and it is clouded by Rouget's own efforts to delineate separate views of the musical modes and especially the notions of homeopathy (Plato, especially in the *Laws*) and allopathy (Aristotle). Perhaps the conflation of trance and possession, or *epoidos* and *mania*, is another way of describing the underlying contrariety at work in the Orphic poet: the "shamanic contradiction." *Epoidos* works from an interior divining power; *mania*, through possession by the god.

30. Plato used the terms *Orphicoi* and *Orpheotelestai*. *Orphism*, a convenient modern term, was coined by Erwin Rohde.

31. He is also critical of the Orpheus of legend, saying that Orpheus failed to retrieve Eurydice because he was not willing to die for her love, as Alcestis did in a similar situation (*Symposium*).

32. Originally, "Know thyself" had more to do with man's knowing his "place"—better, his *modality* as man, humble and subject to *thanatos*. It was a cautionary remark coming from the god of order, limits, and just proportion warning of the offense of *hubris* before the gods.

33. Kirk et al., *Pre-Socratic Philosophers*, p. 316 (Frag. 126, Stobaeus *Anth* 1, 149, 60).

34. Perceval Frutiger, *Les mythes de Platon* (Paris: Librairie Alcan, 1930), p. 152.

35. Compact Edition of the *Oxford English Dictionary*, s.v. 1.

36. Where Socrates looks forward to "discoursing" with eudae-monic heroes, which would inevitably lead to yet another insurrection, trial, and the meting of a fate not unlike that of Lucifer! This is brilliantly parodied in Lucian's *Dialogue of the Dead*.

37. It is striking to compare this passage with Goethe's Platonic poem "Höhere und Höechtest," where the speaker mounts into heaven in full possession of senses that become more finely wrought through the upward passage, merging with the apperceptive faculty of the demiurge.

38. Friedländer has a particularly lucid discussion of the geography of the *Phaedo* (Paul Friedländer, *Plato: An Introduction*, tr. Hans Meyerhoff, Bollingen series [New York: Pantheon, 1958]), pp. 262–69.

39. Walter Pater, *Plato and Platonism* (London: Macmillan, 1910), p. 143.

40. Friedländer, p. 198.

41. *Phaedrus* 259c.

42. It should be noted that the Muses, as authors of musical enchantment, are focal in this operation as well, corroborating in part Boyancé's argument. Indeed, they assume the role of judges, echoing the function of the arbiters of the differential fates of souls in the myth of Er, when the cicadas report to them concerning how and by whom they are severally honored.

The myth of the cicadas also admirably fits as well the structuralist analysis of the Orpheus myth, which focuses upon the extremes of too much sweetness, where a surfeit of sex in the "lune de miel" of the Orpheus-Eurydice bond sets up the necessity of the swing to the opposite pole of dismemberment, *sparagmos*, and conversion to ash, the logical antipode of honey. (Honey, in Virgil's version, is the free gift that Aristaeus forfeits in his pursuit of Eurydice. Whether this pursuit is "unlawful" or not depends upon one's interpretation of the farmer's identity. My sense of him is that he is a double of Orpheus, who is left "pure" by never actually consummating the bond with Eurydike, which Aristaeus does in his stead. Thus her death is the "dying" of both Shakespeare and Freud.) The range covered by the logical opposition and mediation involved here is given in Levi-Strauss's work, *From Honey to Ashes*. See also the work of Marcel Détienne, especially *Dionysos Slain*.

43. Richmond Lattimore, *Greek Lyrics* (Chicago: University of Chicago Press, 1960), pp. 39–40.

44. Friedländer, pp. 190ff.

45. Boyancé, p. 84.

46. Perhaps the rarely used *fluxion* better describes this process and medium.

47. Arrowsmith, "Aristophanes' Birds," pp. 119–68.

48. Cited from Eisler, *Weltenmantel*, in Cornford, p. 178.
49. Guthrie, *Orpheus*, 242.
50. Cornford, pp. 124ff.
51. Shakespeare, *The Two Gentlemen of Verona*, act 3, sc. 2. I am indebted to Elizabeth Sewell for drawing my attention to this line. See *The Orphic Voice*, p. 58.
52. Otto, *Homeric Gods*, p. 80.
53. Aeschylus, *Bassarides*, a fragment given in Kern, *Orph. fr.*, p. 33. Cited in Guthrie, *Greeks and Their Gods*, p. 315. This, though, is Orpheus after he has "reformed," swearing off relations with the opposite sex, trying to distance himself from his bereavement over the second loss of Eurydice. The image emphasizes an Apolline Orpheus, in contradistinction to the distinctive Orphic image of the severed chanting head and sounding lyre floating down the Hebrus—which unites both the Apolline and the Dionysian.

Chapter 3. Brothers in Decadence: Mallarmé, Neitzsche, and the Orphic Wagner

1. Interestingly, Elizabeth Sewell argues in *The Orphic Voice* that Francis Bacon and Shakespeare reveal a shift in consciousness in their writing during the first decade of the seventeenth century, closely contemporaneous with the birth of opera.
2. In this sense, he *reverses* the classical order, as argued by Mihai Spariosu in his *Dionysus Reborn* (Ithaca: Cornell University Press, 1989). In the development of aesthetics at the end of the eighteenth century, Kant (Aristotle) precedes Schiller (Plato), who precedes Nietzsche (Herakleitos).
3. As is helpfully illustrated in Adrean Del Caro's *Nietzsche Contra Nietzsche* (Baton Rouge: Louisiana State University Press, 1989). Del Caro's study situates Nietzsche's struggle to define himself against the romantics in a thorough analysis of his sources, measured against Nietzsche's progressive statements about romanticism.
4. Schelling in his late philosophy had developed an idea that was strikingly similar to that which we find in *BT*, in the "Dionysiology" of his *Philosophy of Revelation*, but this conception is subsumed, a prolegomena to its proper consummation in Christ. Whereas Nietzsche stresses Dionysus, Schelling stressed the role of Apollo (cf. note 40 for Schelling citation).
5. Nietzsche, *Philosophy in the Tragic Age of the Greeks*, p. 62.
6. Allan Megill, *Prophets of Extremity: Nietzsche, Heidegger, Foucault, Derrida* (Berkeley and Los Angeles: University of California Press, 1985), p. 2.

7. As enumerated by Spariosu, p. 38.

8. Spariosu, p. 66.

9. Benjamin Bennett, "Nietzsche's Idea of Myth: The Birth of Tragedy out of the Spirit of Eighteenth Century Aesthetics," *PMLA* 94 (1979), p. 425.

10. Bennett, p. 422.

11. Contrast with Plato, a "mixed" type; both terms are from Nietzsche, *Philosophy in the Tragic Age of the Greeks*.

12. Friedrich Nietzsche, *The Birth of Tragedy and The Genealogy of Morals*, tr. Francis Golffing (New York: Doubleday, 1956), p. 143. Hereafter cited as *BT*, Golffing.

13. *BT*, Golffing, p. 24.

14. Otto, *Dionysus*, pp. 86–91.

15. *BT*, Golffing, p. 39.

16. Compare Mallarmé, who argues for the "disparition élocutoire du poëte, qui cède l'initiative aux mots" (a revolutionary formulation to which we shall return at the end of the next chapter), replacing the "direction personnelle enthousiaste de la phrase"—presumably a dig at the romantics, and perhaps Hugo as well, though he would keep any attacks on the latter veiled ("Crise de vers," in Stéphane Mallarmé, *Oeuvres complètes*, ed. Henri Mondor, G. Jean-Aubry [Paris: Gallimard, 1945], p. 361. Hereafter cited as *OC*).

17. Friedrich Nietzsche, *The Birth of Tragedy and The Case of Wagner*, tr. Walter Kaufmann (New York: Random House, 1967), p. 50. Henceforth cited as *BT*, Kaufmann. Golffing, who enjoys the catchy phrase, translates this as the "ground of being" (*BT*, Golffing, p. 39).

18. The contrasting claims of *physis* and *nomos* were at the center of the fifth-century revolution in Greece. When I use *nomos* here as a "law of being," I realize that I transgress this distinction (natural law versus cultural law). But in doing so I am following Nietzsche, who said that these "artistic energies . . . burst forth *without the mediation of any human artist*" (*BT*, Golffing, p. 24).

19. The terms of analysis are different, but this is precisely what Hegel had predicted in his treatise "Romantic Art" (ca. 1807).

20. *BT*, Golffing, p. 28.

21. This characterization of Mallarmé as anti-bourgeois must be qualified, however, because of the aspect of ritual, performance, and "theatricality" involved with the presentation of "le Livre." In this ritual-theatrical sense, "la Foule" (the Crowd) is absolutely essential, as Peter Dayan points out in *Mallarmé's Divine Transposition* (Oxford: Oxford University Press, 1986), pp. 47–95.

22. Cf. especially *The Antichrist* and *Ecce Homo*, both written during his last productive year, 1888.

23. Stéphane Mallarmé, *Correspondance. 1862–1871*, ed. Henri Mondor (Paris: Gallimard, 1959), p. 242.

24. Stéphane Mallarmé, *Correspondance*, (letter to Cazalis, 1865), p. 151.

25. Guy Michaud, *Mallarmé* (Paris: Hatier, 1958), p. 148: "Je veille vingt-quatre heures par jour," in a letter to J-H Rosny.

26. Friedrich Nietzsche, "On Truth and Lie in an Extra-Moral Sense," in *The Portable Nietzsche*, Walter Kaufmann, ed., tr. (New York: Penguin, 1976), pp. 46–47.

27. *OC*, Translation: "The first is for narrative, instruction or description (even though an adequate exchange of human thoughts might well be achieved through the silent exchange of money). The elementary use of language involves that universal *journalistic style* which characterizes all kinds of contemporary writing, with the exception of literature" (Stéphane Mallarmé, *Mallarmé: Selected Prose Poems, Essays and Letters*, tr. Bradford Cook [Baltimore: Johns Hopkins Press, 1956], p. 42; henceforth cited as Cook).

"What good is the marvel of transposing a fact of nature into its almost complete and vibratory disappearance with the play of the word, however, unless there comes forth from it, without the bother of a nearby or concrete reminder, the pure notion" (Mary Ann Caws, *Stéphane Mallarmé: Selected Poetry and Prose* [New York: New Directions Publishing, 1982], pp. 75–76).

28. Mallarmé, unlike Nietzsche, is a dualist who accepts the "ordinary world" described in the "journalistic language" of the first paragraph of the Ghil preface above. His radical transformation of the poetic idiom, to "purifier les mots du tribau," does not attempt to call into question the nature of "truth" in its ordinary usage. This point is argued particularly well in Peter Dayan's *Mallarmé's Divine Transposition*. I shall address this dualism further in chapter 4.

29. But this is not the case in *The Birth of Tragedy*, where metaphysics and aesthetics are viewed as essentially the same, answering Anaximander's demand by the dictum that stands at the head of this chapter: existence is *justified* through aesthetics. Nietzsche's position here is still quite close to Schopenhauer's.

30. Gilles Deleuze, *Nietzsche and Philosophy*, tr. Hugh Tomlinson (New York: Columbia University Press, 1983).

31. Friedrich Nietzsche, *Early Greek Philosophy and Other Essays*, tr. Max Mügge (New York: Russell and Russell 1964), p. 108.

32. Deleuze, p. 33.

33. See my discussion of "La Musique et les lettres" at the end of chapter 4.

34. The question of whether Mallarmé was a Schopenhaurean,

with his insistence upon the music before music and upon the special status of music among the arts, is a valid one. Baillot's study claims that there is no possibility of influence in this case (Alexandre Baillot, *Influence de la philosophie de Schopenhauer en France [1860–1900]* [Paris: J. Vrin, 1927]). He is probably right that Mallarmé never read Schopenhauer (or the popularized Schopenhauer of Hartmann, widely read by the European bourgeosie). Yet there remains a common heart to their insights into the privileged place of music among the arts. The extended scholarly argument about Mallarmé's supposed "Hegelianism" seems to me overblown. It needs to be balanced by more attention to the common concern, if not influence, manifested in the deliberations on the special status of music in Schopenhauer and Mallarmé. This is partially addressed in Thibaudet's comments to the effect that Mallarmé evokes the "Platonic aesthetic" of Schopenhauer, which is further developed in Bergson (Alfred Thibaudet, *La Poésie de Mallarmé*, new ed. [Paris: Gallimard, 1926]).

35. Philip Grundelehner, *The Poetry of Friedrich Nietzsche* (New York: Oxford University Press, 1986), has written the first book-length study in English of Nietzsche's poetry. Considering the quality of the verse, these three hundred pages represent an inflation. What could have been the most fruitful aspect of the book, discussing the verse in conjunction with the life, reveals much less than have corresponding studies of Nietzsche's prose. Another recent book, Alexander Nehamas, *Nietzsche: Life as Literature* (Cambridge: Harvard University Press, 1987), accomplishes this admirably.

36. In the original text of *The Birth of Tragedy*, section 12, he speaks of Socrates as the "new Orpheus who rose against Dionysus" (*BT*, Kaufmann, p. 86).

37. Francis Bacon, "Orpheus, or Philosophy," *The Wisdom of the Ancients. Selected Writings of Francis Bacon*, ed. Hugh G. Dick (New York: Random House [Modern Library], 1955), p. 410.

38. Though Gerard Else mounts a strong argument for a civically motivated kind of *simulation* of Dionysian religion in the theater of Athens (Gerard F. Else, *The Origin and Early Form of Greek Tragedy* [Cambridge: Harvard University Press, 1965]).

39. This is yet a third polarity, Dionysos/Christ, as Kaufmann notes (Walter Kaufmann, *Nietzsche: Philosopher, Psychologist, Antichrist* [Cleveland: World Publishing, Meridian Books, 1956], chapter 12).

40. Max Baeumer, "Nietzsche and the Tradition of the Dionysian," in *Studies in Nietzsche and the Classical Tradition*, tr. Timothy Sellner, ed. James O'Flaherty, T. Sellner, R. Helm (Chapel Hill: University of North Carolina Press, 1976), pp. 165–89. Though Winckelmann had initially formulated the aesthetic principles inaugurating the "tyranny of Greece over Germany" in Apolline terms, the Dionysian tra-

dition in German letters developed for nearly a century before adumbrated in Nietzsche. In a description of the "Dionysian Circle"—what we might call the chthonic realm—Müller speaks of the nature of the god as one that "overwhelms human feelings and shakes man out of the clear repose of self-awareness." Though Goethe was the first to use the god's name as an adjective, Müller first applied it consistently in place of "the Bacchic." As Baeumer summarizes, the adjective "Dionysian" "was abstracted from the god himself, his being and his myths, and was generalized in psychological terms by Müller, aestheticized philosophically by Schelling, and finally made by Nietzsche into the substantive, "the Dionysian," whereupon it attained the status of a legitimate ancient and modern phenomenon" (Baeumer, 182).

Perhaps most surprising in Baeumer's account is his demonstration that the ideas of Schelling already carried the essential character of the Dionysian-Apolline polarity, both in terms of natural "potencies" and as the fundamental forces behind the creative process of art. Dionysos is the ancient's "divine madness" (conflating the specified forms of *mania* in the *Phaedrus*), which "even yet is the innermost part of things . . . the real power of nature and all of her creations" (Friedrich Schelling, *Die Weltalter* [cited in Baeumer, 184]). The remark "Dionysos *is* genius" summarizes Bruno Snell's analysis of the phenomenon in the philosophical-literary nexus of Schiller-Schlegel-Goethe-Schelling (Bruno Snell, *The Discovery of the Mind,* tr. T. G. Rosenmeyer [New York and Evanston: Harper and Row, 1960], p. 216). Schelling vigorously described the working of this intoxicated, unrestrained power along with its complement, the reflective power of form as the Apolline in his late *Philosophie der Offenbarung,* where he observed that:

> Indeed, not only in God, but even in men—to the extent that they have been blessed with the slightest glimmer of creative power—the same relationship is to be found, this same contradiction: a blind creative power, by its very nature unrestrained, opposed by a reflective, and thus in reality a negative power, residing in the same subject, which restrains and forms this blind power. . . . To be intoxicated and sober not at different times, but simultaneously—this is the secret of true poetry. It is this which differentiates between Apollinian inspiration and the merely Dionysian. An infinite content, and thus a content in its most complete, that is, in its most finite form, is the highest calling of art. (Book 2, lect. 26; cited and translated by Baeumer, p. 186)

As Baeumer points out, this characterization is essentially the same as that of Nietzsche's two forces in the opening of the *BT*. As in Bachofen, whose ideas were closely reflected in Nietzsche's handling of the polarity, no direct influence can be traced. But it is clear that in the light of the evidence marshalled by Baeumer, Nietzsche is the culmination of a tradition, not, as he asserts, its progenitor.

41. Both Baeumer and Silk and Stern point to the following journal notation of Wagner's as primary data for this identification: "Birth out of music: Aeschylus. Decadence-Euripides" (Baeumer, p. 189).

42. Nietzsche sees Euripides and Socrates as co-conspirators undercutting the "tragic age" of Aeschylus (and, to a lesser extent, of Sophocles) in which the old myths lived in the public tragic spectacle. He calls the age that they inaugurate "Alexandrian"—the beginning of a long decline into decadence (*BT*, sections 11-14). But in an important article, Albert Henrichs argues that Nietzsche never read, and thus did not really know, Euripides; instead, Henrichs demonstrates that Nietzsche only parroted the opinions about Euripides of the Schlegel brothers. Albert Henrichs, "Nietzsche and Euripides," *Greek Roman and Byzantine Studies*, 26, no. 4 (1986), pp. 369-97.

43. for Schelling's aesthetics, see note 40.

44. Arthur Schopenhauer, *The World as Will and Representation*, vol. 1, tr. E. F. J. Paine (Indian Hills, Colo.: Falcon's Wing Press, 1958), p. 257. Hereafter cited as Schopenhauer, *WWR*, vol. 1.

45. Schopenhauer, *WWR*, vol. 1, p. 262.

46. As Silk and Stern point out, his position as a father figure made him much more difficult to break with than was Schopenhauer, who was already criticized in the middle section of *The Birth of Tragedy* (Silk and Stern, p. 29).

47. As have such later terms as "metaphysical" music in the terminology of Dahlhaus. See Klaus Kropfinger, "Wagners Musikbegriff und Nietzsches 'Geist der Musik,'" *Nietzsche-Studien*, 14 (1985), p. 8.

48. Two excellent articles on Nietzsche, Wagner, and the "Gesamtkunstwerk" are (1) the Kropfinger article just cited and (2) Klaus-Detlef Bruse, "Die Griechische Trägodie als 'Gesamtkunstwerk'—Anmerkungen zu den musikästhetischen Reflexionen des frühen Nietzsche," *Nietzsche-Studien*, 13 (1984), pp. 156-77.

49. To avoid confusion Wagner distinguished his work from opera as "music drama." Wagner denied any positive influence from his operatic predecessors. Ironically, in its origins in Italy in the first years of the seventeenth century, opera focussed upon the theme of Orpheus and Eurydice. But it is true that Wagner had virtually nothing in common with the Italian opera of the Florentine Camerata (1594-1605).

50. In *Der Fall Wagner*, Nietzsche calls Wagner "This Klingsor of all Klingsors." Klingsor is the old magician in *Parsifal* (*BT*, Kaufmann, p. 184).

51. *The Case of Wagner*, in *BT*, Kaufmann, p. 171. Mallarmé is of course also a "miniaturist," though in a different medium.

52. Friedrich Nietzsche, "Nietzsche contra Wagner," in *The Portable Nietzsche*, Walter Kaufmann, ed., tr. (New York: Penguin, 1976), p. 663.

53. *OC*, p. 71. Translation:

> The silence now funereal of a pall
> Spreads more than one fold on this furniture
> Which must with lack of memory bestir
> A collapsing of the central pedestal.

Hubert Creekmore, Caws, p. 55

54. Both Mallarmé and Nietzsche ironize Hugo. Like Wagner, he was his own biographer, creating and living a heroic self-myth, and thus, in Nietzsche's eyes, putting truth last. Nietzsche says that Wagner *"has increased music's capacity for language to the point of making it immeasurable*: he is the Victor Hugo of music as language" *(The Case of Wagner,* in *BT*, Kaufmann, p. 173). Nietzsche speaks of the "immeasurable, . . . infinite melody" of the composer's "royal largess." But the kingly metaphor cloaks the rhetorical theatricality of both men, who are "shrewd hosts." "Nobody equals their talent for presenting a princely table at modest expense." Mallarmé speaks of the passing of Hugo, which is the occasion for a "Crise de Vers," in terms of an "inquiétude du voile dans le temple" ("Crise," *OC*, p. 361). He is a "Monument en ce désert," the cultural wasteland that he further impoverished by dying. This was cause for discomfiture on the part of "Un lecteur française, ses habits interrompues à la mort de Victor Hugo," who "ne peut que se déconcerter. Hugo, dans sa tâche mystérieuse, rabbit toute la prose, philosophie, éloquence, histoire au vers, et, comme il était le vers personnellement, il confisqua chez qui pense, discourt ou narre, presque le droit à s'énoncer." Even more extreme, Mallarmé adds, "Le vers, je crois, avec respect attendit le géant qui identifiait à sa main tenace et plus ferme toujours de forgeron, vint à manquer; lui, pour se rompre." A shrewd host, indeed.

55. "Richard Wagner: Rêverie d'un poète français," *OC*, pp. 541–46.

56. *OC*, p. 541. Translation: "Oh strange defiance hurled at poets by him who has usurped their duty with the most open and splendid audacity: Richard Wagner!" (Cook, p. 73).

57. "Crise de vers," *OC* 361. I believe poetry waited respectfully to break asunder until the giant who identified it with his blacksmith's hand had passed (author's translation).

58. See Judy Kravis' brief analysis of "Richard Wagner" in *The Prose of Mallarmé* (Cambridge: Cambridge University Press, 1976), pp. 34–38.

59. *OC*, p. 543.

60. *OC*, p. 545.

61. *OC*, p. 544. Translation: "the secret of origins, even as it is being acted out. Some strange, new primitive happiness keeps them seated there before that mobile veil of orchestral delicacy, before that magnificence which adorns their genesis" (Cook, p. 76).

62. The "decorative" holds, however, a place of some honor in Mallarmé's aesthetic universe—along with ceremony and formal gatherings, sites for "occasional" verse. Still, in the present instance, the decorative masks.

63. "Crise de vers," *OC*, p. 361.

64. *OC*, pp. 543–44. Translation: "[music that] is obedient to its own most complex laws, above all to the vague [floating] and the intuitive. First it mingles its colors and forms of the actor with its own timbres and motifs, thereby creating a richer atmosphere of Revery than would be possible for any earthbound melody; creating a deity draped in the invisible folds of a musical texture. And then it sweeps him away in a wave of Passion which is too furiously unleashed to be borne by one alone; hurls him down, twists him about, and even robs him of his senses (they are lost in this superhuman rush), only to give them back again, so that he may be all-victorious in a song which bursts through the agony of creative thought" (Cook, pp. 75–76).

65. "Hero" is my interpretation of "vers un seul"—the perenially ambiguous referent in Mallarmé: the "personnage" at the beginning of the passage, and the precipitate of the divine *afflux* at the end. The preposition "vers" is a fulcrum in Mallarmé's lexicon, indicating the opening toward the unknown, the boundary of the infinite, the limit of this world, "ici-bas." It has a commanding position in his enigmatic masterpiece, the first installment, as it were, of "Le Livre": "Un Coup de dès." The agitation of the hero cast upon the wave, especially with the "twisting," recalls the entry of the soul into the torrential river of the lower, ephemeral world in Plato's *Timaeus*, only here the hero is being cast *out*. "Tordre" also points to a figure of Mallarmé's personal mythology, the Chimera.

66. Here we have again an echo of tattering and ripping the veil of the temple in "Crise."

67. Judy Kravis, *The Prose of Mallarmé* (Cambridge: Cambridge University Press, 1976), p. 34. Kravis cites as her source Suzanne Bernard, *Mallarmé et la Musique* (Paris: Nizet, 1959), p. 24.

68. Kravis, p. 37.

69. *OC*, p. 542. Translation: "Now that Music has been added, everything is completely changed. The central principle of the old Theater has been annihilated. Now stage performance has become strictly allegorical, empty, abstract, impersonal; now in order to rise up and resemble truth, it must be revived in the life-giving breath poured out by Music" (Cook, p. 74).

70. *OC*, p. 546. Translation, my own: [These disciples, in order to find . . .] the definitive salvation, go straight to the summit of your Art, for them the goal of the search.

71. For example, in "La Musique et les lettres": "la renovation de rites et de rimes . . . par la retrempe et l'essor purifiants du chant" (*OC*, pp. 644, 648).

72. Everything retempers itself in the primitive stream, but [doesn't go] so far as the source (author's translation).

73. *BT*, Kaufmann, p. 72.

74. Schopenhauer, *WWR*, vol. 1, pp. 352–53.

75. *OC*, p. 544.

76. Nietzsche, "Nietzsche contra Wagner," p. 666.

77. Nietzsche, "Nietzsche contra Wagner," p. 666.

78. Nietzsche, "Nietzsche contra Wagner," p. 666.

79. Nietzsche, "Nietzsche contra Wagner," p. 667.

80. *OC*, p. 541. Translation: "by virtue of the conciseness of its writing, only the Dance can translate the fugacious and the sudden into the Idea" (Cook, p. 73).

81. The "Spectacle futur" is of course an allusion to Wagner's claim to having created "die Musik der Zukunft."

82. Michael Haar, "Nietzsche and Metaphysical Language," in *The New Nietzsche*, ed. David B. Allison (New York: Dell, 1977), p. 6. Another of Nietzsche's "dancing" remarks: how "to dance in chains" (*Human, All-too Human*).

83. See Mallarmé's "le précipiter, le tordre" (*OC*, p. 544).

Chapter 4. The Orphic Moment of Stéphane Mallarmé

1. Sewell, chapter 1.

2. Here I am leaving out the scientific side of the moment, which Sewell adumbrates in the work of Linnaeus, Erasmus Darwin, and Goethe. Her theme widens here to embrace what Emerson (the first American Orphic voice) called "a natural history of the intellect."

3. The tradition of Orphism in France has received extensive study. The most important contributions are: Eva Kushner, *Le Mythe d'Orphée dans la littérature française contemporaine* (Paris: Nizet, 1961); Gwendolyn M. Bays, *The Orphic Vision: Seer Poets from Novalis to Rimbaud*

(Lincoln: University of Nebraska Press, 1964); Georges Cattaui, *Orphisme et prophétie chez les poètes français 1850-1950* (Paris: Plon, 1965); Hermione B. Riffaterre, *Orphéus dans la poésie romantique* (Paris: Nizet, 1970); Brian Juden, *Traditions orphiques et tendances mystiques dans le romantisme français (1800-1855)* (Paris: Kliencksieck, 1971).

4. Hugo is the summation of the Romantic Orpheus, as Mallarmé, who patiently awaited the moment for the next phase, realized. He represented the end of a tradition in poetry, just as Beethoven had for music. Nothing more was left to say in their respective idioms.

5. Illuminism was an anti-rational reaction to the perceived excesses of the *philosophes* of the Enlightenment, emphasizing at all costs that nature was "spiritual" rather than mechanical. Its roots were in Neoplatonism, kabbala, and alchemy. In the modern era Swedenborg was a major figure, and phrenology, Rosicrucianism, and mesmerism were related movements. It was an "atmosphere of muddled intellectual reaction" (Walter Strauss, in a personal conversation, Sept. 1988), which provides a sharp contrast with the Cartesian precision of Mallarmé's versification. Strauss discusses illuminism in the context of Nerval (pp. 52-53) and again in the context of Rimbaud (pp. 219-20). Quite rightly, he places Bays's *The Orphic Vision: Seer Poets from Novalis to Rimbaud* in this tradition. His use of Herbert Marcuse's distinction, in *Eros and Civilization*, between two main currents in modern literature, the Promethean (Blake, Shelley, Hugo, Rimbaud and on to the surrealists) and the Orphic (the poets he treats in *Descent*: Novalis, Nerval, Mallarmé, Rilke—looking beyond them to Valéry, Yeats, and Trakl), is helpful. But the most germane distinction, it seems to me, remains that made by Marcel Raymond between the "voyant" (Nerval, Rimbaud) and the "artiste" (Mallarmé, Valéry): Marcel Raymond, *From Baudelaire to Surrealism* (New York: Wittenborn, Schultz, 1950).

6. Strauss, 276n.

7. Strauss, p. 117

8. Strauss, p. 117.

9. "Crise de Vers," *OC*, p. 361.

10. Cited in Morris Abrams, *The Mirror and the Lamp* (New York: Oxford University Press, 1953), p. 212.

11. Charles Segal's *Orpheus: The Myth of the Poet* (Baltimore: Johns Hopkins University Press, 1989), while a valuable addition to criticism of Orphic poetry (Virgil, Ovid, Rilke, Marcel Camus's *Orfeo Negro* and Cocteaus's *Orphée*), omits discussion of Mallarmé altogether.

12. Sewell, p. 403.

13. Sewell, p. 404.

14. "Les dieux antiques," Mallarmé's translation with introduction to Cox's *Manual of Mythology* (1882). "Cantique de Saint Jean" has

an implicit confirmation of this schema. There the moment of the beheading is consonant with the moment of the setting sun. The Baptist is to the Christ-sun as Orpheus is to Apollo/Helios. See discussion, page 85 below.

15. "as if volatilized by an intellectual chemistry."

16. *OC*, p. 1160. Translation: "to fix for an instant in the mind the image of the gods before their disappearance."

17. "Crise de Vers," *OC*, p. 367. Translation: "disintegration in articulated shudders close to instrumentation."

18. "Mystère," *OC*, p. 386. Ttranslation: "vibratory center of suspense . . . being that which doesn't say itself in discourse."

19. As Mallarmé wrote Verlaine in the celebrated letter of November 1885.

20. Preface to Ghil's "Traité du verbe," *OC*, p. 857. Translation: "What good is the marvel of transposing a fact of nature into its almost complete and vibratory disappearance with the play of the word, however, unless there comes forth from it, without the bother of a nearby or concrete reminder, the pure notion." (Caws, pp. 75–76).

21. *OC*, p. 858.

22. *OC*, p. 857.

23. Letter to E. Lefebure, May 27, 1867, (Mallarmé, *Correspondance*, p. 249). Translation: "It was not until yesterday that I heard in the young wheat that sacred voice of the innocent earth, already more unified than that of the bird, that son of the trees in the solar night, which has something of the stars and the moon, and a little of death. But above all how much more unified it is than the voice of a woman, who walked and sang before me, and through whose voice one could see a thousand words in which it vibrated—a voice pregnant with the Void! All the happiness the earth possesses in not being broken down into matter and spirit was contained in the unique sound of the cricket" (*Selected Letters of Stéphane Mallarmé*, tr. Rosemary Lloyd (Chicago: University of Chicago Press, 1988), p. 81.

24. Plato's marvelous parable of the cicadas as autochthonous men from the *Phaedrus* has never seemed closer than in the text of this letter.

25. This lovely little passage is quite close to the tone and thematics of the *Chandos-Brief* of Hofmannsthal: a retreat into *little things*, which is to anticipate the next stage of modern poetry, the figure of Chandos acceding to the period of Rilke's *Dinggedichte*.

26. The moment, and its subsequent elaboration, is exemplary of what Nietzsche had to say about the lyric poet: "The Dionysiac musician, himself imageless, is nothing but original pain and reverberation of the image" (*BT*, Golffing, p. 39).

27. "I . . . recognized in the sound *nul,* the taut strings of the musical instrument: it had been forgotten, and now, surely, glorious Memory had just visited it with His wing or with a palm-branch, [the finger on the artifice of the mystery]" (Cook, p. 2).

28. "The instrument's string, stretched taut in forgetfulness over the sound *nul,* would seem to break, and I would add in a sort of litany: *'est morte'* (Cook, p. 3).

29. *"est morte,* detached from that fateful suspension, ran uselessly on into the resulting emptiness of meaning" (Cook, p. 2).

30. *OC,* pp. 272–73. Translation: "But the moment at which there took place the irrefutable intervention of the supernatural and the beginning of the anguish beneath which my once lordly spirit agonizes, was when I saw, raising my eyes, in the street of antique dealers which I had followed instinctively, that I was in from of a lute-maker's shop selling old musical instruments hung on the wall, and, on the ground, some yellow palms and the wings of old birds hidden in the shadow. Like an eccentric, I fled, a person probably condemned to wear mourning for the inexplicable Penultimate" (Anthony Hartley, *Mallarmé* [Baltimore: Penguin, 1965], p. 125).

31. The forgotten instrument with the singular string recalls the *ektara,* the "one-string" (cf. guitar, sitar/cithera/zither), which I witnessed wandering Hindu holy men play (singers of *nirguni bhajans,* devotional songs to the *nirgun* [formless one]) while learning Hindustani classical singing (1968–69). I eagerly asked my singing master (Kumar Gandharva) where I could obtain one. He laughed and said one must make this instrument oneself, showing me the one he had made. The same tension is here between the *formless one* and the *Ur-Eine,* the negation of existence and the only existent, which we have in Mallarmé and Nietzsche. Mallarmé must make his own instrument; he is his only instrument. As "Musician of silence," he outdoes even the ascetic singers of the one-string.

32. In "Le santal vieux qui se dédore / De sa viole étincelant," "étincelant" echoes the Greek word *ailoos:* shimmering, gleaming, glistening, flickering, iridescent. It is the quality of many-faceted light, a vision that is always of the perishable moment. It is thus another Mallarméan word, to be classed with "glissant," "presque vibratoire," "frisonne," "frottait," and, later in this sonnet, "ruisselant" and "frôle."

33. Mallarmé, *Correspondance,* p. 151.

34. *OC,* p. 74. Translation:

> But where, limned gold, the dreamer dwells,
> There sleeps a mournful mandola,
> Its deep lacuna a source of song,

Of a kind that toward some window,
formed by that belly or none at all,
Filial, one might have been born.

—Patricia Terry and Maurice Shroder, in Caws, p. 59

35. *OC*, p. 74. Translation: I feel as if shadows were spreading in my vertebae all in a shudder at one and the same time, / and my head emerging, a solitary look-out, in the triumphant flights of this scythe." (Hartley, p. 49)

36. *OC*, p. 49.

37. *OC*, p. 1468.

38. At the window ledge concealing
the ancient sandalwood gold-flaking
Of her viol dimly twinkling
Long ago with flute or mandore,

Stands the pallid Saint displaying
The ancient missal page unfolding
At the Magnificat outpouring
Long ago for vesper and compline:

At the monstrance glazing lightly
Brushed now by a harp the Angel
Fashioned in his evening flight
Just for the delicate finger

Tip which, lacking the ancient missal
Or ancient sandalwood, she poises
On the instrumental plumage,
Musician of silence.

—Herbert Creekmore, in Caws, p. 41

39. This "axis" is extraordinarily close in form to the bats who turn on their "autochthonous wing tips" as they brush the gates of the underworld (in "Théodore de Banville," *OC*, p. 521).

40. Charles Mauron, cited in the note to the variant "Sainte Cécilia" (*OC*, pp. 1468–69). In the same set of notes, Aubanel writes back to Mallarmé concerrning the poem that "cela ressemble à une vieille peinture de missel, a un vitrail ancien" (*Mallarmé, Correspondance*, Letter for Aubanel, Dec. 21, 1865).

41. *OC*, p. 40. Translation: I bring you the child of an Idumaean night! Dark, with bleeding wing and pale, its feathers plucked, through the glass burned with spices and gold, through the icy panes, still dreary, alas! the dawn threw itself on the angelic lamp. O palms! and when it

showed this relic to the father trying out a hostile smile, the blue, sterile solitude shuddered (Hartley, p. 33).

42. In the notes to this poem, in remarks taken from D. Seurat (*OC*, p. 1439), the poet is seen as self-creating, as Jacob was in Idumea, the land he took from Esau, the hairy "humanité monstreuse," the two "hommes pre-adamiques, rois d'Idumée..êtres sans sexe, se reproduisant sans femmes." The poem is thus a "naissance monstrueuse," denied the breast "Par qui coule en blancheur sibylline la femme / Pour les lèvres que l'air du vierge azur affame?" I get the image of the poet/child/bird, its mouth pressed against the glass from the inside, waiting eternally for milk from the impossible: the azur, male, and virginal.

43. *OC*, pp. 67–68. Translation:

> Will new and alive the beautiful today
> Shatter with a blow of drunken wing
> This hard lake, forgotten haunted under rime
> By the transparent glacier, flights unknown!
>
> A swan of long ago remembers now that he,
> Magnificent but lost to hope, is doomed
> For having failed to sing the realms of life
> When the ennui of sterile winter gleamed.
>
> His neck will shake off the white torment space
> Inflicts upon the bird for his denial,
> But not this horror, plumage trapped in ice.
>
> Phantom by brilliance captive to this place,
> Immobile, he assumes disdain's cold dream,
> Which, in his useless exile, robes the Swan.

—Patricia Terry and Maurice Shroder, in Caws, pp. 45–46

44. In the *Republic, book 10*, the "Myth of Er," Plato has Orpheus choose to return to earth as a swan, eschewing further pollution by being borne in a human womb.

45. Strauss, p. 45.

46. This despite Mallarmé's occasional use of such phrases as "Moi projété absolu" (*Igitur*) and "qui déchaîna l'Infinité" ("Musique").

47. As Michaud says, "La Poésie est l'expression par le langage humain ramené à son rhythme essentiel" (Poetry is expression in the human language returned to its essential rhythm) (Michaud, *Mallarmé*, p. 114).

48. "Musique et lettres," *OC*, p. 648.

49. Both Richard and Poulet conduct interesting discussions of Mallarméan space: Georges Poulet, *La Distance intérieure* (Paris: Plon,

1952), pp. 298ff.; Jean-Pierre Richard, *L'Univers poétique de Stéphane Mallarmé* (Paris: Editions du Seuil, 1961).

50. Mallarmé, *Correspondance*, pp. 224–25. Lloyd J. Austin points out that Mallarmé has borrowed the sacred spider image from the letters of Keats. (Lloyd J. Austin, *Poetic Principles and Practice* [New York: Cambridge University Press, 1987], p. 28).

51. Letter to Cazalis, in Mallarmé, *Correspondance*, p. 242. The poetics of Edgar Allan Poe, and their enthusiastic adoption and further elaboration by Baudelaire, thoroughly soak these thoughts. Mallarmé speaks in this passage of the "arabesque" as the agent enacting the figure upon the coordinates. This term, an excellent figure for the mathematical and impersonal creation of form, also comes via Poe and Baudelaire. See Hugo Friedrich, *The Structure of Modern [Lyric] Poetry*, tr. Joachim Neugroschel (Evanston: Northwestern University Press, 1974), p. 37.

52. *OC*, p. 643.

53. In the opinion of Paul Claudel, Mallarmé belonged to the "pure tradition classique et française, et l'on peut même dire qu'il en est le couronnement" (pure French classical tradition, and one could even say he is its crown). Cited in Jacques Scherer, *L'Expression litteraire dans l'oeuvre de Mallarmé* (Paris: Librairie A. G. Nizet, 1957), p. 42.

54. Alternative translation: We have disturbed poetry.

55. *OC*, p. 649. Translation: evocative of prestiges located at the limit of hearing and almost of abstract vision.

56. "Crise de vers, *OC*, p. 365. Translation (author's): To hear the indescribable ray—like those flashes that gild and tear apart a meander of melodies: where music rejoins the line to form, since Wagner, poetry. This piece was written slightly before the more ambiguous "Wagner" piece, which I discussed in the third chapter. Clearly, Wagner's ambition contributed to Mallarmé's hopes for a new marriage. But what transpired was the colossal simulacram of such a wedding, staged and inauthentic. I think back to Mallarmé's contrast between the "grillon" and the multiply cracked voice of the woman singing in the field. It is the cricket who bears the new note, not the "endless melody."

57. Such a seeing/hearing shares the quality that Walter Pater describes so inimitably, saying that Plato is a "seer who has a sort of sensuous love of the unseen," with an "aptitude of things visible [that] empowers him to express, as if for the eyes, what except for the eye of the mind is strictly invisible" (Pater, p. 143). This is the moment just before that from which Baudelaire writes, which is the posterior, materially perceptible side of primary synesthesia.

58. *OC*, p. 649. Translation: the alternative face enlarged here towards the obscure, there, scintillating . . . of a phenomenon, the only one that I will call the Idea.

59. But Judy Kravis is right to point out that the two faces continually do a *volte face*, so that one cannot say that one side of the coin is "music," the other "letters" (Kravis, p. 213).

60. *OC*, p. 649.

61. A dualist in the tradition of his forebears, Pascal and Descartes, Mallarmé uses "l'Idée" and its analogues in a way that evokes Platonic idealism. The Platonic position was central in Mallarmé criticism until about 1964, as rather neatly summarized in the work of Delfel and Michaud (Guy Delfel, *L'Aesthétique de Mallarmé* [Paris: Flammarion, n.d.]). But with a new generation of critics, notably the deconstructionists, this position has been subject to concerted attack, and Mallarmé's poetics has been offered as model for a new program for razing the foundations of the republic of letters. To an extent I agree with the more recent critics, especially in the refusal to see Mallarmé as a classical Platonic idealist. As I have said earlier, he never (after the poems of his youth) invokes the other world in anything like the plenitude that Plato grants the world of Forms; it is rather the horizon or limit of this one. But that horizon always sparkles with the bewitching possibility of something *more* and *other* than ordinary reality has to offer. It is the oft-successful evocation of this *possibility* that gives Mallarmé's poetry its "idealistic" flavor. In granting a space for this possibility, Mallarmé, I believe, leaves a door open, at least tentatively, to the metaphysical tradition that recent French theorists eschew. In honoring Mallarmé as a fulcrum or bridge between the old metaphysics and the minimalist postmodern position, I part company with these theorists.

62. Strauss, p. 93.

63. *OC*, p. 646.

64. Coleridge also worked upon an ambitious project, the *Encyclopedia Metropolitana*, which was to have been self-referencing, a true *encyclical*, containing all knowledge in a format that only Coleridge could manage. Since he was unable to convince his partners and backers of its necessary cyclical structure, they abandoned the project, but not before Coleridge had produced his remarkable *Preface* (1819). Both Coleridge and Mallarmé projected twenty years for their life-poems, and both produced only fragments. At the end of his life, Mallarmé resigned himself to this paltry production, realizing that even his fragments, the "éparpillement en frissons articulés proches de l'instrumentation," each contained the whole. "Le livre, instrument spirituel," was the analogue, for the human race in its entirety, of the constellated night sky, his final image of the cosmos.

65. Compare the imprisoned, iron-clad book of "Prose pour Des Esseintes." Cf. especially Poulet's interpretation in *The Metamorphoses of the Circle* (Baltimore: Johns Hopkins University Press, 1966), pp. 290–306.

66. "Defence of Poetry" (1821).

67. *OC*, p. 645. Translation: everything that emanates from the spirit reintegrates itself. Mallarmé's use of "émaner" here must be distinguished from the Plotinian or Shelleyan "emanation." That which returns, the ray of spirit returning to spirit, is not the same as that which first departed. The self-reflexive quality of words—as the context of the reintegration—and the radical alienation from experience of the modern poet (since Nerval and Baudelaire) insure that the *epistrophe* is not a return of the Prodigal. The late nineteenth century discovery of the physical principle of entropy came to poetry before it did to theoretical physics.

68. *OC*, p. 361. This is of course the culmination of a movement, growing out of illuminism, romanticism, and the work of Baudelaire, who staked out the theoretical ground before Mallarmé. I would argue, however, that Mallarmé's own poetry better demonstrates musicality of the sort that he attempts to define in "Musique"—what might be called a "unified field theory" of music. An excellent book that fully explores Mallarmé's sense of poetry as a "music" that is ontologically prior to music intself is David Hillery, *Music and Poetry in France from Baudelaire to Mallarmé* (Bern: Lang, [University of Durham Publications], 1980).

69. *OC*, p. 204. Translation: The air or song beneath the text, conducting the divination from here to there, applies its motif to it in invisible fleurons and cul-de-lampes.

70. *OC*, pp. 647–48.

71. Such is the position of Yves Bonnefoy in a remarkably perspicacious essay on Mallarmé's poetics ("Mallarmé's Poetics," tr. Elaine Ancekewitz, *Yale French Studies*, 54, pp. 9–21). Bonnefoy argues that either term alone is flat—either an unexperienced, uninterpreted nature, or a preposterous, naked Literature claiming, like the Emperor, to wear the coat of all possible colors—and that it is remarkably easy to demonstrate a "modernist" prejudice by reading the second remark (about literature) while forgetting the first (about nature). This "modernist prejudice" is Vico's "conceit of scholars," who would ignore the fact that Mallarmé's thought was "established in fact between two ages of the world" (recall Mallarmé's remark that he lived in an "interregnum") (Bonnefoy, p. 17).

To Bonnefoy, "le hasard" (chance) has to do with the "fact of language," which prevents us from "converting the contingent into the universal." But Mallarmé stubbornly adheres to the hope that, despite the essential irreality of words, their contingency can be overcome through the poetic text, specifically, as *"site"* for the appearance of a reality. For him, the Mallarméan text is a "fact, manifest, undeniable, irreducible to anything else." When Mallarmé speaks of the "transposition divine, qui va du fait à l'Idée," it is the moment of transposition that the verse defines, captures as a "bloc." But both the "fact" and the "Idea" are themselves "real"—just inaccessible to ordinary language. Again Bonnefoy cautions us that in our modern climate of prejudice toward the reality of "facts of nature," we forget that "Mallarmé is fundamentally attached to objects"—objects seen as embedded within the "nature" of the eighteenth century—"in her [nature's] own language, unfortunately poorly transcribed by men's tongues" (p. 17). Moreover, "Objects that can be identified . . . are not only facts to his eyes, but potential names, at the heart of the Intelligible" (the "model examples" being the family of Iridées of "Prose pour des Esseintes") (p. 17).

The practice of poetry for Mallarmé is, then, the reconciliation of two attitudes: "the transposition of current accepted notions and the indication of the pure notion"—a reconciliation effected by the line of verse as "mot nouveau" ("Crise"). This is not a matter of mimesis; the line of verse describes the object, reproduces it, no better than does the language of ordinary reporting. "The word" (or "the Verb," the "new word"), however, grasps as a "'bloc', a possible verse" (p. 18), the state of the soul at the moment in which the poet experiences it, and renders it, albeit enigmatically, as a "fait," an unquestionable phenomenon in its own right. In my terms, the "momentary god" as an *état de l'âme*, is yoked under the tension of original language: "*when the impression is authentically experienced*, it evokes a fact of the universe, makes it present, in its own way, more clearly and completely than any definition tainted with prior notions. . . . The impression, enunciated by the *mot nouveau*, is a specific response of consciousness to *the fact of nature*" (pp. 18–19). Bonnefoy goes on to assert that in this process nature "is becoming conscious of itself through Verse." This is a bit too Heideggerian for my taste, but the essential is here, namely, of one reciprocating movement. In the language of Mallarmé's lecture, this is the unitary place of "musique et lettres." The tools with which the poet accomplishes this elusive feat are better expressed in phenomenological terms, not by paraphrasing Heidegger, but in the words of Goethe: "Every new object, when carefully observed, unlocks a new organ in us."

72. *OC*, pp. 647–48. Translation:

> Nature exists; She will not be changed, although we may add cities, railroads, or other inventions to our material world.
>
> Therefore, our eternal and only problem is to seize relationships and intervals, however few or multiple. Thus, faithful to some special vision deep within, we may extend or simplify the world at will.
>
> To create is to conceive an object in its fleeting moment, in its absence.

To do this, we simply compare its facets and dwell lightly, negligently upon their multiplicity. We conjure up a scene of lovely, evanescent, intersecting forms. We recognize the entire and binding arabesque thus formed as it leaps dizzily in terror or plays disquieting chords; or, through a sudden digression (by no means disconcerting), we are warned of its likeness unto itself even as it hides. *Melodic encoding [*chiffration*] quietens with our very fibers motifs that compose [the soul's] logic. Whatever agony the Chimera brings forth, pouring through Her golden wounds the evidence that she is always wholly Herself, no vanquished throe can falsify or transgress the omnipresent Line drawn from every point to every other for the purpose of instituting the idea; perhaps beneath the level of human vision, like some pure Harmony.*

To habitually surprise [this ideal] constitutes our obligation to him who once unleashed Infinity–Whose rhythm, as when one refingers by touch the keys of the verbal keyboard, gives itself over to the use of apt, everyday words.

For in truth, what is Literature if not our mind's ambition (in the form of language) to define things; to prove to the satisfaction of our soul that the natural phenomenon corresponds to our imaginative understanding of it. And our hope, of course, is that we may ourselves be reflected in it. (Cook, pp. 48–49, except the italicized text, which is my own translation)

Mallarmé's "chiffration" is a neologism that I interpret as "melodic encoding," i.e., the opposite of "déchiffrement," decoding.

73. Friedrich, p. 21.

74. James R. Lawler, *The Language of French Symbolism* (Princeton: Princeton University Press, 1969), p. 149.

75. Or unchain, unmoor. This rich image recalls, for me, the "Spindle of Necessity" by which the world is suspended at the end of the *Republic*: the final vision of Er. It also recalls Schopenhauer's image of the *principium individuationis* as a boat awash upon the vast sea, the *Wille*. The source for that analogy, which Wagner reworked in *Tristan*, is that of Tristan harping while adrift upon the sea in his rudderless bark. This is an unmistakenly Orphic image, out of another tradition with a wealth of Orphic lore of its own, the Celtic.

76. This space however, always suggests at its limits another dimension, as Peter Dayan argues in an excellent study of Mallarmé's prose (*Mallarmé's Divine Transposition*. Oxford: Clarendon Press, 1986). The argument deserves summarizing, for Dayan's reading charts a path

between the traditional, overly Platonic interpretation of the poet and Derrida's revisionist one. Dayan's strategy is to read Mallarmé thrice: first according to the "tradition" of Mallarméan criticism ("thesis"), then in the antithetical manner of Derrida, and finally by a "synthesis" in which he points out the fallacies of each of the prior readings. The procedure is cumbersome, and the claims overly grand (that the author has invented a new method of reading), but the resultant insights justify the effort required to follow his argument.

The problem with the "straight" reading of Mallarmé is its discursive realism, where the "fait" and "idéal" are readily transposable (as in Michaud, who is a convenient reference point because he reads Mallarmé well—in the manner of traditional idealism). For Dayan, the "realistic" is the hallmark of the "referential." Thus he would provisionally define the realistic not only as the physical and bourgeois worlds but also as a whole set of "ideals," including several that he claims Mallarmé rejects: "the occultist's alchemical one, the Christian's mystical ideal, the naturalist's scientific ideal . . ." All of these are "deconstructible" in their referentiality. However, and this is where the Derridean method is lacking, the refusal of the discursive, the "realistic," is from an external viewpoint. From *within* the figure—and each of these ideals is contained within a figure constituted by an implicit set of operative principles—the ideal works, not in the referential manner of the "correspondence" theory of truth, but in a figured manner. Dayan thus posits a "Mallarméan" or "figured" ideal that is "non-realistic, non-metaphysical, extra-dimensional." In a sense, Dayan is offering a more elaborate, self-conscious model for what Keats simply called "Negative Capability." The important difference is that his "figured ideal' involves not only the entry into nature's sympathetic web but also the multiple imagined wholes of the human universe (thus entire "paradigms," including the natural-scientific, the mystical, etc.).

Refreshingly, Dayan points out that Mallarmé is interested not in "Discourse," as is Derrida, but only in a particular instance of it, namely poetry. The "disruption" of linear discourse in his poetry "is due to an ambition to do something other than describe reality or its discourse; it is due to the attraction of something entirely outside reality, entirely (structurally) foreign to it: the ideal, which in its latent form pre-dates language, and refuses to be reduced to discursive logic" (p. 146). The "disruption" then, is not simply the play of *différance*, one more semiotic act in the endless series of the web of language; there is something "latent," "out-side" the web. The old Zen saying is apt here: one must not confuse the moon with the finger that points to it.

In the final two chapters Dayan performs an elegant analysis of a certain "crux" to which Mallarmé repeatedly leads the reader. At this point, incompatible (but felt to be necessary discursively) arguments abut, and one is forced, in order to make sense of the text, to enter the "extra dimension." Dayan thinks that Mallarmé consciously employs two mutually incompatible logical fallacies to effect this crux, particularly in his critical prose. One is "dispositional," the other "essentialist." In sum, the larger linguistic-structural pattern that Dayan's argument demonstrates in the prose writings is the same characteristic oscillation that I find minutely in the particular images of individual poems.

77. "Une inquiétude du voile dans le temple avec des plis significatifs et un peu sa déchirure" ("Crise de vers," *OC*, pp. 360–61).

78. *OC*, p. 361.

79. Or so Mallarmé would have us believe. Following his scenario, Hugo would be a French analogue of Homer, prolonging by more than a half century the break with the old "mimetic" order. (The situation as Mallarmé presents it here is similar to our original "Orphic moment": the birth, in Onomacritus, Pherecydes, and Plato of literature and the intellectual.) In fact, he is hiding another figure behind the veil of his own rhetoric: Baudelaire. Though Hugo was the national poet, and the repository of taste in verse style and the "traditional" poetic voice or persona, twenty-five years had already passed since Baudelaire had published the first edition of *Les Fleurs du mal*. Hugo was never a serious model for Mallarmé's verse, whereas reading Baudelaire at eighteen was the *coup de foudre* that galvanized Mallarmé into poetry. The young Mallarmé emulated him until the years of the Tournon nightmare, which Walter Strauss thinks was in large part provoked by his necessity to move beyond his master, Baudelaire, whose "Spleen" led to a suffocating encroachment of matter upon the younger poet.

80. "Musique," *OC*, p. 644.

81. *OC*, p. 648.

82. *OC*, p. 367. Translation: a breaking of the great literary rhythms . . . and their dispersion in articulated shudders close to instrumentation. The phenomenon of atomism in Mallarmé is discussed in terms of his concept of *time* in an article by Bettina Knapp, "'Igitur or Elbehnon's Folly': The Depersonalization Process and the Creative Encounter" (*Yale French Studies*, 54 (1978), p. 204.

83. *OC*, p. 367.

84. *OC*, p. 366. Translation: from a fistful of dust or reality without enclosing it, into the book, even as text, the volatile dispersion which we call spirit, which has nothing to do with anything but the musicality of everything.

85. I realize that the terms of my analysis move here into those of anthropology, and thus continue the tradition, since the shift from the Frazerian to the Durkheimian, of anthropological reading of ancient

myth. This may indeed be another example of the "conceit of scholars," but the wedding of the disciplines of philology, anthropology, archaeology, and historiography continues to be one of the most fruitful in the era of modern scholarship. The best example of this method, I think, is Walter Burkert, *Homo Necans* (Berkeley and Los Angeles: University of California Press, 1983), where the sacrificial ritual of the *sparagmos* is examined as the single most important datum of primitive Greek religion: an old idea, certainly, but given here with a wealth of newly integrated evidence.

86. Cf. especially John Block Friedman, *Orpheus in the Middle Ages* (Cambridge: Harvard University Press, 1970).

87. The astonishing figure is carried even further. At the head of a host, an Islamic man blows upon a battle horn. Immediately in front of him is a composite Christ/Orpheus figure, one trunk of whom bears on his back a Renaissance oboe, with a flute inserted in his anus (the other branch is a dead Christ figure, arms outstretched). Below him, another figure is trapped within a drum being beaten by a demon. An androgynous satyr figure is perched atop a cithara, turning the hurdy-gurdy handle, but there is the suggestion that he, too, is screwed into the instrument by the fact of the detail of handle protruding from his anus. Bosch's awareness of the background of the figure in the theogonies is apparent by his painting, just behind this figure, at the apex of the entire group (which rides upon the Boschian flood of humanity, interlaced with demons) a crouched, bent young man, delicately balancing an egg upon his back. This latter image provides an analogue for the "balancing" ("un balancement prévu d'inversions") that is central to my interpretation of Orpheus as the delicately balanced dancer between the realms of Apollo and Dionysos.

88. *OC*, p. 363. Translation: anyone, with his playing and his ear, can turn himself into an instrument as soon as he blows, strokes, or strikes it with skill; wearing it out in the process, and dedicating it also to language.

89. *OC*, p. 869. Translation: This is the perfect use of the mystery which the symbol contitutes: to evoke little by little an object to show a state of the soul, or inversely to choose an object and disengage from it a state of the soul by a series of decodings.

90. The theme of this "passion play" is at least as old as Philo, who said that G-d was present in the world as "a vowel amid consonants." In the more restrained (modernist) words of Mallarmé's only consensus disciple, Paul Valéry, this is the play of "le mot," which, "en se rapprochent de l'organisme dépositaire de la vie, . . . présente dans ses voyelles et ses dipthongues comme une chair et dans ses consonnes comme une ossature délicate à disséquer" (cited in Cattaui, p. 116).

Chapter 5. Tombs, Fans, Cosmologies: A View from the Prison House

    1. Again, it is tempting to go against Socrates and see the soul as an "attunement."

    2. Derveni Theogony (ca. 450 B.C.); Eudemian Theogony (ca. 400 B.C.); Platonic Dialogues (405–350 B.C.). Source: West, *Orphic Poems*, p. 264.

    3. "Tombeaux de Poe," *OC*, p. 70.

    4. Mallarmé, *Correspondance*, p. 242 (As fragile as my earthly apparition is, I can only submit to the absolutely necessary developments which would enable the universe to refind its identity in me).

    5. Rodenbach, *L'Elite*, cited in Richard, p. 424.

    6. See the discussion at the beginning of the conclusion.

    7. "Le Tombeau de Charles Baudelaire," *OC*, p. 70. Translation:

> The buried temple through the sewer's dark
> Sepulchral mouth that drools out mud and rubies.

(Caws, p. 51)

    8. Compare the *ptyx* of "Ses purs ongles" in the discussion at the end of the chapter.

    9. An absence that is, nevertheless, palpable in its "frissons"—key term in the Orphic vocabulary of vibration. Compare Baudelaire's "frisson galvanique" (Friedrich, p. 26).

    10. Kravis, p. 171.

    11. These boneplates from Olbia (Scythia) are capital examples of Orphism in the fourth to third centuries B.C. Inscriptions engraved in bone, such as "Son of earth and starry heaven," serve to highlight the radically mixed nature of the wearer. The bone, as medium, has a quality similar to that of the fan, each being pure white, yet materiality. (Compare Rilke's "Hetären-Gräber" and Eliot's chirping bones from "Ash Wednesday.")

In another vein, "Un baiser flambant se déchire" is the complement to the image of potential energy in "Vierge," the "swan sonnet": "Va t'il nous déchirer avec un coup d'aile ivre?"

    12. *OC*, p. 57. Translation:

> With for language nothing except a beating in the skies the future line of poetry frees itself from the most precious dwelling-place,
>
>   wing swooping low, the messenger, this fan if it is the same through which behind you some mirror has shone
>
>   limpidly (where a little invisible ash is going to fall pursued in every grain, the only thing to trouble me),
>
>   let it appear always the same between your ever busy hands.

(Hartley, p. 65)

13. Compare the cigar's bright kiss of "Toute l'âme résumée" (*OC*, p. 73) and the ashes of "Igitur," to which we shall turn at the end of this chapter.

14. *O.C.*, p. 58. Translation:

Oh dreamer, that I may plunge
Pathless to pure delight,
Learn by a subtle lie
To keep my wing within your hand.
A twilight coolness comes

Upon you with each beat
Whose caged stroke lightly
Thrusts the horizon back.

Now feel the space shivering
Dizzy, some great kiss
Which, wild to be born in vain,
Cannot break forth or rest.

Can you feel paradise
Shy as a buried laugh, slip
from the corner of your mouth
Down the concerted fold!

The scepter of pink shores
Stagnant on golden eves is
this white shut flight you pose
Against a bracelet's fire.

—Peter Caws and Mary Ann Caws (Caws, p. 43)

15. *OC*, pp. 58–59.
16. *OC*, p. 62.
17. *OC*, p. 521.
18. *OC*, p. 67. Translation:

When shadow threatened with the fatal law
One old dream, desire and pain of my spine,
Grieved at persihing beneath ceilings funereal,
It folded its indubitable wing within me.

Luxury, O ebony room where, to charm a king,
Celebrated garlands writhe in their death,
You are but a proud lie spoken by darkness
In the eyes of the lone man dazzled by his faith.

Yes, I know that, far in deep night, the Earth
Casts with great brillliance the strange mystery
Under the hideous centuries that darken it less.

Space ever alike if it grow or deny itself
Rolls in that boredom vile fires as witnesses
That genius has been lit with a festive star.

—James Lawler (Caws, p. 45)

19. Richard poses a number of questions meant to expose the "incomplete" thematics of this poem, which necessitate a study of "Igitur" to elucidate its context. They include the following: "Nous comprenons mal aussi comment le reploiement d'une aile a pu concrètement aboutir au surgissement d'un feu" (Richard, p. 183). But it is clear to me that reading the poem with the erotics of the *Phaedrus* as a background shows the relation between the "folded wing" and the surging forth of fire at the end. The wing folded into the spinal column is a charging of the consciousness of the poet, which smolders underneath the obscuring centuries of the earth's time. Another daimonic effect is suggested by Mallarmé's image. Namely, the caduceus as double-winged emblem for traffic through the central nervous system: the hidden, subtle, and unexpected action of Hermes. In the end, the "Astre en fête" is lit by the fires of poetry and literature, consistent with Mallarmé's poetics. Though rooted in the earthly and the material, the "éclat" of "l'insolite mystère" is the bursting into flame of the torch of Hermes/Thoth, an inner light.

20. *OC*, pp. 67–69.

21. This figure of Nyx, her stars as jeweled fingernails, strongly evokes Apuleius's vision of Isis in book 11 of *The Metamorphoses (The Golden Ass)*. Cf. *The Golden Ass of Apuleius*, tr. William Adlington (New York: Horace Liveright, 1927).

22. *OC*, pp. 68–69. Translation:

The onyx of her pure nails offered high,
Lampadephore at midnight, Anguish bears
Many a twilight dream the Phoenix burned
To ashes gathered by no amphora.

On the credence, in the empty room: no ptyx,
Curio of vacuous sonority, extinct
(The Master's gone to dip tears from the Styx
With the unique delight of Nothingness).

But near the vacant northern window, gold
Expires, conformed perhaps to the motif
Of unicorn flames rearing at a nymph,

> She, in the mirror, nude, defunct, although
> Within the framed oblivion at once
> Appears, all scintillation, the Septet.

—Patricia Terry and Maurice Shroder (Caws, p. 49)

23. See the discussion that concludes this chapter.

24. I have consulted the following interpretations of "Ses purs ongles": Richard, pp. 167–69, 215–16; Robert G. Cohn, *Mallarmé: Igitur* (Berkeley and Los Angeles: University of California Press, 1981), p. 30; and Richard Goodkin, *The Symbolist Home and the Tragic Home: Mallarmé and Oedipus* (Amsterdam and Philadelphia: John Benjamins, Purdue University Monographs in Romance Languages, vol. 13 (1984), pp. 159–75. Goodkin's in particular is a brilliant reading. His overall context is to compare the efforts of both Oedipus and Mallarmé to overcome contingency, the illusion of permanence, by establishing a "home," either as a house/family name or within language. The paradigm for this process, both in Sophocles' tragedy and in Mallarmé's symbolist aesthetic, is the search of the two halves of the *symbolon* to reunite. Goodkin demonstrates that this poem brings together the twin themes of house and language in a uniquely successful way. He identifies the "Dream" as that of establishing a purely metaphoric language, replacing the need for the *anaphoric* function of language (a play on *amphore* [amphora]). This dream of a purely metaphoric transfer constitutes a reconsecration of language in poetic utterance (the "Orphic purification"). His etymological analysis of the Greek terms in the poem in the service of this project is particularly masterful.

25. Austin, p. 217.

26. *OC*, p. 386.

27. *OC*, p. 379.

28. But in Richard's interpretation, the "pli" fills the inner space of the Book, and it is intimately self-connected throughout. Readers of Richard will have recognized by now the closeness of my thematics to his. In a study which is a tour de force, never to be surpassed, none is more brilliant than his section on the reflexive Mallarméan erotics of the family of birds: the static equilibria of constellations and flowers, and dynamic equilibria of fans, folds, and wings—with their aerodynamic relations: butterflies and smiles. This "aller-retour" is enroute to his penultimate chapter, which my use of the term *Aufhebung* also signals: subsumed under the title "Idée," he moves through an impressive series of operations: an alchemical transformation of "sommation" and "évènement" (or "vaporisation") into its synthesis, "l'abstraction"—all on their way "Vers une dialectique de totalité." But instead of rushing headlong into this totality—which I judge to be an overzealous pursuit of a

Hegelianism that trembles in Mallarmé's work, but does not drive it—I want to linger with the relation of tomb and fan, which, though implicit in Richard's analysis, is not directly stated.

29. Mondor, *Propos sur la Poésie*, p. 149. Cited in Lawler, pp. 14–15. Mondor's text consists of a collection of occasional remarks by Mallarmé: "all [made] of pages in a subtle state, which are there like the precious bottom of a grotto which remains the beautiful burial place in order to live there with an enchanting idea."

30. Richard speaks of this process as the infinite "papillotage" (blinking) of things (Richard, p. 424). The image occurs as part of an extraordinary conflation of Mallarméan images; this deserves further commment in the concluding chapter, where I examine the continuation of Mallarmé's Orphic moment in his critics. The traditional topos for the metaphor of words as angels is Philo, who explicitly draws the connections that are implicit in Plato.

31. *L'Amitié de Stéphane Mallarmé et de Charles Rodenbach*, p. 143. Cited in Richard, p. 424 (no other publication details given). This is a key moment in Richard's argument, "Vers une dialectique de la totalité" (pp. 419–437). In the conclusion, we will return to the "homeopathic" image of Mallarmé as grotto and center of the universe.

32. He does use *sépulcre* at the end of "Prose pour Des Esseintes" and in the sonnet of the "Tombeaux" series, "Sur les bois oubliés" (*OC*, p. 69).

33. Dayan, p. 187.

34. *OC*, p. 386. Translation: "The words, of their own accord, are exalted at many a facet acknowledged as the rarest and most significant for the mind, the centre of vibratory suspense; which perceives them independently from the ordinary sequence, projected like the walls of a cavern, as long as their mobility or principle lasts, being that part of discourse which is not spoken: all of them, before their extinction, being quick to take part in a reciprocity of fires, either at a distance or presented obliquely as a contingency" (Hartley, p. 203).

35. Compare the remark at the end of "Mystère," "L'air ou chant sous le texte, conduisant la divination d'ici là, y applique son motif en fleuron et cul de lampe invisibles." Compare as well: "brût, immédiat ici, . . . là essentiel . . ." *OC*, p. 387. The "mobility or principle" of words— the "unsayable"—is grounded in the Platonic ideas that all soul is in motion and that it is self-moving. The "motif" of the song beneath the text, which invisibly guides it, is like the architectural principle, whereby the "fleurons" of columns (*corbélés*), are supported by the deeper, hidden structure of the arch that the "fleurons" bring to bear on the columns. This is a virtually perfect example of Mallarmé's use of the "decorative" in a structural manner. The musical motif for the formation of the text

has its analogue in the unhearable (compare "invisibles") music of the spheres, guiding the movement of the heavenly bodies. Both of these are forms of *divination*.

36. Compare for example: "Les monuments, la mer, la face humaine, dans leur plénitude, natifs, conservant une vertu autrement attrayante que ne les voilera une description . . ." ("Crise," *OC*, p. 366).

37. "Mystère," *OC*, p. 386. Translation: The abrupt, high play of wings, mirrors to itself . . . raises itself up as some superior equilibrium, to the foreseen balancing of inversions.

38. Richard talks extensively about this process, which he calls "vaporization" (Richard, p. 392ff.). Music is the "instrument de vaporisation" and the reciprocal of "sommation." Their resolution (*Aufhebung*) is "abstraction." Baudelaire, though, says it best in the following: "De la concentration de la vaporisation du moi, tout est là . . ." (cited in Cattaui, p. 124).

39. Kravis, p. 178. This statement is the inverse of Pater's comment on Plato as "sensuous seer of the unseeable."

40. "Crise," *OC*, p. 366. Translation: "The pure work implies the disappearance of the poet as speaker, yielding his initiative to words, which are mobilized by the shock of their difference; they light up with reciprocal reflections like a virtual stream of fireworks over jewels, restoring perceptible breath to the former lyric impulse, or the enthusiastic personal directing of the sentence" (Caws, p. 75).

41. Richard, p. 175. Compare Mallarmé's "interillumination" of words in this passage with the following description by Mikhail Bakhtin comparing the play of words with the activity of particles of light in a spectral dispersion chamber:

> And into this complex play of light and shadow the word enters—it becomes saturated with this play. . . . If we imagine the *intention* of such a word, that is, its *directionality toward the object*, in the form of a ray of light, then the living and unrepeatable play of colors and light on the facets of the image it constucts can be explained as the spectral dispersion of the ray-word, not within the object itself (as would be the case in the play of an image-as-trope, in poetic speech taken in the narrow sense, in an "autotelic word"), but rather as its spectral dispersion in an atmosphere filled with alien words, value judgments and accents through which the ray passes on its way towards the object; the social atmosphere of the word, the atmosphere that surrounds the object, makes the facets of the image sparkle. (Mikhail Bakhtin, *The Dialogic Imagination,* ed. Michael Holquist, tr. Michael Holquist and

Caryl Emerson [Austin: University of Texas Press, 1981], p. 277.)

42. "Musique," *OC*, p. 649.

43. Mikhail Bakhtin (cited in note 41) is the modern critic who has perhaps ceded the most to words, "hero-ideologists": ideas in the process of formation. The last few pages of this document should make apparent his debt to Mallarmé.

44. Bonniot explains this term in the context of other uses that clearly represented failed or shelved projects (*OC*, pp. 423–24).

45. Georges Poulet, *La Distance intérieure* (Paris: Plon, 1952), p. 325.

46. Leo Bersani, in *The Death of Stéphane Mallarmé* (Cambridge: Cambridge University Press, 1982), speaks of "Igitur" as the death of the poet.

47. Other analyses include those of Kristeva, already mentioned, and Bettina Knapp's potpourri of Jungian-alchemical-kabbalistic elements, "'Igitur or Elbehnon's Folly': The Depersonalization Process and the Creative Encounter." *Yale French Studies*, vol. 54 (ch. 4, note 82). Cohn's *Igitur*, thought somewhat marred by overwriting, is nevertheless immensely helpful.

48. The full title is "Igitur, ou la folie d'Elbehnon." Due to considerations of space and context, I will not go into all the peregrinations of the critics in quest of the answer to "wherefore Igitur?" The association of Elbehnon and Elsinor seems apropos.

49. Richard denies this "Cratylism" (p. 576).

50. Roland de Renéville, *L'expérience poétique*, cited in Cohn, *Igitur*, p. 20.

51. Cohn, *Igitur*, p. 21.

52. The French "ne . . . point" (not at all) bears an equally important meaning for the alternative name that Cohn proffers. As for the feather, he goes so far as to interpolate (apparently, for I cannot find it in the text) a "feather duster" (*plumeau*).

53. Cohn, *Igitur*, p. 14.

54. *OC*, p. 433. At least in the critical tradition. But in Mallarmé's introduction, he is described as "tout enfant." Perhaps those who read Igitur as Hamlet neglect this phrase.

55. *OC*, p. 438. Translation: this perfection of my certainty bothers me . . . the necessity to inhabit the heart of this race.

56. One of the more ingenious is that of the structuralist, Marcel Detienne, who interprets the boiling and roasting as significant mediations of the culturally significant processes of preparing food. By these actions, the Orphics emphasized dramatically their refusal of the exist-

ing societal mores (the same is true, in a different context, of their vege-
tarianism) (Marcel Detienne, *Dionysos Slain*, tr. Mireille Muellner and
Leonard Muellner (Baltimore: Johns Hopkins University Press, 1979).

The book, "le grimoire," which Igitur closes with finality, reminds
me of another book from another midnight dream, that which
Descartes entertained the night before coming to his infamous dictum.
The book, a dictionary, lies open on the table. As the dream proceeds,
the table starts to tilt to the left, and the book starts to slide off. Anx-
iously looking at it again, the dreamer finds that it has fewer words than
it contained before (recounted by Karl Stern, *Flight from Woman* [New
York: Farrar, Straus, and Giroux, 1965]).

57. For a review of the segment of the Rhapsodic Theogony
which provides a background for this discussion, see chapter 1, pp.
21–23.

58. Giving Aristophanes his occasion to ridicule the *Orpheotelestai*
and their ilk in *The Birds*.

59. This is her primary mode of appearance in the *récit*. But Nyx
has many names in "Igitur": Nuit, Minuit, l'Ombre, Chaos de l'Ombre.

60. *OC*, pp. 445–51.

61. Maurice Blanchot, *The Space of Literature*, tr. Ann Smock (Lincoln: University of Nebraska Press, 1982), p. 113.

62. It also represents the extreme movement of the pendulum,
when it must begin the return oscillation, or, defying gravity, "over-
swing" into it opposite, like Apollo into Dionysos, as I indicated in chapter 3.

63. *OC*, p. 443.

64. *OC*, p. 450.

65. But, unlike Nietzsche's "last man," in full cognizance of the
meaning of his act. To use again Nietzsche's phrase from his reconsid-
ered reflections on Wagner, Igitur is rather a "miniature," a fore-inkling
of the *Übermensch*.

66. Cohn, *Igitur*, p. 8.

67. *OC*, p. 43. Translation: The crescent, yes the only crescent is
on the iron dial of the clock, hanging Lucifer as a weight, ever wounds,
ever a new hour's time wept by the dark drops of the water-clock (Hartley, p. 37).

68. Cohn, *Igitur*, pp. 27–28. See also Richard's fertile discussion
of the "licorne" (Richard, pp. 215–16).

69. Goodkin notes that the Greek *nyx* is embedded in "onyx." He
refuses to associate, however, the "nix" from Phénix with the Greek
spelling (Goodkin, p. 162). He convincingly indicates Mallarmé's famil-
iarity with the Greek term by referring to the entry under the letter N in
"Les mots anglais" (*OC*, p. 962).

70. René Ghil, *Les Dates et les oeuvres* (Paris: Crès, 1923), p. 222. Cited in Robert G. Cohn, *Toward the Poems of Mallarmé* (Berkeley and Los Angeles: University of California Press, 1965), p. 139.

71. Once again, I am indebted to William Arrowsmith for this correction to the Mallarmistes' collective latinate ignorance (and my own, of course) of this Greek word.

72. Cohn, *Toward the Poems of Mallarmé*, p. 141.

73. As Kerenyi puts it in his *Dionysos*, Orphism is "a masculine, speculative tendency within a religion [Dionysian] having women's cults at its core." (Kerenyi, p. 262)

74. *OC*, p. 437.

75. *OC*, p. 653.

76. "Banville," *OC*, p. 521.

77. In Phillip Wheelright, *The Burning Fountain* (Bloomington: Indiana University Press, 1959), p. 134, the author alludes to the *uraeus*, a sacred Egyptian figure consisting of a winged black orb (earth) with a serpent protruding underneath. It reminds me, again, of Plato's *Pteros*. The protruding snake in this figure has both autochthonous and phallic connotations.

Conclusion

1. As Paul Friedländer says, Hades and the Intelligible realm are synonomous (Friedländer, p. 183).

2. George Rodenbach, "L'Élite." The original French-language statement, used as the epigraph of this chapter, is cited in Michaud, p. 133.

3. These are the two basic logical operations that Richard finds in Mallarmé's *oeuvre*. (Richard, esp. chapter 8, pp. 373–465). As Baudelaire summed it up, "De la concentration et de la vaporisation du moi, tout est là" (cited in Cattaui, p. 124).

4. "Musique," *OC*, p. 647. Trans.: cf. chapter 4, note 72.

5. Though when man is the operator, the universe appears as a human being—so my point is more logical than phenomenological. Against my metaphor of poet-as-magus, Blanchot makes the following remark: "The 'omission of self,' the 'anonymous death' of the poetic ritual, turns poetry into a true self-immolation, not for the purpose of questionable magical transports, but for almost technical reasons: since he who speaks the language of poetry is exposed to the kind of dying which true speech inevitably involves" (Maurice Blanchot, *The Sirens' Song,* ed. Gabriel Josipovici, tr. Sacha Rabinovich (Bloomington: University of Indiana Press), "Le livre à venir," pp. 231–32). But we are really not that far

apart. There is precision involved in my notion of Mallarmé as "operator." Mallarmé's art is neither a matter of divine afflatus nor of a vague mysticism of the sort in which Novalis immersed himself. As I said in defining the Orphic moment in chapter 4, the appearance of Orpheus/Mallarmé was at the moment when the Apollinian forms collapsed; it was a *reflex* emitted by that collapse. See also my discussion of words as self-reflexive within the context of the poet's "death" later in the same chapter.

6. Richard, p. 424. Translation: But the fact is that Mallarmé dreamed of himself as a grotto, because he imagined himself a kiosk, vault, shell; as Rodenbach said it so well, "bringing it all back to himself and to unity, because he lived at the center of nature."

7. Poulet says that the artistic material must "reoriginate" in the thought of the critic, who is the "prey" of the artist. Georges Poulet, "The Phenomenology of Reading," in *Critical Theory Since Plato*, ed. Hazard Adams (New York: Harcourt, Brace, 1971), pp. 1214-16. Genette seizes a particularly characteristic phrase where Richard speaks of Mallarmé's own kind of creative revery: "Il ne pense pas, il caresse des idées, s'enivre de raisonnements" (cited in Gérard Genette, "Bonheur de Mallarmé?" *Figures I* [1966], p. 94).

8. Richard, p. 424. More directly than the *coquille*, the image of the Master-as-grotto transgresses Plato's cave, because unlike the latter, its operator turns back upon himself, an act of "autoallumage," rather than turning toward the light of the sun for the illumination that the cave, its fire, and its flickering shadows withhold. However, this passage must be tempered by reading it in the light of the eclipse of the clarity of "solar" truth, replaced, especially in German Romanticism, by the effort to see the "midnight sun" within. Translation: Perfect image of a beauty 'turned within,' type of hollow diamond that, while respecting the infinite blinking of things, succeeded in utilizing this dispersion even as a means of individual awakening and global harmonization. Happy enclosure of an egg, brilliance of the diamond, pleasure of prismatic incisiveness, joy of reflexive self-lighting, the Mallarméan grotto reunited all these joys in a single beneficent form.

9. *BT*, Kaufmann, p. 71 (sect. ix). Goffman transposes the verbs in two consequtive clauses, emerging with "the tragedy at the heart of things . . . the contrariety at the center of the universe" (*BT*, Golffing, p. 64).

10. Richard, pp. 419-37.

11. The *type* of the traditional image is the flaming sword guarding the entrance to the Garden of Eden. This was Philo's analysis, one that was typical of the Neoplatonists as well.

12. Coleridge's point is apt here: one must "discriminate without dividing."

13. Jacques Derrida, *Dissemination*, tr. Barbara Johnson (Chicago: University of Chicago Press, 1981).

14. Christopher Middleton, *The Pursuit of the Kingfisher* (Manchester: Carcanet Press, 1984), p. 11.

15. A distinguished predecessor to Blanchot is Paul Valéry, whose work I have unfortunately had to slight.

16. The question on the possiblity of literature, though, is posed in Maurice Blanchot, *Faux pas* (Paris: Gallimard, 1943).

17. Blanchot, *Space of Literature*, inside title page (as in the French original). This quest for a center is similar to Poulet's method of approaching an author. Poulet has an insightful piece on Blanchot: "Maurice Blanchot, Critique et Romancier" *(Critique,* no. 229 [1966]), pp. 485–97.

18. Blanchot, *Space of Literature*, p. 171.

19. Blanchot, *Space of Literature*, p. 163.

20. Blanchot, *Space of Literature*, p. 171.

21. In Schiller's poem, a novice creeps into the shrine of the goddess in the middle of night, removes the veil, and is struck dumb as a consequence.

22. Compare the Pharoah, after the model of Osiris, going to his coffin where the painted image of Isis, with arms outstretched, receives him in death.

23. Blanchot, *Space of Literature*, pp. 172–73.

24. From the line of one of Rilke's *Sonnets to Orpheus*: "Be infinitely [forever] dead in Eurydice."

25. Blanchot, *Space of Literature*, p. 173.

26. This is the central theme of James Hillman's remarkable work on the domain of Hades, *The Dream and the Underworld* (New York: Harper and Row, 1979). Hillman argues that the fantasy of mastery with which the Freudian ("heroic") ego tries to penetrate the dream is inappropriate, because when one drags the dream-images up to the light of day, they become other than the image that attracted the analytic ego in the first place. Instead, one must adopt an "imaginal ego" that learns to be comfortable with the dream-images by meeting them in the murky light of the "bridge" between night and day. Blanchot's description of the Orpheus persona in the language of "power" and "mastery" is somewhat misleading, for the moment when Orpheus dwells with Eurydice as "song" (*epoidos, epodé*) is one not of mastery, but of mutual submission.

27. Blanchot, *Space of Literature*, p. 175.

28. Blanchot, *Space of Literature*, p. 176.

29. Maurice Blanchot, *The Sirens' Song*, (Bloomington: Indiana University Press, 1982), pp. 237–38.

30. Blanchot, *Sirens' Song*, p. 247n.

31. Blanchot, *Sirens' Song*, p. 231.

Works Cited

Abrams, Meyer H. *The Mirror and the Lamp*. New York: Oxford University Press, 1953.

Alderink, Larry. *Creation and Salvation in Ancient Orphism*. University Park, Pa.: American Philological Association, 1981.

Apuleius. *The Golden Ass*. Tr. William Adlington. New York: Horace Liveright, 1927.

Aristophanes. *The Birds*. Tr. William Arrowsmith. *Three Comedies*. Ed. William Arrowsmith. Ann Arbor: University of Michigan Press, 1969.

Arrowsmith, William. Introduction to *Alcestis*, by Euripides. New York: Oxford University Press, 1974.

——. "Aristophanes' Birds: The Fantasy Politics of Eros." *Arion*, n.s. 1, no 1 (1973), pp. 119-67.

——. "A Greek Theater of Ideas." *Arion*, 2, no. 3 (1963), pp. 32-56.

——. "Nietzsche on Classics and Classicists." *Arion*, 2, no. 1, pp. 5ff.; 2, no. 2 (1963), pp. 5ff.

Austin, Lloyd J. *Poetic Principles and Practice*. Cambridge: Cambridge University Press, 1987.

Bachelard, Gaston. "La Dialectique dynamique de la rêverie mallarméene." *Le Point*, 29-30 (1944), pp. 40-44.

——. *The Poetics of Reverie*. Boston: Beacon, 1971.

Bacon, Francis. *Wisdom of the Ancients*. In *Selected Writings of Francis Bacon*. Ed. Hugh G. Dick, pp. 410-13. New York: Random House [The Modern Library], 1955.

Baeumer, Max L. "Nietzsche and the Tradition of the Dionysian." In *Studies in Nietzsche and the Classical Tradition,* tr. Timothy Sellner, ed. James O'Flaherty, T. Sellner, and R. Helm, pp. 165–89. Chapel Hill: University of North Carolina Press, 1976.

Baillot, Alexandre. *Influence de la philosphie de Schopenhauer en France (1860–1900).* Paris: J. Vrin, 1927.

Bakhtin, Mikhail. *The Dialogic Imagination.* Ed. Michael Holquist, tr. Michael Hoquist and Caryl Emerson. Austin: University of Texas Press, 1981.

Bays, Gwendolyn. *The Orphic Vision: Seer Poets from Novalis to Rimbaud.* Lincoln: University of Nebraska Press, 1964.

Behler, Ernst. "Nietzsche und die Frühromantische Schule." *Nietzsche-Studien,* 7 (1978), pp. 59–96.

Bennett, Benjamin. "Nietzsche's Idea of Myth: The Birth of Tragedy out of the Spirit of Eighteenth Century Aesthetics." *PMLA* 94 (1979), pp. 420–33.

Bersani, Leo. *The Death of Stephane Mallarmé.* Cambridge: Cambridge University Press, 1982.

Blanchot, Maurice. *L'Espace littéraire.* Paris: Gallimard, 1955.

——. *Faux pas.* Paris: Gallimard, 1943.

——. *The Sirens' Song.* Ed. Gabriel Josipovici, tr. Sacha Rabinovitch. Bloomington: Indiana University Press, 1982.

——. *The Space of Literature.* Tr. Ann Smock. Lincoln: University of Nebraska Press, 1982.

——. *Thomas the Obscure.* Tr. Robert Lamberton. New York: David Lewis, 1973.

Bloch, Ernst. *Essays on the Philosophy of Music.* Cambridge: Cambridge University Press, 1985.

Böhme, Robert. *Orpheus: Der Sänger und seine Zeit.* Bern: Francke, 1970.

Bonnefoy, Yves. "The Poetics of Mallarmé." Tr. Elaine Ancekewicz. *Yale French Studies,* 54 (1978), pp. 9–21.

Bowie, Malcolm, Alison Fairlie, and Alison Finch. *Baudelaire, Mallarmé, Valéry.* Cambridge: Cambridge University Press, 1982.

Boyancé, Pierre. *Le culte des Muses chez les philosophes grecs.* Paris: Editions E. de Boccard, 1972.

Bréhier, Emile. *The Hellenic Age.* Tr. Joseph Thomas. Chicago: University of Chicago Press, 1963.

Broch, Herman. *Hugo Von Hoffmansthal and his Time.* Tr., ed.

Michael Steinberg. Chicago: University of Chicago Press, 1984.

Bruse, Klaus-Detlef. "Die Griechische Trägodie als 'Gesamtkunstwerk'—Anmerkungen zu den musikästhetischen Reflexionen des frühen Nietzsche." *Nietzsche-Studien*, 13 (1984), pp. 157–77.

Burkert, Walter. "Craft versus Sect: The Problem of Orphics and Pythagoreans." In *Jewish and Christian Self-Definition.* Vol. 3 of *Self-Definition in the Greco-Roman World.* Ed. Ben F. Meyer and E. P. Sanders. Philadelphia: Fortress, 1982.

——. *Greek Religion.* Tr. John Raffan. Cambridge: Harvard University Press, 1985.

——. *Homo Necans.* Berkeley and Los Angeles: University of California Press, 1983.

——. *Lore and Science in Ancient Pythagoreanism.* Tr. Edwin Minor, Jr. Cambridge: Harvard University Press, 1972.

——. "Orphism and Bacchic Mysteries." Colloquy at Center for Hermeneutical Studies in Hellenistic and Modern Culture, Berkeley. March 1977.

Campbell, Joseph, *Primitive Mythology.* Vol. 1 of *The Masks of God.* New York: Viking, 1969.

——. ed. *Myths, Dreams, and Religion.* New York: Dutton, 1971.

Cassirer, Ernst. *An Essay on Man: An Introduction to a Philosophy of Human Culture.* New Haven: Yale University Press, 1944; Toronto: Bantam, 1970.

——. *Language and Myth.* Tr. Suzanne Langer. New York: Harper, 1946; New York: Dutton, 1953.

Cattaui, Georges. *Orphisme et la prophétie chez les poètes français 1850–1950.* Paris: Plon, 1965.

Caws. See Mallarmé, *Selected Poetry and Prose.*

Champigny, R. "Mallarmé's Relation to Platonism and Romanticism." *Modern Language Review,* July 1956, pp. 348–58.

Chiari, Joseph. *Symbolisme from Poe to Mallarmé.* London: Rockcliff, 1956.

Clement of Alexandria. "The Exhortation to the Greeks." In *Clement of Alexandria.* Tr. G. W. Butterworth. London: Loeb Classics Library, 1919.

Cohn, Robert G. *Igitur.* Berkeley: University of California Press, 1981.

——. "The Mallarmé Century." *Stanford French Review.* Winter 1978.

———. "Mallarmé contre Genette." *Tel Quel* 69 (1977), pp. 51–54.

———. *Toward the Poems of Mallarmé.* Berkeley and Los Angeles: The University of California Press, 1965.

Coman, Jean. "Orphée, civilisateur de l'humanité." *Zalmoxis*, 1 (1938), pp. 130–76.

Cook. See Mallarmé, *Selected Prose Poems, Essays and Letters.*

Cornford. Francis M. *From Religion to Philosphy.* London: Edward Arnold, 1912.

Davies, Gardner. "The Demon of Analogy." *French Studies*, July 1955, pp. 197–211; Oct. 1955, pp. 326–47.

———. *Les Tombeaux de Mallarmé.* Paris: J. Corti, 1950.

Davis, Gladys. *The Asiatic Dionysus.* London: G. Bell, 1914.

Dayan, Peter. *Mallarme's Divine Transposition.* Oxford: Oxford University Press, 1986.

Del Caro, Adrean. *Nietzsche Contra Nietzsche.* Baton Rouge: Lousiana State University Press, 1989.

Deleuze, Gilles. *Nietzsche and Philosphy.* Tr. Hugh Tomlinson. New York: Columbia University Press, 1983.

Delfel, Guy. *L'Aesthétique de Mallarmé.* Paris: Flammarion, n.d.

De Man, Paul. *Blindness and Insight.* Minneapolis: University of Minnesota Press, 1983.

Derrida, Jacques. *Dissemination.* Tr. Barbara Johnson. Chicago: University of Chicago Press, 1981.

Detienne, Marcel. *Dionysos Slain.* Tr. Mireille Muellner and Leonard Muellner. Baltimore: Johns Hopkins University Press, 1979.

Dodds, Ernest R. *The Greeks and the Irrational.* Berkeley and Los Angeles: University of California Press, 1951.

Eliade, Mircea. *Shamanism: Archaic Techniques of Ecstasy.* Tr. Willard Trask. Princeton: Princeton University Press, 1972.

———. *Zalmoxis.* Chicago: University of Chicago Press, 1972.

Eliot, T. S. *The Complete Poems and Plays.* New York: Harcourt, Brace, 1958.

———. *From Poe to Valéry.* New York: Harcourt, Brace, 1948.

Else, Gerald F. *The Origin and Early Form of Greek Tragedy* Cambridge: Harvard University Press, 1965.

Euripides. *The Bacchae,* Tr. William Arrowsmith. *Euripides III.* Ed. David Grene, Richmond Lattimore. New York: Modern Library, 1959.

Feldman, Burton, and Robert D. Richardson. *The Rise of Modern Mythology.* Bloomington: Indiana University Press, 1972.

Friedländer, Paul. *Plato: An Introduction.* Vol. 1. Tr. Hans Meyer-hoff. Bollingen series. New York: Pantheon, 1958.

Friedman, John B. *Orpheus in the Middle Ages.* Cambridge: Harvard University Press, 1970.

Friedrich, Hugo. *The Structure of Modern Poetry.* Tr. Joachim Neugroschel. Evanston: Northwestern University Press, 1974.

Frutiger, Perceval. *Les mythes de Platon.* Paris: Librairie Alcan, 1930.

Genette, Gérard. "Bonheur de Mallarmé?" In *Figures: essais.* Vol. 1. Paris: Editions du Seuil, 1966, pp. 91–100.

Gill, Austin. 'Du fait à l'idéal': la transposition Mallarméenne." *Revue de Linguistique Roman,* 32 (1968), pp. 291–304.

Godwin, Joscelyn. "The Golden Chain of Orpheus." *Temenos,* 4 (1983), pp. 7–25.

——. "The Golden Chain of Orpheus." Pt. 2. *Temenos,* 5 (1984), pp. 211–39.

Goodkin, Richard. *The Symbolist Home and the Tragic Home: Mallarmé and Oedipus.* Purdue University Monographs in Romance Languages, vol 13. Amsterdam and Philadelphia: John Benjamins, 1984.

Gould, Thomas. *Mythical Intentions in Modern Literature.* Princeton: Princeton University Press, 1981.

Grundelehner, Phillip. *The Poetry of Friedrich Nietzsche.* New York: Oxford University Press, 1986.

Guépin, J. P. *The Tragic Paradox.* Amsterdam: Adolf Hakkert, 1968.

Guthrie, W. K. C. *The Greeks and Their Gods.* Boston: Beacon, 1955.

——. *Orpheus and Greek Religion.* 2d. ed. London: Methuen, 1952.

Haar, Michael. "Nietzsche and Metaphysical Language." In *The New Nietzsche,* pp. 5–36. Ed. David B. Allison. New York: Dell, 1977.

Harrison, Jane E. *Prolegomena to the Study of Greek Religion.* London: Merlin Press, 1961.

Hartley. See Mallarmé, *Selected Poetry.*

Hassan, Ihab. *The Dismemberment of Orpheus.* New York: Oxford University Press, 1971.

Havelock, Eric. *Preface to Plato.* Cambridge: Harvard University Press, 1963.

Heller, Eric. *The Disinherited Mind.* Cambridge: Cambridge University Press, 1952.

Henrichs, Albert. "Loss of Self, Suffering, Violence: The Modern View of Dionysus from Nietzsche to Girard." *Harvard Review of Classical Philology*, 88 (1984), pp. 205–40.

———. "Nietzsche and Euripides." *Greek Roman and Byzantine Studies*, 26, no. 4 (1986), pp. 369–97.

Hesiod. *Theogony.* In *Theogony and Works and Days,* tr. Dorothea Wender. Harmondsworth: Penguin, 1973.

Hillery, David. *Music and Poetry in France from Baudelaire to Mallarmé.* Berne: Lang, 1980.

Hillman, James. *The Dream and the Underworld.* New York: Harper and Row, 1979.

———. "Psychology: Monotheistic or Polytheistic?" Appendix to *The New Polytheism,* by David Miller, pp. 109–42. Dallas: Spring Publications, 1981.

———. *Re-Visioning Psychology.* New York: Harper and Row, 1975.

Hultkrantz, Ake. *The North American Indian Orpheus Tradition.* Stockholm, 1957.

Juden, Brian. *Traditions orphiques et tendances mystiques dans le Romantisme français (1800–1855).* Paris: Kliencksieck, 1971.

Kaufmann, Walter. *Nietzsche: Philosopher, Psychologist, Antichrist.* Cleveland: World Publishing, Meridian Books, 1956

Kerenyi, Carl. *Dionysus: Archetypal Image of Indestructible Life.* Tr. Ralph Mannheim, Bollingen series, 65. Princeton: Princeton University Press, 1976.

Kirk, G. S., J. E. Raven, and M. Schofield. *The Pre-Socratic Philosophers.* Cambridge: Cambridge University Press, 1983.

Knapp, Bettina. "'Igitur or Elbehnon's Folly': The Depersonalization Process and the Creative Encounter." *Yale French Studies* 54 (1978), pp. 188–213.

Kravis, Judy. *The Prose of Mallarmé.* Cambridge: Cambridge University Press, 1976.

Kristeva, Julia. *Revolution in Poetic Language.* Tr. Margaret Waller, New York: Columbia University Press, 1984.

Kropfinger, Klaus. "Wagners Musikbegriff und Nietzsche's 'Geist der Musik.'" *Nietzsche-Studien,* 14 (1985), pp. 1–12.

Kushner, Eva. *Le Mythe d'Orphée dans la littérature française contemporaine.* Paris: Nizet, 1961.

Lattimore, Richmond, *Greek Lyrics.* Chicago: Chicago University Press, 1960.

Lawler, James R. *The Language of French Symbolism.* Princeton: Princeton University Press, 1969.

Lévi-Strauss, Claude. *From Honey to Ashes.* Tr. John Weightman and Doreen Weightman. New York: Harper and Row, 1973.

Lindsay, Jack. *The Clashing Rocks.* London: Chapman and Hall, 1965.

Linforth, Ivan. *The Arts of Orpheus.* Berkeley and Los Angeles: University of California Press, 1941.

Link, Margaret Schevill. *The Pollen Path: A Collection of Navajo Myths Retold by Margaret Schevill Link.* Stanford: Stanford University Press, 1956.

Macchioro, Vittorio. *From Orpheus to Paul.* New York: Henry Holt, 1930.

Mallarmé, Stéphane. *Correspondance 1862-1871.* Ed. Henri Mondor. Paris: Gallimard, 1959.

——. *Oeuvres complètes.* Ed. H. Mondor and G. Jean-Aubry. Paris: Gallimard, 1965.

——. *Propos sur la Poésie.* Bibliotheque de la Pleíade, 65. Ed. Henri Mondor. Monaco: Editions du Rocher, 1946.

——. *Selected Letters of Stéphane Mallarmé.* Ed., tr. Rosemary Lloyd. Chicago: University of Chicago Press, 1988.

——. *Selected Poetry.* Ed., tr. Anthony Hartley. Baltimore: Penguin, 1965.

——. *Selected Poetry and Prose.* Ed. Mary Ann Caws. New York: New Directions, 1982.

——. *Selected Prose Poems, Essays and Letters.* Tr. Bradford Cook. Baltimore: Johns Hopkins Press, 1956.

Marcuse, Herbert. *Eros and Civilization.* Boston: Beacon, 1955.

Megill, Allan. *Prophets of Extremity. Nietzsche, Heidegger, Foucault, Derrida.* Berkeley and Los Angeles: University of California Press, 1985.

Meuli, Karl, "Scythia." *Hermes* 70 (1953), pp. 153–64.

Michaud, Guy. *Mallarmé.* Paris: Hatier, 1958.

Middleton, Christopher. *The Pursuit of the Kingfisher.* Manchester: Carcanet press, 1984.

Miller, David. *The New Polytheism.* Dallas: Spring Publications, 1981.

Moulinier. *Orphée et L'Orphisme.* Paris: Société D'Edition "Les Belles Lettres," 1955.

Murray, Gilbert. *Five Stages of Greek Religion.* New York: Columbia University Press, 1925.

Nehamas, Alexander. *Nietzsche: Life as Literature.* Cambridge: Harvard University Press, 1985.

Nietzsche, Friedrich. *Beyond Good and Evil.* Tr. Marianne Cowan. Chicago: Henry Regnery and Co., 1955.

———. *The Birth of Tragedy and The Case of Wagner.* Tr. Walter Kaufmann. New York: Random House, 1967.

———. *The Birth of Tragedy and The Genealogy of Morals.* Tr. Francis Golffing. New York: Doubleday, 1956.

———. *Early Greek Philosophy and Other Essays.* Tr. Max Mügge. New York: Russell and Russell, 1964.

———. "Nietzsche contra Wagner." In *The Portable Nietzsche.* Ed., tr. Walter Kaufmann, pp. 661–83, New York: Penguin, 1976.

———. "On Truth and Lie in an Extra-Moral Sense." In *The Portable Nietzsche,* Ed., tr. Walter Kaufmann, 46–47. New York: Penguin, 1976.

———. *Philosophy in the Tragic Age of the Greeks.* Tr. Marianne Cowan. Chicago: Henry Regnery and Co., 1937.

———. *Unmodern Observations.* Ed. William Arrowsmith. New Haven: Yale University Press, 1990.

Noulet, Emilie. *Vingt Poèmes de Mallarmé.* Paris: Librarie Droz, 1940.

O'Flaherty James C., T. F. Sellner, and R.M. Helm. *Studies in Nietzsche and the Classical Tradition.* Chapel Hill: University of North Carolina Press, 1976.

Otto, Walter F. *Dionysus: Myth and Cult.* Tr. Robert B. Palmer. Bloomington: Indiana University Press, 1973.

———. *Homeric Gods.* Tr. Moses Hadas. Boston: Beacon, 1954

Ovid. *Metamorphoses.* Tr. A. D. Melville. Oxford and New York: Oxford University Press, 1986.

Pater, Walter. *Plato and Platonism.* London: Macmillan, 1910.

Plato. *The Collected Dialogues.* Ed. Edith Hamilton and Huntington Cairns. Bollingen series, 71. New York: Random House, Pantheon Books, 1963.

Poulet, Georges. *La distance intérieure.* Paris: Plon, 1952.

———. "Maurice Blanchot: Critique et romancier." *Critique* 229 (1966), pp. 485–97.

———. *The Metamorphoses of the Circle.* Baltimore: Johns Hopkins University Press, 1966.

———. "Phenomenology of Reading." In *Critical Theory since Plato.* Ed. Hazard Adams, pp. 1213–22. New York: Harcourt, Brace, 1971.

Raymond, Marcel. *From Baudelaire to Surrealism.* New York: Wittenborn, Schultz, 1950.

Richard, Jean-Pierre. *L'univers poétique de Stéphane Mallarmé.* Paris: Editions du Seuil, 1961.

Riffaterre, Hermione B. *Orphéus dans la poésie romantique.* Paris: Nizet, 1970.

Robbins, Vernon. "Famous Orpheus." In *Orpheus: The Metamorphosis of a Myth.* Ed. John Warden, pp. 5–16. Toronto: University of Toronto Press, 1982.

Rohde, Erwin. *Psyche.* New York: Harcourt, Brace, 1925.

Rouget, Gilbert. *Music and Trance: A Theory of the Relations between Music and Possession.* Tr. Brunhilde Biebuyck (in collaboration with the author). Chicago: University of Chicago Press, 1985.

Scherer, Jacques. *L'expression littéraire dans l'oeuvre de Mallarmé.* Paris: Nizet, 1957.

Schopenhauer, Arthur. *The World as Will and Representation.* Vol. 1. Tr. E. F. J. Payne. Indian Hills, Colo.: The Falcon's Wing Press, 1958.

———. *The World as Will and Representation.* Vol. 2. Tr. E. J. F. Payne. Indian Hills, Colo.: Falcon's Wing Press, 1958; New York: Dover, 1966.

Segal, Charles. *Orpheus: the Myth of the Poet.* Baltimore: Johns Hopkins University Press, 1989.

Ségond, J. "La vocation platonicienne de Stéphane Mallarmé. *Fontaine,* 5 (1943), pp. 382–407.

Sewell, Elizabeth. *The Orphic Voice.* London: Routledge and Kegan Paul, 1960.

Seznec, Jean. "Les Dieux antiques de Mallarmé." In *Baudelaire, Mallarmé, Valéry.* Ed. Malcolm Bowie, A. Fairlie, and Alison Finch. Cambridge: Cambridge University Press, 1982.

Silk, M. S. and J. P. Stern. *Nietzsche on Tragedy.* Cambridge: Cambridge University Press, 1984.

Snell, Bruno. *The Discovery of the Mind.* Tr. T. G. Rosenmeyer. New York and Evanston: Harper and Row, 1960.

Spariosu, Mihai. *Dionysus Reborn.* Ithaca: Cornell University Press, 1989.

Stern, Karl. *The Flight from Woman.* New York: Farrar, Strauss, and Giroux, 1965.

Stewart, J. A. *The Myths in Plato.* New York: Macmillan, 1905.

Strauss, Walter A. *Descent and Return: The Orphic Theme in Modern Literature.* Cambridge: Harvard University Press, 1971.

Thibaudet, Alfred. *La Poésie de Mallarmé,* new ed. Paris: Gallimard, 1926.

Vico, Giambattista. *The New Science of Giambattista Vico.* Tr. Thomas G. Bergin and Max H. Fisch. Ithaca: Cornell University Press, 1984.

Virgil. *Georgics.* Tr. Smith Palmer Bovie. Chicago: University of Chicago Press, 1956.

Warden, John, ed. *Orpheus: The Metamorphosis of a Myth.* Toronto: University of Toronto Press, 1982.

West, Martin L. *Early Greek Philosophy and the Orient.* Oxford: Oxford University Press, 1971.

———. *The Orphic Poems.* Oxford: Oxford University Press, 1983.

Wheelright, Phillip. *The Burning Fountain.* Bloomington: Indiana University Press, 1959.

Yates, Frances. *Giordano Bruno and the Hermetic Tradition.* Chicago: University of Chicago Press, 1964.

Index

Soul: as attunement *(continued)*
    dualism of, 28–30; fate of, 35, 38; inner
    music of, xiv, 36, 48; pluralistic images
    of, 30; and primary synesthesia, 46;
    purified, 38, 39; and stars, 39; as
    winged *daimon*, 38; as winged mystery,
    43–47, 49, 103. *See also* Comet-souls;
    Empsychon; Psyche
Sparagmos, xv, xvi, 14, 15, 22, 117, 119,
    154n; and death of Dionysos, 22, 117,
    119; and death of Orpheus, 18, 19, 77,
    78, 98–99
Spariosu, Mihai, 155n
Spell: literature as, 97–98
Spindle of Necessity, xvii, 35, 36–37, 173n
Star-*daimones*: and souls, 39
Stimmung, 95
Stofftrieb, 54
Strauss, Walter: *Descent and Return*, 76,
    142n; on Orphic moment, 76–78
Styx: in hydrostatic system, 40; in Mal-
    larmé, 109, 122, 123, 124, 127
Sub-limus, 48
Swan: Orpheus as, 33, 90, 152n; song of, 2,
    49
Symbolisme: defined, 100
Symbolist poet. *See* Mallarmé, Stéphane
Symplegades (clashing rocks), xiii, 8, 36
Symposium (Plato), 33, 37, 41, 44
Syncretism: Gnostic, 45; Hellenistic, 10, 45

Tartarus, 40, 46, 142n
Telestic madness, 21, 31
Teletai, 21, 38. *See also* Orpheotelestai
Tetraktys, 45
Thamus, 42
Thanatos, 153n
Theogony (Hesiod), 142n
Theoi/theos (gods), 23–24; and law of
    being, 24, 25; as *maniai*, 31
Thespis aoidos, 32
Thoth, 42
Thumos (appetitive self/affective will), 3,
    28, 30, 31, 138; vs. *nous*, 30; and
    paideia, 31; and *psyche*, 28
Thyiades, 14–15, 147n. *See also* Maenads
Thyrsus, 118
Timaeus (Plato), 5, 36, 39, 41, 45, 48, 151n
Time: to Mallarmé, 175n
Tiresias: as *daimon*, 25
Titanic: vs. divine, xiii–xiv, 6, 23; in

humans, 6, 23, 147n
Titanos, xiii, 22
Titans: and Dionysos, 22–23; and male ini-
    tiation rites, 147n
Tombeaux: as metaphor in Mallarmé,
    102–5, 111, 112, 115
Tragedy: and music, 26, 64; and shamanic
    tradition, xiii, 7, 8, 9
Tragodeia (goat-song), 145n
Traité du Verbe (Ghil), 60, 80–81
Tristan (Wagner), 173n
Truth: and language, 59–60
Typos, 41

Ubermensch, 60
Underworld: fates of souls in, 35; journey
    to by Orpheus, 7, 36
Upanishads, 37
Ur-Eine, xv, 19, 57, 80, 115–17, 120. *See also*
    Dionysos
Uraeus, 185n
Uranos, 22, 23
Urgund, 63
Usener, Herman K., xii, 23

Va-et-vient, 138
Valéry, Paul, 76, 176n
Veil: moving, in Wagnerian music, 68–69
Verlaine, Paul, 103
Vico, Giambattista, 5–6; on imaginative
    universals, 140n; *New Science of
    Giambattista Vico*, xix, 5, 140n; on
    Orpheus as monstrous, xix, 5, 139n; on
    Orpheus as poetic character, 5; on
    titanic within, 147n
Virgil, 16, 17, 141n
Volatilization, 113
Voyage, finite, 71

Wagner, Richard: and Mallarmé, 67–72,
    73; *Gesamtkunstwerk*, 66; *Meistersinger*,
    69; music drama of, 66, 160n; and Niet-
    zsche, 64, 66–67, 72–74; and Schopen-
    hauer, 65–66, 173n; *Tristan*, 173n
Way-song. *See* Oima
Welt als Wille und Vorstellung, Die
    (Schopenhauer), 65
West, Martin, 147n
Widerspruch (contradiction), xiv, 56, 129

3797216R00132

Printed in Great Britain
by Amazon.co.uk, Ltd.,
Marston Gate.